CREATIVE KNITTING

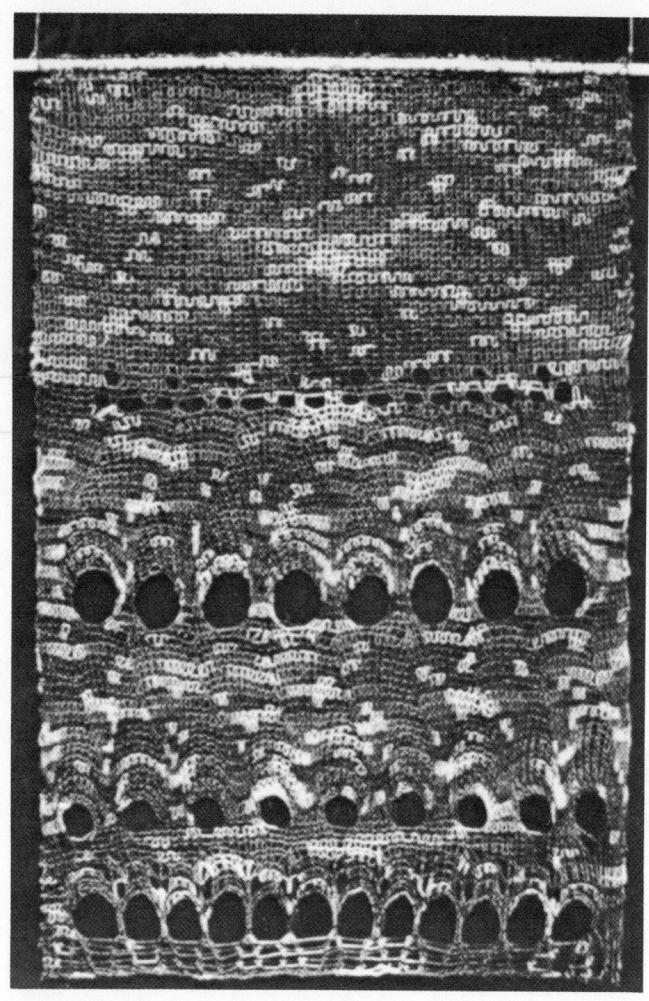

Wall hanging, 20" × 30". Bell-like motif knit in 5/1 natural linen, which was ikat-dyed dark green, bronze, and natural. (Collection of Jack Lenor Larsen.)

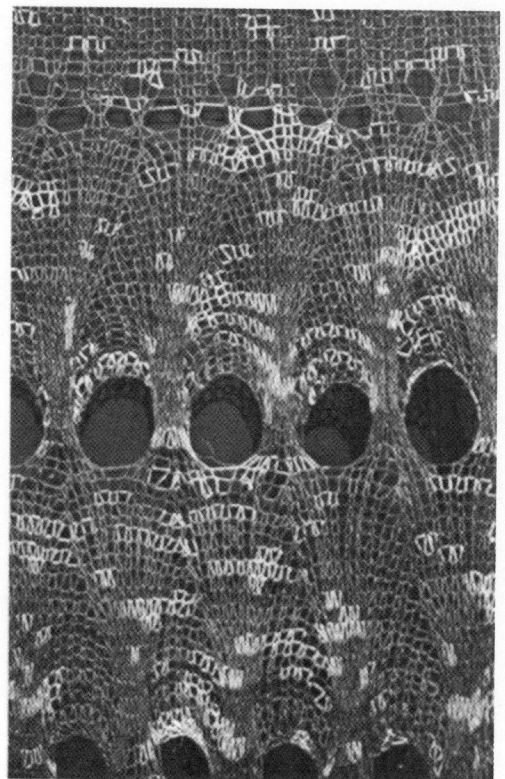

Detail of wall hanging above shows strong diagonal effect of decreasing done on just one side of the increased area.

Mary Walker Phillips
CREATIVE KNITTING
A New Art Form

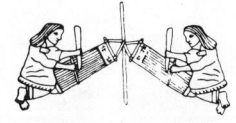

DOS TEJEDORAS FIBER ARTS PUBLICATIONS
St. Paul, Minnesota

"IMITATION WILL FASHION WHAT IT HAS SEEN, BUT
IMAGINATION GOES ON TO WHAT IT HAS NOT SEEN"

APOLLONIUS OF TYANA

Also by Mary Walker Phillips
Step-by-Step Knitting. New York: Golden Press, 1967.
Step-by-Step Macrame. New York: Golden Press, 1970.
Knitting. Franklin Watts, 1977.

Dos Tejedoras Fiber Arts Publications
3036 N. Snelling Avenue, Saint Paul, MN 55113

Library of Congress Catalog Card Number 72-110061
ISBN 0-932394-06-X

Revised Edition published by Dos Tejedoras Fiber Arts Publications, 1986.
Previous editions were published by Litton Educational Publishing, Inc. (1971),
and Van Nostrand Rinehold Co.(1980).

Photographs by Ferdinand Boesch, unless stated otherwise.
Diagrams by William Sayles
Interior Design by Rose Delia Vasquez
Cover Design by Nancy Leeper

Acknowledgements
There are many people who have encouraged me and
have graciously given their constructive comments.
Without their help I am sure this book would never have
come into being. To all of my friends, thank you. I am especially grateful to the American Craft Council, Jean Ko-
foid, Shirley and William Sayles and Milton Sonday. Jack
Lenor Larsen, by his remarks concerning knitting, reacti-
vated my knitting needles and is one of the persons most
responsible for my in-depth involvement with knitting.
To Jack, my special thanks.

This book is dedicated to my mother, Mrs. John P. Phillips, and also to my sister, Martha Phillips Stackhouse;
to my brother, William David Phillips; and to their
respective families.

Contents

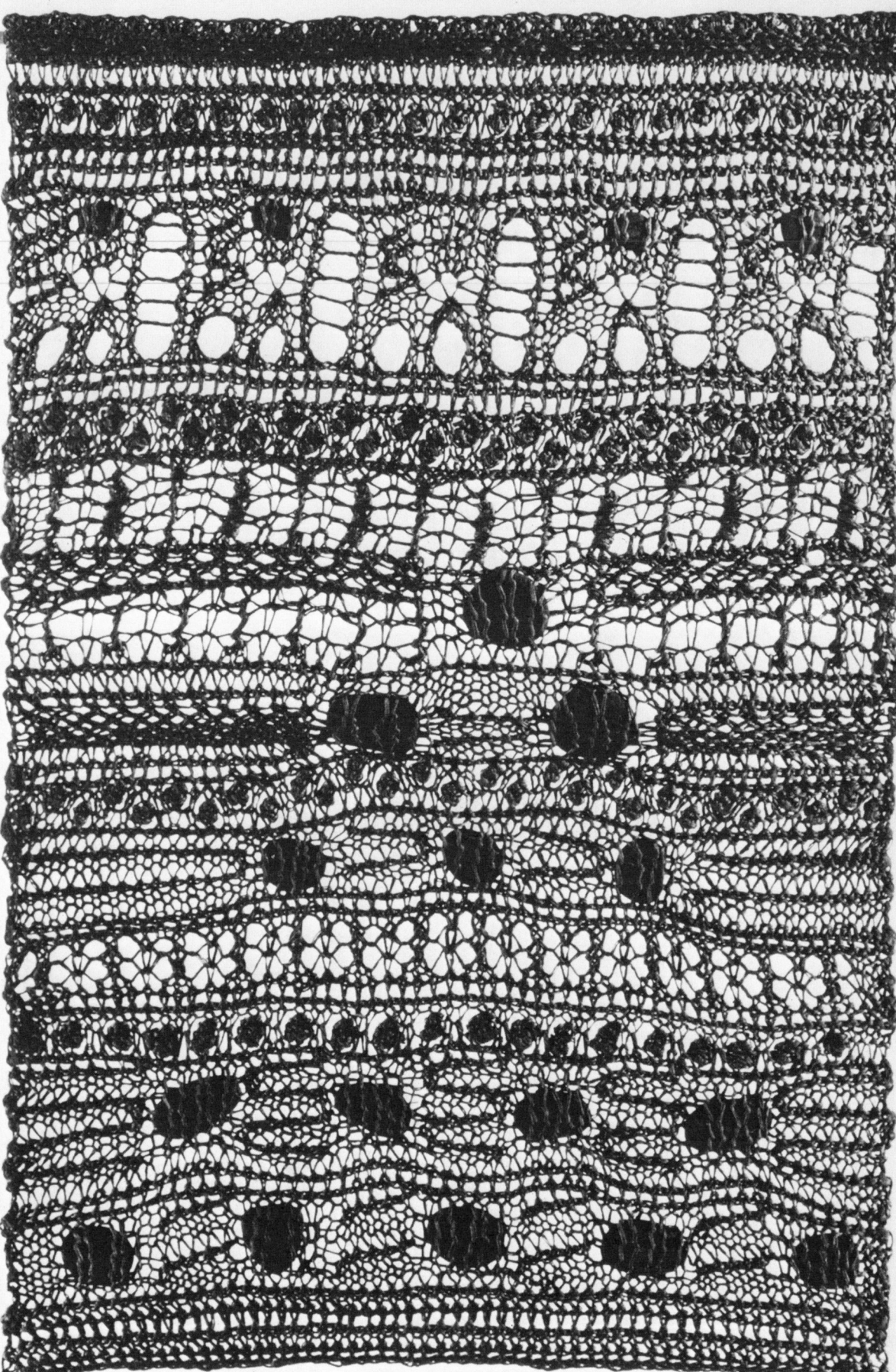

Foreword

I grow dissatisfied with the word "art."

Depending on your age, your standards, or your life-style, the word has come to include more and more—or less and less. Nor can I any longer be reconciled to the separation between "fine" and "applied" art. At best it is now an artificial dividing line. At worst it is pretentious. And on both scores it is usually attached to a price tag.

Feeling as I do, I come more and more to rely on such words as "skill," "craft," "taste." These are the words I think of when I look at the work of Mary Walker Phillips. She takes thread and with it she makes beautiful things with her hands. They are marvelously crafted. They have taste. That is, they seem absolutely right. I do not want to change them. I find them satisfying. She is a good artist and her medium is thread.

It is a disappearing craft she practices. She acquired her skill as a weaver and she now applies it to knitting. There are very few people in the world who can do that today on her level. Perhaps a few venerable women on the Shetland Isles can still create beautiful spider-web structures out of fine wool. It is those Shetland shawls I think of when I see the knitwork of Mary Walker Phillips. She keeps alive one of the world's great folk crafts and she gives it new meaning in this noisy world of machinery.

That, I think, is the message in her book.

Cecil Lubell
Editor, *American Fabrics Magazine*

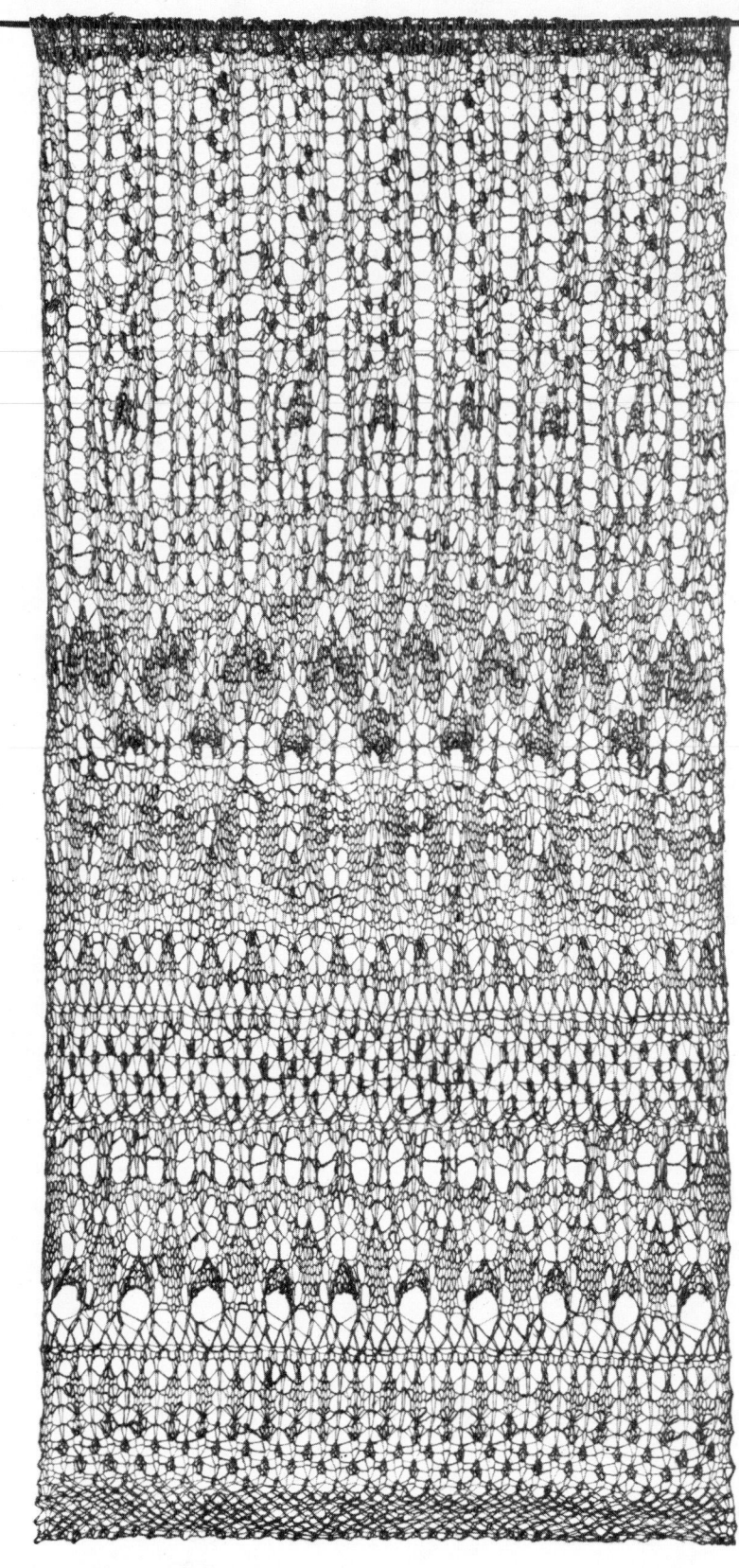

Illus. 1. Wall hanging, 19″ × 40″, (1968). Collection of Helen Richards. Red Scandinavian linen. Fine, lacy construction is achieved by using a variety of the stitches and patterns detailed in Chapter 5.

1. Introduction

For years now the movement in crafts has been towards exploring new ways of seeing and doing the traditional techniques so as to afford more pleasure to the eye and to the touch. Not only are we accustomed to weaving as a traditional way of making cloth, but we can also go to a museum to view woven constructions; we associate ceramics with casseroles and vases as well as with wall panels and sculpture; and, while we are familiar with the functional purposes of metal, we also recognize it as a valid art medium. But, what about knitting? Even though it is an ideal medium for self-expression, many knitters still consider it mainly as a means of making clothes.

The purpose of this book is to establish an awareness of knitting as an independent art style and to describe its many diverse qualities. Most of all, it is to ask the knitter to rethink the long-accepted practice of developing someone else's designs and, by taking a new view, to see knitting as a fresh experience in creative expression.

In 1962, when I started experimenting with knitting as a creative craft, I had only a few indications of its possibilities (I was a weaver at the time and already had a love for yarn and for designs created by the stitches). Through experimenting with knitting a whole new world opened up to me. Knitting became an art worthy of study, and I forsook the loom for the soft clicking of needles.

It was with the purchase of *Mary Thomas's Book of Knitting Patterns,** discovered while rummaging through a secondhand book store, that I really became involved in creative knitting. The book is full of information and contains many patterns that I still have not fully explored. At a later date, I bought *Mary Thomas's Knitting Book* which, even though I had been knitting for years, supplied me with the technical knowledge that I needed. The more involved I became, the more I realized that knitting had potential as an entirely new creative medium.

The intervening years have brought increased recognition of this medium, and now knitted structures, such as wall hangings, are exhibited by museums, galleries, and contemporary craft shows throughout the country. Creative knitting has become part of textile courses and is taught at workshops. It has become a legitimate medium for artistic expression. There are also practical applications of creative knitting—blankets, afghans, draperies, lampshades, pillow covers, place mats, room dividers, screens, and so on.

Knitting is an effective medium through which you can express your individuality; there is almost no limit to the amount of patterns available and to the variations on those patterns. Many variations are yet to be made and still new patterns to be discovered. You can work with graphs, plotting your

Personal expression in knitting, as in any other creative medium, is not achieved by copying

* See Bibliography at back of book.

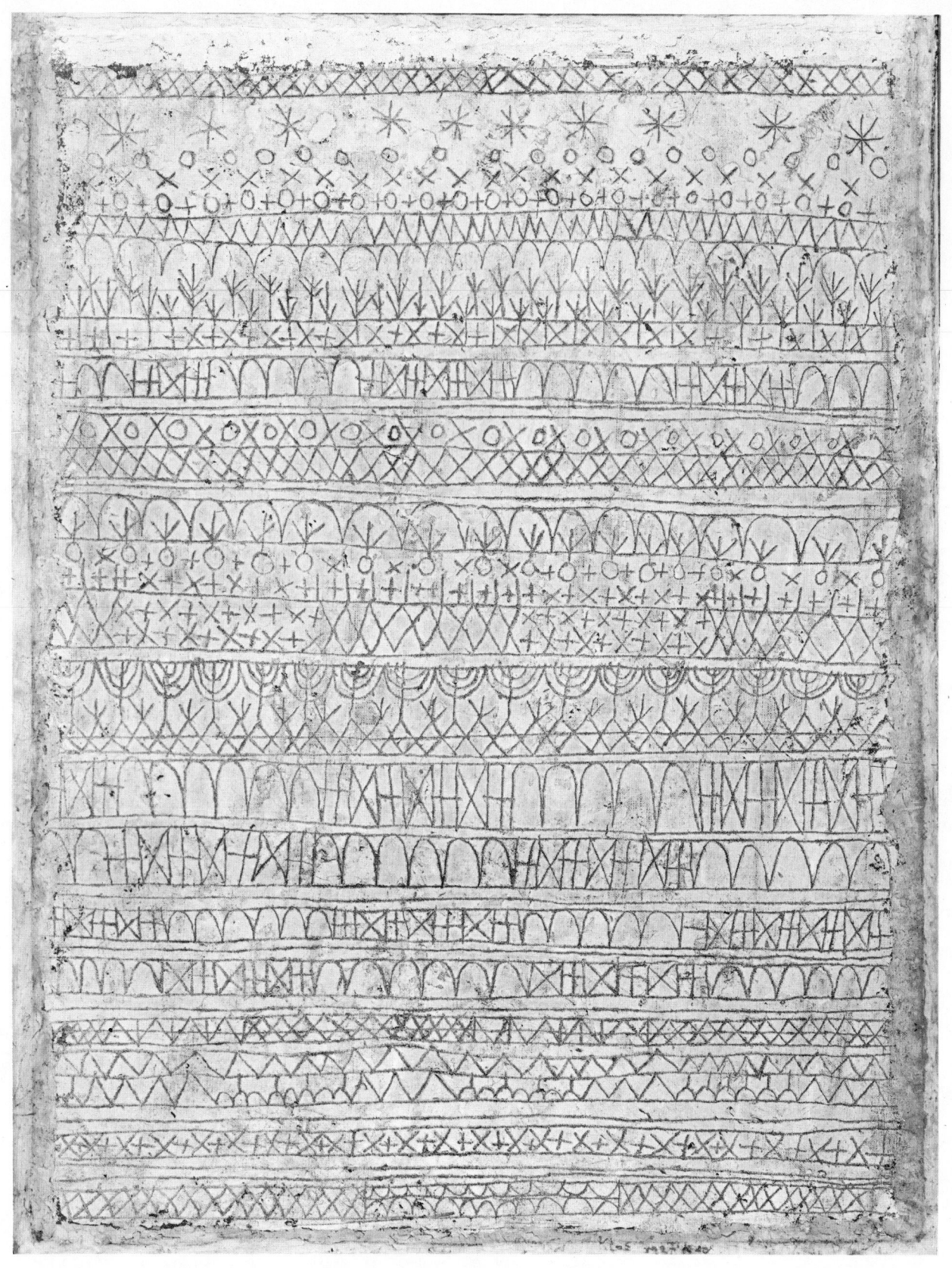

Illus. 2. Sources of inspiration for knitted constructions are everywhere. One example with beautiful, linear qualities is this painting, "Pastorale," by Paul Klee. (Tempera on canvas mounted on wood, 27¼" × 20⅝", 1927. Collection of the Museum of Modern Art, Abby Aldrich Rockefeller Fund.)

Detail of knitted purse from Sicily, possibly a seventeenth-century work. Silk with metallic wrapped silk yarn. Features a pair of eagles as a decorative element. (Collection of Cooper-Hewitt Museum of Decorative Arts and Design, Smithsonian Institution.)

Knitted wool glove from India, eighteenth to nineteenth century. (Collection of Cooper-Hewitt Museum of Decorative Arts and Design, Smithsonian Institution; purchased in memory of Mrs. John Innes Kane.)

Example of lace knitting done by Maria Flodor, Germany, 1836. Sampler was knit with cotton threads and glass beads. (Collection of Cooper-Hewitt Museum of Decorative Arts and Design, Smithsonian Institution; bequest of Mrs. Henry E. Coe.)

Knitted miniature figures shown next to a penny to indicate scale. Example of cross-knit looping characteristic of the Paracas period. (third century B.C. to third century A.D.) Found at Cerro Uhle, Ocucaje, Ica Valley, on south coast of Peru. (Collection of The Textile Museum, Washington, D.C.)

exactly what someone else has done. Rather, the aim is to translate with yarn the atmosphere of the inspiration. There are many sources of inspiration. The works of Paul Klee (1879–1940) never fail to give me new ideas. Many of his compositions are harmonious lattices of verticals and horizontals—the linear qualities that are so inherent to knitting. The first reaction I had to the knitted piece in Illus. 3 was that it resembled a Klee drawing.

The paintings of Wassily Kandinsky (1866–1944) and of Piet Mondrian (1872–1944) also captured my imagination and have provided an influence in my work. The architectural works of Antonio Gaudí (1852–1926) alone can supply a lifetime of ideas; the undulating lines of his creations can be incorporated so naturally into a knitted structure. Everywhere we look we find inspiration: forged iron grillwork, lacelike in design; cross sections of stem structures; spider webs; elevated train trestles and their shadow patterns—we are surrounded by a fertile field of ideas.

As any knitter knows, this craft requires little equipment and few materials, making it a natural medium for many who have neither the space for large projects nor the money for extensive equipment. All that is needed is a spool of yarn, a pair of knitting needles, a box of T pins, and a blocking surface.

Included in this book are diagrams for a variety of stitches and directions for still other stitches and patterns. These stitches and patterns, along with their variations, represent many of the ones that I use in my own work. The elementary steps of knitting, such as casting on to begin a piece and binding off, and such simple stitches as Garter, Stockinette, and Cable are not described in this book. The experienced knitter will know them, and the beginner can refer to the books listed in the Bibliography for this information. A good representation of my wall hangings are included, together with other pieces of mine, and they are described as to stitches and materials used. Some are analyzed so that you can follow the progression of the stitches in their variations and see how they combine to produce a unique construction.

This book is directed to the person who is curious about a variety of approaches and design potentials, to those who find conventional knitting too limited and want to use their talents in a more creative way; to craftspeople in allied arts—such as weaving, embroidery, and needlepoint; to textile designers and students who want to add another medium of expression to their backgrounds; to art teachers, therapists, decorators, architects; and all creative persons everywhere.

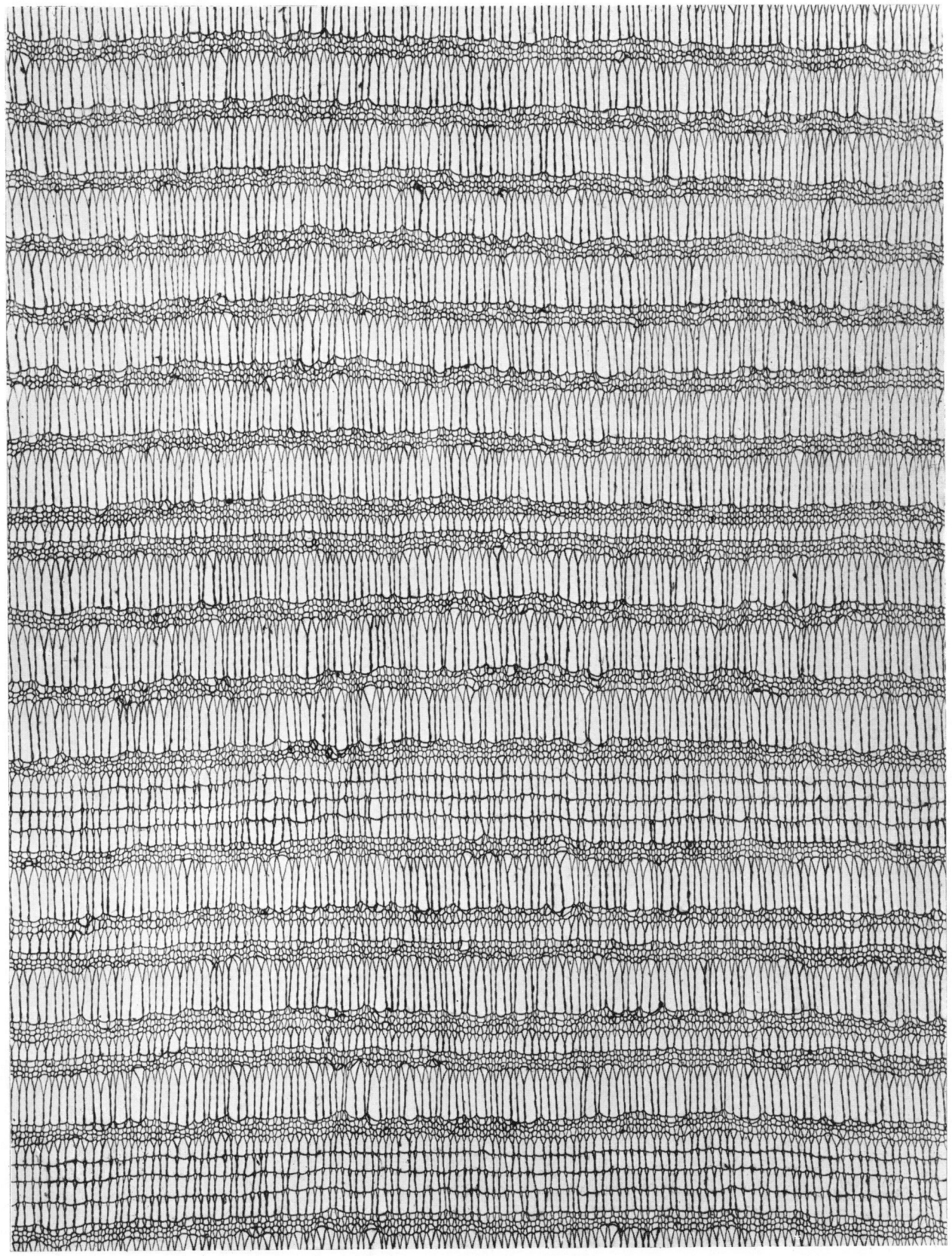

Illus. 3.   Casement, 4′ × 9′, (1963). Knit in 5/1 natural linen with a #7 circular needle. Fancy Crossed Throw and alternating rows of Garter Stitch provide composition of vertical and horizontal lines. See detail (Illus. 29) on page 44.

2. History

A curiosity about knitting of the past will not only make you aware of the vast and resourceful scope of this craft but will also disclose a rich, inspirational source. Museums and historical societies around the world have impressive collections of knitting that astound the viewer by revealing the versatility of the early knitters.

Although the actual origin of knitting is not known, it is said to have been brought to Spain by Arab traders, from where it spread to other European countries. The technique uses two or more needles to produce a fabric. The needles repeatedly interloop a single element—yard, thread, etc.—with itself, each loop securing the corresponding loop in the previous row so that all loops are vertically aligned.

One of the oldest known fragments of single-element construction was found at Dura-Europos (ancient city of Syria) through excavations conducted by Yale University and the French Academy of Inscriptions and Letters. While the fragment appears to have been knit in the Cross Eastern Stitch, current studies suggest that the method of construction may have been cross-knit looping. In that method, a single needle with an eye takes a loop around the crossing of the loop in the previous row. One disadvantage to cross-knit looping is its slowness; it is worked with a short length of yarn, and when that

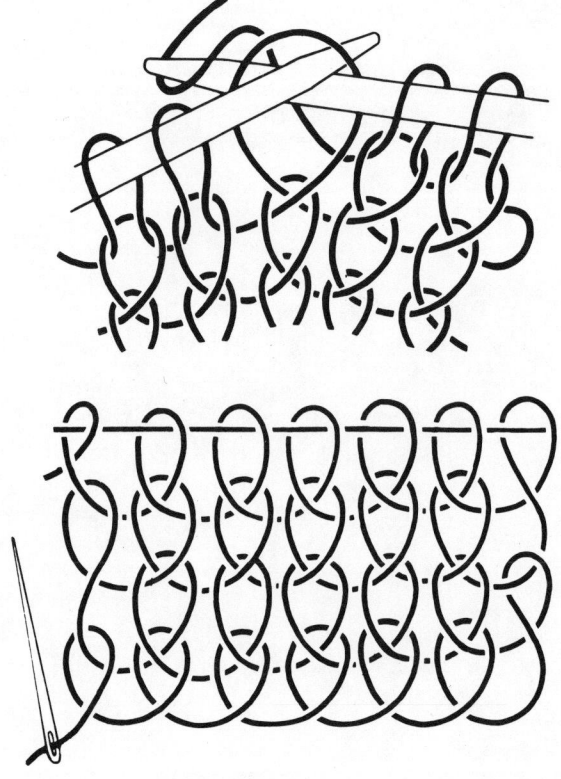

Illus. 4. Diagrams show identical structures produced by two different techniques; crossed Eastern knitting (top), cross-knit looping (bottom).

length is used up, additional yarn is either spliced or spun on.

Even though crossed Eastern knitting and cross-knit looping are two different methods of construction, the fabrics they produce are identical in structure (illus. 4). One difference, which is an important consideration when attempting to analyze a piece, is that knitting is unraveled from the cast-off edge and cross-knit looping from the beginning edge. Therefore, when a fragment lacks top and bottom edges and has no tool or tools attached, it is seldom possible to know for certain which method was used.

Woolen sandal socks, dating from pre-Islamic Egypt (fourth to fifth centuries), that were discovered in tombs of the Copts (Christian descendants of ancient Egyptians) are also thought to be cross-knit looping rather than crossed Eastern knitting, particularly since numerous needles with eyes have been found from that period. Excellent examples of such sandal socks are in the Royal Ontario Museum, Toronto, Canada and the Victoria and Albert Museum, London, England.

The sock shown in illus. 5 is an example of Arabian color knitting (Islamic period, twelfth to fifteenth centuries). The construction is uncrossed knitting (page 40.) and seems to have been worked with four needles. The use of two colors suggests that the yarns could have been held in both hands during the knitting process.

Arabian color knitting has played an important part in the evolution of this craft and, no doubt, was a source of inspiration to knitters of Spain and Italy during the twelfth to sixteenth centuries when color knitting in those countries reached its peak.

The introduction of silk to Europe changed the appearance of knitting. Previously many fabrics had been knit with natural-color wool and had been felted to resemble weaving. (In the felting process, the fabric is soaked in water for days, then pummeled with stones, causing it to shrink and thus to felt; stitches are completely obliterated.) With the increased availability of silk, however, expensive and luxurious clothes were knit in colors and designs that closely resembled brocaded or embossed fabrics. Gold and silver metal threads were often used to knit areas or to outline patterns.

Illus. 5. Example of Arabian color knitting (twelfth to fifteenth centuries). Top of a blue and white cotton sock. (Collection of the Textile Museum, Washington, D.C.)

An example of color knitting during the sixteenth century in Italy is the pair of bishop's gloves shown in Illus. 6. (The Spanish also were knitting ecclesiastical gloves of equal beauty during this period.) This pair is laced at the sides and is knit in crimson silk and gold thread. There is an added decorative touch of gold tassels at the wrists. On the back of each glove is a sacred monogram.

Illus. 6. Example of color knitting from sixteenth-century Italy. Bishop's gloves, 11½″ × 6″. Crimson silk and gold thread. (Collection of The Metropolitan Museum of Art, Rogers Fund, 1926.)

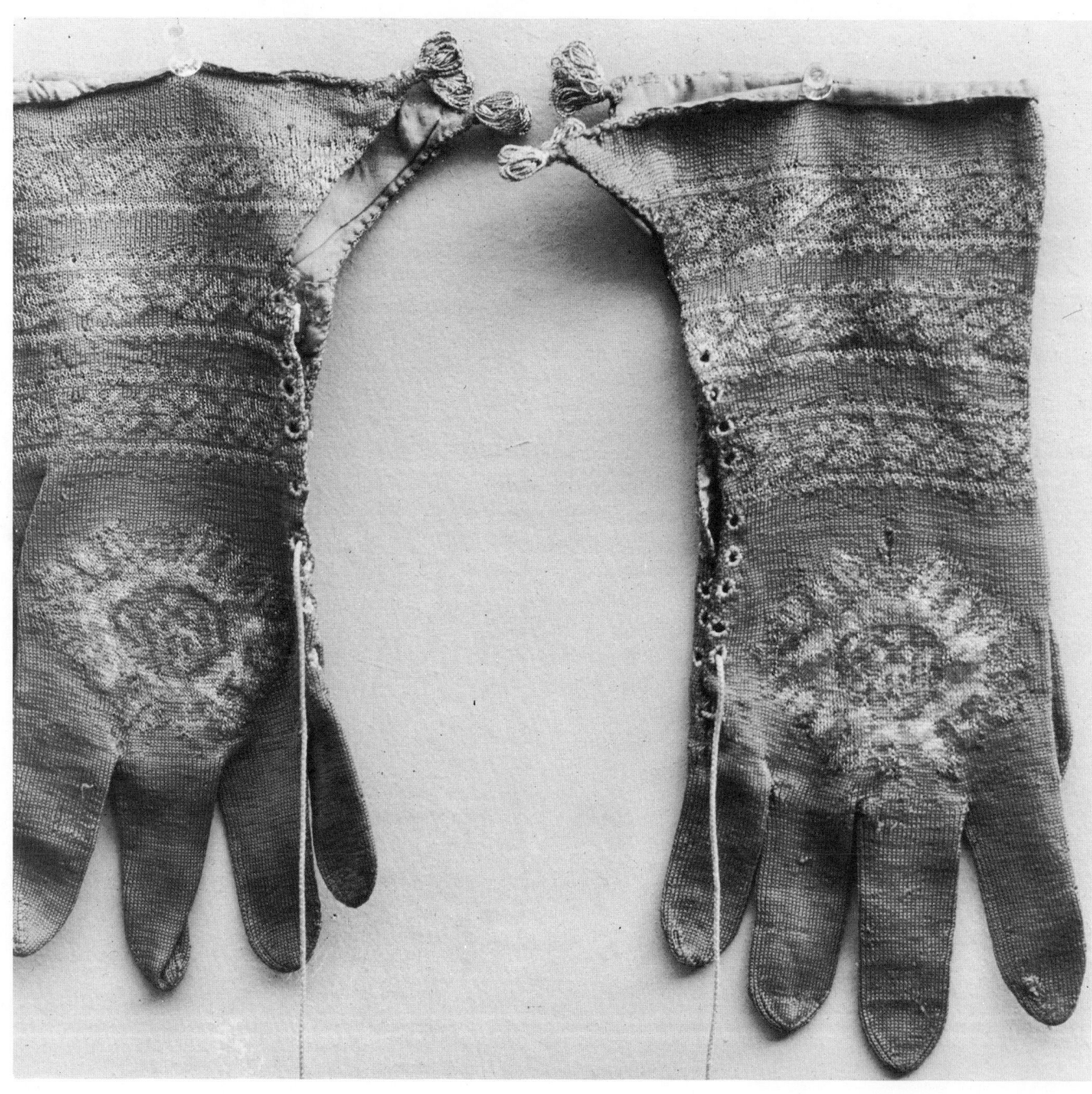

With the thriving of the color tradition in Italy, many beautiful fabrics continued to be knit, most particularly handsome coats for men that were patterned in floral designs and used silk and metal threads. A fine example of pattern knitting during the first half of the sixteenth century is the sleeveless waistcoat from Venice (illus. 7). The ground color is a golden yellow and is in the Stockinette Stitch. The floral pattern is outlined in purple silk, and the pattern itself is of silver gilt thread and yellow silk twisted together. The textural effect of high relief or embossed knitting within the pattern was achieved with a reverse Stockinette Stitch.

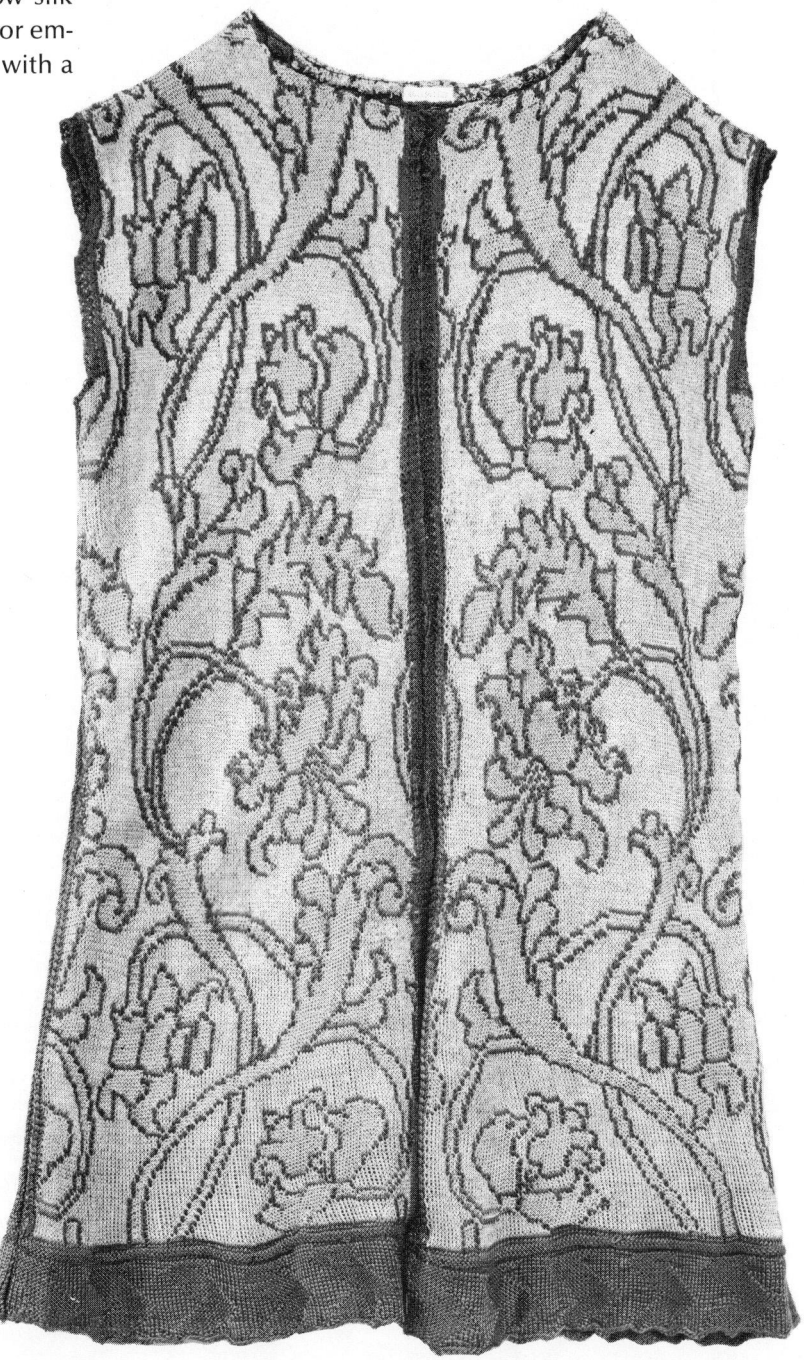

Illus. 7. Example of embossed knitting. Waistcoat has floral pattern in high relief against gold background. Done in gold and purple silk and silver thread. Venice, early sixteenth century. (Collection of The Metropolitan Museum of Art, Fletcher Fund, 1946.)

17

Illus. 8. Example of stranded knitting. Jacket of green and gold silk. Italy or Spain, late sixteenth century. (Collection of The Metropolitan Museum of Art, Hewitt Fund, 1914.)

Illus. 9. Knitted nightcap. Green and white silk. Italy, late seventeenth century. (Collection of The Metropolitan Museum of Art, Rogers Fund, 1926.)

In some instances of color knitting, the yarns were stranded (left "floating") on the back of the fabric. Perhaps the technique of using both English and Continental knitting methods was applied so that the left and right hands could each hold a different color. Such a technique would make it less difficult for knitters to work elaborate patterns. A pillow cover dating from the thirteenth century and found in a coffin of the royal family of Castile in the Convent of Santa Maria de las Huelgas at Burgos, Spain contains motifs in superb stranded knitting: groups of birds, eight-pointed stars, fleurs-de-lis, and geometric patterns. In the sixteenth-century jacket (from Italy or Spain) shown in illus. 8, green and gold silk threads are used with the Garter and Stockinette Stitches. Stranded knitting was also used in the Italian nightcap (illus. 9) of the late seventeenth century. Stylized birds and flowers in green and white silk form the intricately stranded pattern.

Holland, as well as Italy, had a tradition of embossed knitting, and it was through the presentation of a pair of knitted hose to the King of Denmark in the sixteenth century that the craft traveled from Holland to Denmark. The King was delighted with his gift, and he became determined that his own people should become knitters. He invited a group of knitters from Holland to settle outside of Copenhagen, extending to them full rights as citizens, and they, in turn, taught the Danish women how to knit.

Henry VIII received a pair of much-prized hose from France and was fond of boasting that they had been brought over especially from Paris for him to wear. The portrait medallion stockings in illus. 10 are examples of sixteenth-century French hosiery. They are knit with silk in green, blue, yellow, and pink alternating, vertical bands, separated by white bands. The white bands contain the portrait medallion of Jacques Necker (1732–1804), a French financier, and letters spelling out his name.

The Tudor and Elizabethan periods (1485–1603) marked the era of the golden age of knitting, a time of great excellence in craftsmanship. Knitting and hosiery guilds were formed in England and throughout Europe to maintain high standards; requirements and rules for membership were rigid. A young man had to serve an apprenticeship for six years; three years were spent in learning the fundamentals of the craft and another three years in traveling to other countries for exploratory study. At the end of that time, the apprentice had to submit to an examination given by the master craftsmen of his own guild; he had thirteen weeks in which to complete a beret, a woolen shirt, a pair of woolen socks with clocks, and a 5'-x-6' rug of intricate design. Only after the apprentice received the approval of his guild was he admitted as a master knitter.

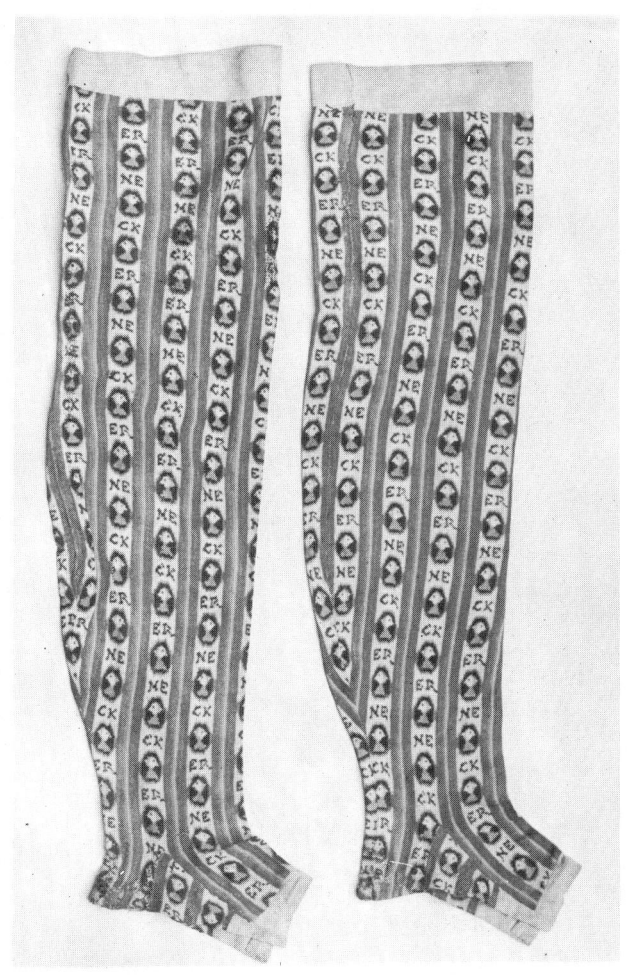

Illus. 10. Knitted silk stockings with portrait medallions. France, eighteenth century. (Collection of The Metropolitan Museum of Art, Rogers Fund, 1925.)

Illus. 11. Knitted wool rug. Germany, late eighteenth century.
(Collection of The Metropolitan Museum of Art, Rogers Fund,
1909.)

An excellent example of the type of rug required of a guild member is shown in illus. 11. It was knit in 1790 by Christof Wagner of Germany. The background is gray with rampant lions in red, unicorns in light brown, and peacocks in dark blue. Design motifs are in shades of rose, blue, crimson, green, yellow, and black. Since guilds in the Upper Rhine and Alsace received their charters from the Hapsburgs, a double-headed eagle, which was the Hapsburg coat of arms, is worked in black in the center of the rug. Most likely a knitting frame, similar to the modern knitting jenny, was used for knitting rugs since work of such weight would have been impossible to hold on two needles.

Wherever knitting was introduced it flourished; colored knitting continued to be popular, particularly in the East, where the colors used were especially brilliant. A late eighteenth-century piece of great interest is the silk sock from Persia shown in illus. 12. The background is black, and the designs are yellow, green, pink, and apricot. The very intricate bird patterns on the front of the sock are outlined with gold metal thread, beautifully worked in chain embroidery. The sole is a diaper pattern.

Illus. 12. Knitted sock. Silk with outlines in chain embroidery of gold metal thread. Persia, late eighteenth century. (Collection of The Metropolitan Museum of Art, Rogers Fund, 1928.)

Illus. 13. Knitted silk stocking. Asia Minor, nineteenth century. (Collection of The Metropolitan Museum of Art, Rogers Fund, 1909.)

A nineteenth-century multicolored silk stocking from Asia Minor (illus. 13) provides interest in that the pattern is carried out in the heel area as well as in the toe. The work in the stocking resembles mid-European and Scandinavian color knitting (the best-known examples of such knitting come from Scandinavia, Spain, Fair Isle, and the Balkan States). A Balkan pattern in the Cross Eastern Stitch was used in the nineteenth-century Greek bag shown in illus. 14.

According to tradition, the people of Fair Isle (an island off the coast of England) learned Spanish color knitting from shipwrecked sailors during the time of the Armada. Another group of islands cut off from England and Scotland by the Atlantic Ocean is Shetland. The delicate lace knitting of Shetland is a wonder to behold, so fine is the handspun thread that is used. The sampler shown in color on page 11, while German in origin, makes use of the types of lace stitches seen in many of the shawls from Shetland. It was knit in 1836 by Maria Flodor and uses cotton thread and glass beads.

The Aran Isles, off the western coast of Ireland, and the ancient fishing ports and villages of Cornwall and Devon also played large roles in the story of knitting. Each port had its own traditional fisherman's sweater, and one could tell where a fisherman was from by the jersey he wore. For everyday wear, a man would don a sweater in plain Stockinette Stitch and, for holidays, one worked in heavy Cables, embossed knitting, and Bobbles. The sweater patterns bear such names as "The Sacred Heart," "Rose of Sharon," "Star of Bethlehem," and "Crown of Glory." Similarly, the intricate lace patterns from Shetland were based on stitches known as "Bird's Eye," "Cat's Paw," "Lace Holes," and so on. A knitter who did nothing else but learn all the patterns used in Shetland shawls and Irish fishermen's sweaters would have a gold mine of ideas to draw on for future knitting projects.

Illus. 14. Detail of knitted wool bag. Use of the Crossed Eastern Stitch. Greece, late nineteenth century. (Collection of the author.)

Knitting in the United States during the period of colonization was done primarily to make plain clothing; there was little time in the lives of those busy people for the decorative. Not only did women knit, but girls six and seven years of age were expected to be proficient in the craft, and boys were required to knit suspenders. As a young man, Benedict Arnold went among the Dutch at the head of the Hudson River, and into Canada, peddling knit goods from Connecticut. Knitters at this time did excellent work and eventually made such goods as bedspreads, lace, and rugs.

The sample shown in Illus. 15 was knit in about 1937 in order to show the method used in 1846 to make a rug. Bits of cloth were worked into a knitted background to make the pile. Some rugs even used old knit pieces cut into strips for pile. Beaded bags were popular projects in the nineteenth century, and the patterns were so made that each bead fell into its proper place during the knitting process.

The Hopi Indians of the Southwest learned how to knit from the Spaniards who came to America in the sixteenth century. A pair of knit leggings done by Hopi men is shown in Illus. 16. They are knit of white cotton. Leggings such as these would be worn by the men as part of their dress or ceremonial costumes.

Illus. 15. Knitted rug sample. Knit in 1937 by Miss Maude M. Fierce as an example of rug making in the United States in 1846. (Collection of The Smithsonian Institution, Washington, D.C.)

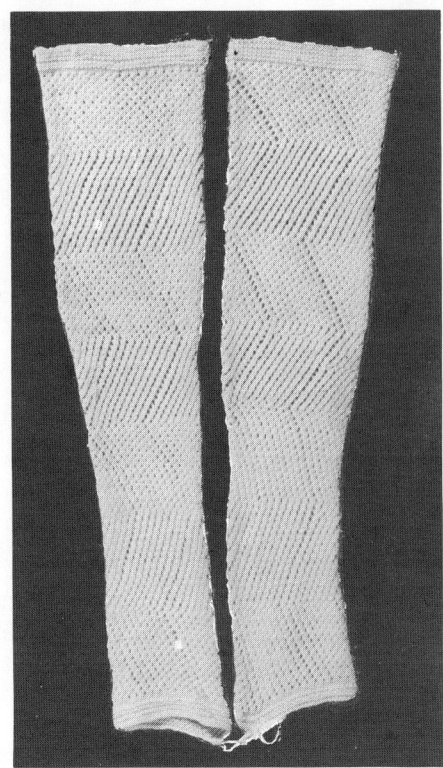

Illus. 16. Knitted leggings of white cotton made by Hopi Indians. (Collection of the Museum of Northern Arizona, Flagstaff.)

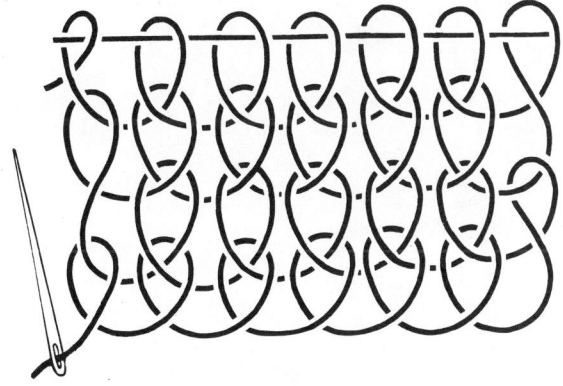

Illus. 17. Cross-knit looping, used in pre-Conquest Peru.

Illus. 18. Fragment of a tubular turban in alpaca. Cross-knit looping. Peru, Paracas period. (Collection of The Textile Museum, Washington, D.C.)

Illus. 19.   Fragment of a Peruvian turban from the Paracas period, done in alpaca with cross-knit looping. (Collection of The Textile Museum, Washington, D.C.)

Illus. 20.   Knitted copy of the Peruvian fragment in Illus. 19. Done in cotton by the late Louise Bellinger. (Collection of The Textile Museum, Washington, D.C.)

Parts of South America also contributed in an essential way to the knitting tradition. One of the richest sources of inspiration to the knitter is the cross-knit looping done by Peruvians of the Paracas and Nazca periods (third century B.C. to third century A.D.). This single-element work closely resembles crossed Eastern knitting but is actually cross-knit looping since the former was not known in Peru until after the Spanish conquest (1533). As had been pointed out, either method will produce a fabric that is identical to the eye.

A fragment of a turban from the Paracas period is shown in illus. 18. It was worked in many colors of alpaca yarn—tan, brown, dark gray, pink, rose, red, red-brown, salmon, yellow, dark green, green, blue, and purple-tan. Its design is of a mythological nature, and its motif is a stylized cat face. The main portion of the fabric is tubular; the figures repeat on the back. The turban was started over a cord, and work progressed as each successive row of loops was built onto the preceding row. When colors were not needed, they were carried over into the inside of the tube. Another fragment of a Peruvian turban from the Paracas period is shown in illus. 19.

The detail of a woven shawl from the Nazca period (illus. 21) shows a border of birds worked in cross-knit looping and alpaca yarn. Unfortunately many of the birds no longer have their beaks. However, in this example, the close resemblance of cross-knit looping to crossed Eastern knitting is very striking.

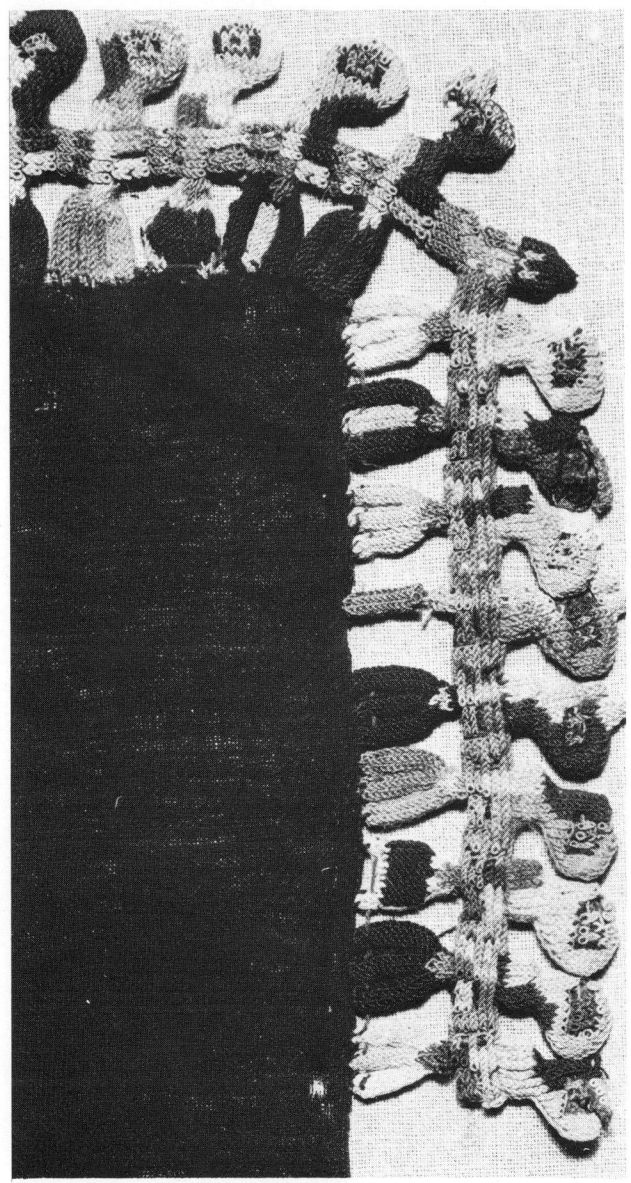

Illus. 21. Woven shawl fragment with border of birds in cross-knit looping. Peru, Nazca period. (Collection of The Textile Museum, Washington, D.C.)

Peruvian gauze weave in its many variations has been a great source of inspiration to me. Gossamer in appearance, some are made of overspun cotton (cotton that has been spun until it kinks and twists over itself) in natural, white, or brown; others are of single weight. One of the pieces in my collection, a design of a highly stylized cat, is also made of overspun cotton.

The cotton fragment shown in illus. 22 is particularly interesting; presumably the fabric was tie-dyed. It is certainly easy to see how such work of open and solid areas can influence lace patterns in knitting. The fragment in illus. 23 shows clearly that the piece was worked in two different weights of yarn. It is "knotless netting" worked in overspun cotton and embroidered with a heavier cotton yarn. The most geometrical and stylized of the three gauze weaves is shown in illus. 24. Its design would certainly lend itself to reproduction by knitting. Such outstanding textiles provide a never-ending source of study to all textile designers. Since there were no written records of work done in previous generations for the ancient Peruvians to refer to, their intuitive ability to produce such inventive work continues to be amazing.

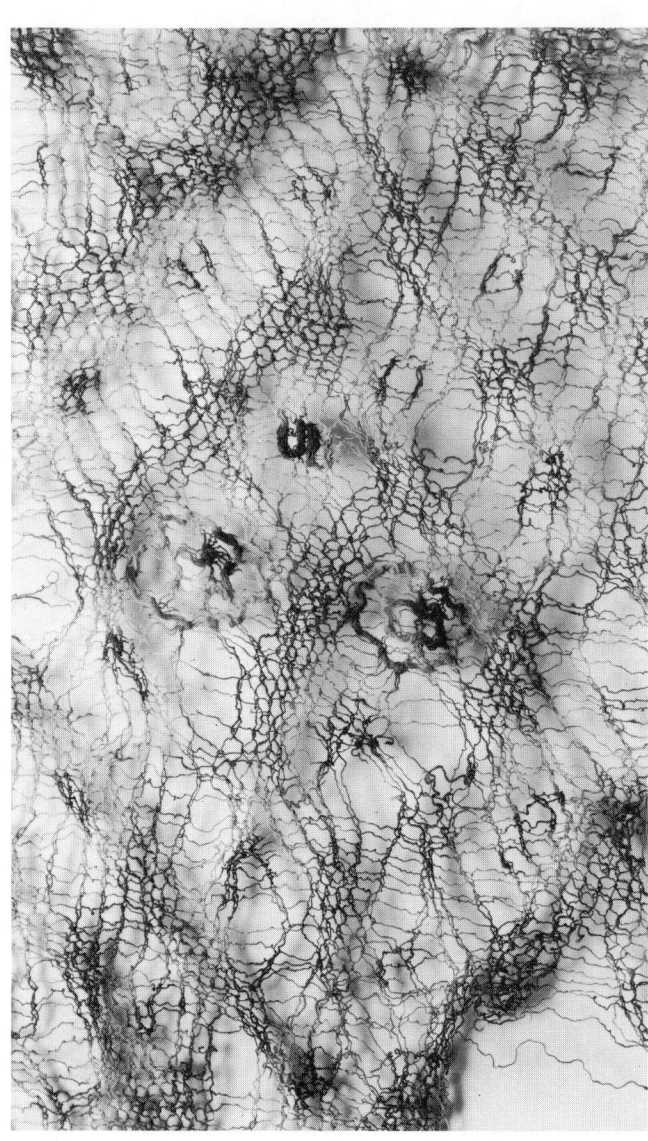

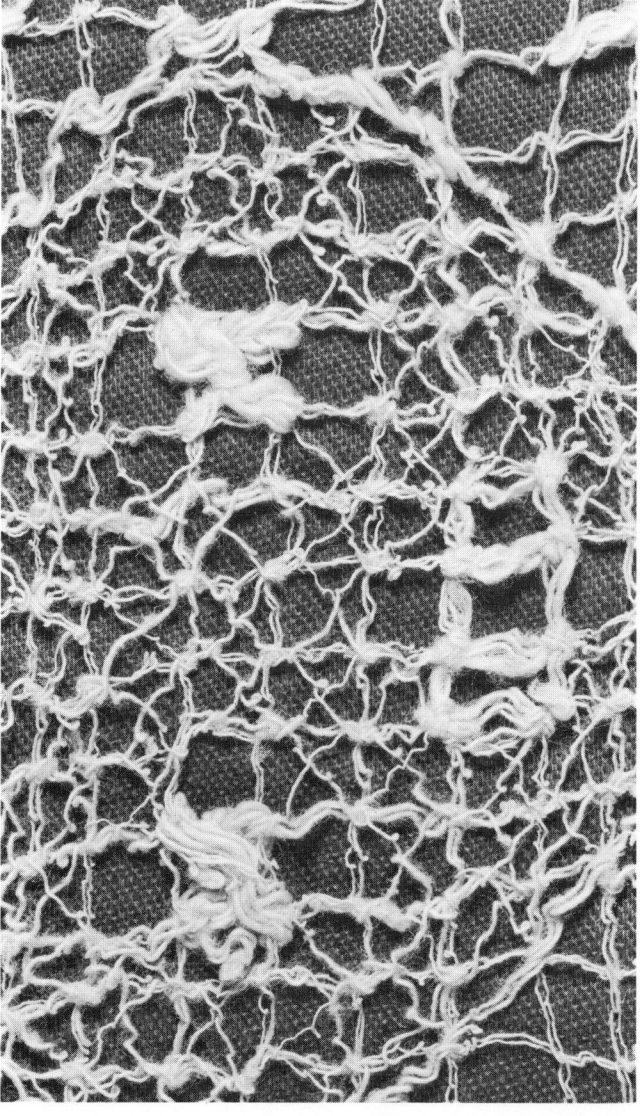

Illus. 22. Peruvian cotton gauze weave (detail); fabric presumably tie-dyed. Lacy construction is ideal source of ideas for creative knitting. (Collection of The Brooklyn Museum.)

Illus. 23. Peruvian cotton gauze weave (detail), embroidered with a heavy yarn. (Collection of The Brooklyn Museum.)

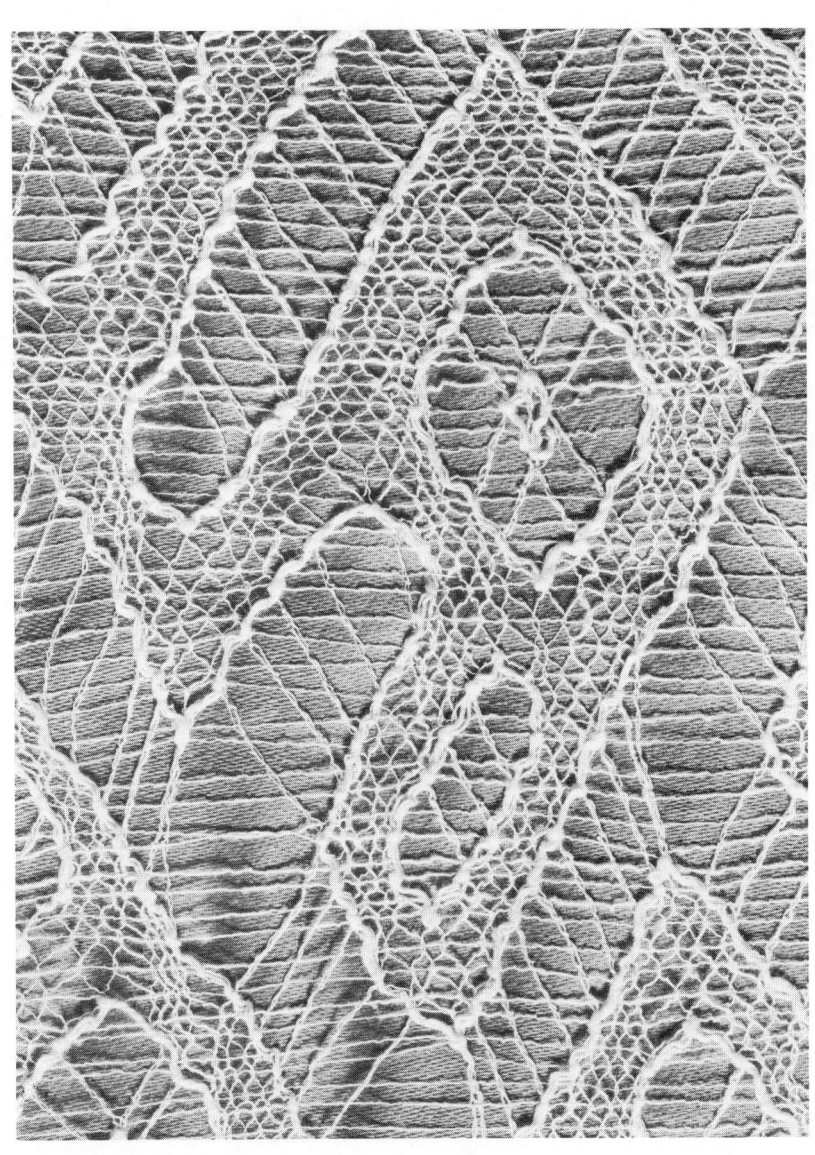

Illus. 24. Example of highly geometrical pattern in a Peruvian cotton gauze weave. The heavy outlines are embroidered. (Collection of The Brooklyn Museum.)

The people of post-Conquest Peru continued the tradition of doing beautiful work, but with a difference, for they had learned knitting. The shepherd's bag (Illus. 25) with a tied fringe on the bottom was knit with alpaca as was the shaped cap (Illus. 26) from the same period. The variation of geometric shapes in the latter blend well with the stylized animals that are worked throughout. They are repeated in the top section which ends with a brushlike tassel.

Knitting of the past is a constant, inspirational joy—and full of surprises. Even with this rich past, there are even richer possibilities for an exciting future.

Illus. 25. Knitted bag of alpaca. Southern Highlands, post-Conquest Peru. (Collection of The Textile Museum, Washington, D.C.)

Illus. 26. Knitted cap of alpaca. Southern Highlands, post-Conquest Peru. (Collection of The Textile Museum, Washington, D.C.)

3. Equipment

The basic tools of knitting are simple, inexpensive, and convenient to obtain. Many readers of this book will already have some of the items listed. Most important is a good selection of knitting needles. You also need several sizes of crochet hooks and cable needles, stitch holders, ring markers, and blunt scissors. Graph paper is necessary if you intend to plot patterns, and a notebook is useful to jot down ideas, yarn information, and so on.

Celotex is recommended as a surface for blocking. It is an insulating material and is obtainable in sheets measuring 4′ × 8′. The sheets can be cut to desired sizes. You will need wrapping paper to cover the Celotex, and masking tape or gummed, paper tape to secure the wrapping paper to the blocking board. A tape measure, a ruler, and rustproof 1½″ T pins (sometimes called wig pins) are useful. The pins are available at notion counters.

Additional items are assorted objects—such as beads, flat rocks, pebbles, seed pods, and mica—that can be incorporated into a knitted structure. A shoe box with a dowel inserted in it makes a convenient spool rack.

NEEDLES

Straight knitting needles are made from almost any material—wood, bone, silver, tortoise shell, plastic, metal, and so on. Double-pointed needles and circular ones are made from plastic or metal, and the latter can be a combination of both materials. Plastic and metal needles are the ones most commonly used; the choice of one over the other is, in most instances, a matter for personal preference. Regardless of the materials the needles are made from, their points must be smooth and well tapered. Blunt-pointed needles have no place in the creative knitter's workbasket. The need for good points will become obvious when you begin knitting with linen, rug wool, silk, synthetics, and other materials that have no stretch factor.

In experimenting with a variety of yarns, I have found that some are apt to be slippery and are better knit with wooden needles, since there is then more control over the yarn. Leather, also seems to knit easier with these needles. You can make your own wooden needles from dowels if you wish. If the dowels are thin enough, their ends can be sharpened in a pencil sharpener; otherwise shave or whittle the ends to well-tapered points. Then sand the dowels until they are completely smooth and finish in any manner desired.

My own collection of needles is extensive and contains duplicate sizes since I am apt to be working on several pieces at the same time, sometimes using the same size needles. Usually I choose 10-inch metal needles for making samples and 24- to 36-inch (depending on the weight of the piece) plastic circular needles for other work. I never use straight needles longer than 10 inches because their ends catch on the arms of chairs and the weight of work on them is awkward. With a circular needle this weight rests in your lap.

YARNS

To a creative knitter, yarn is probably the primary source of inspiration. There is a rich variety of yarns already available and, to these, newly developed ones are constantly being added. Each yarn may differ in properties and characteristics—texture, strength, weight, durability, elasticity, tactile quality, and the ability to absorb light. To know how the yarns differ is important, for this will have a bearing on their selection.

Probably the best way to begin to know the yarns is to make experimental samples using different ones. They can then be evaluated for their possibilities and limitations and their suitability for certain stitches and constructions. For example, yarn that has a minimum of stretch to it is the most satisfactory for wall hangings since there is enough of a stretch factor in the stitch construction itself.

It was through experimenting with synthetics that I found I personally did not respond enough to them to want to work with them. (Perhaps at a later date I will experiment with them again to see if my response has changed.) I feel that natural fibers have a resiliency and character to them that can never be matched by the man-made ones. However, what I consider to be the limitations of synthetics should not prevent anyone else from experimenting, and working, with them. For the most part, I use the handweaving yarns such as linen, silk, wool, and mohair. Their selection is varied, and they are effective in expressing the diverse qualities in the stitches.

Linen varies greatly in quality and texture and has a wide latitude of twists, spins, and colors (soft-spun linen and singles are the most versatile). It has a beautiful finish and sheen, combines well with other materials, as can be seen by the pieces in this book, and possesses a marked strength and diversity of character that few other yarns can match. It also has exceptional durability; a piece knit with linen blocks well and will retain its shape even after hanging for a long period of time.

Linen in its natural state (commonly called "gray unfinished") contains a large portion of gummy resinous pectins and has to be cleaned thoroughly in order to remove this matter. The yarn is skeined, then boiled in hot water with detergent and a small amount of ammonia. In some cases, the water may have to be changed and the yarn reboiled. The yarn must be completely rinsed before drying. I learned the hard way about the necessity for washing gray unfinished linen before combining it with other materials in a knitted piece; if all the pectins are not removed, they will bleed into the other yarns and stain them. It is almost impossible to remove these stains from silk or wool yarn. Also, dye will not take evenly if any pectins remain. However, if gray unfinished linen is the only yarn used in the piece, then, instead of cleaning the yarn beforehand, the piece can be boiled after it has been knit, or, at least, washed well in hot soapy water. Other linen, natural or dyed, is available in what is called a "finished yarn." No boiling is necessary.

Silk is a highly favored yarn but difficult to find because of its limited quantity. Some handweaving supply houses carry it, but it has to be searched for. Its use in a piece adds a high luster and an elegance not achieved by the use of any other yarn. The other desirable qualities of silk are high tensile strength and some elasticity.

Wool comes in a great variety of weights and twists; its characteristic qualities are springiness and softness. Some wools have a great luster and sheen, while others are dull and heavy by comparison; but all radiate a special kind of warmth. An interesting property of wool is its natural tendency toward felting.

In "Popcorn" (Illus. 27) linen, silk, and wool are used in three distinct areas, giving the piece an interest created not only by the different stitches used but also by the sharp contrast of the materials next to one another.

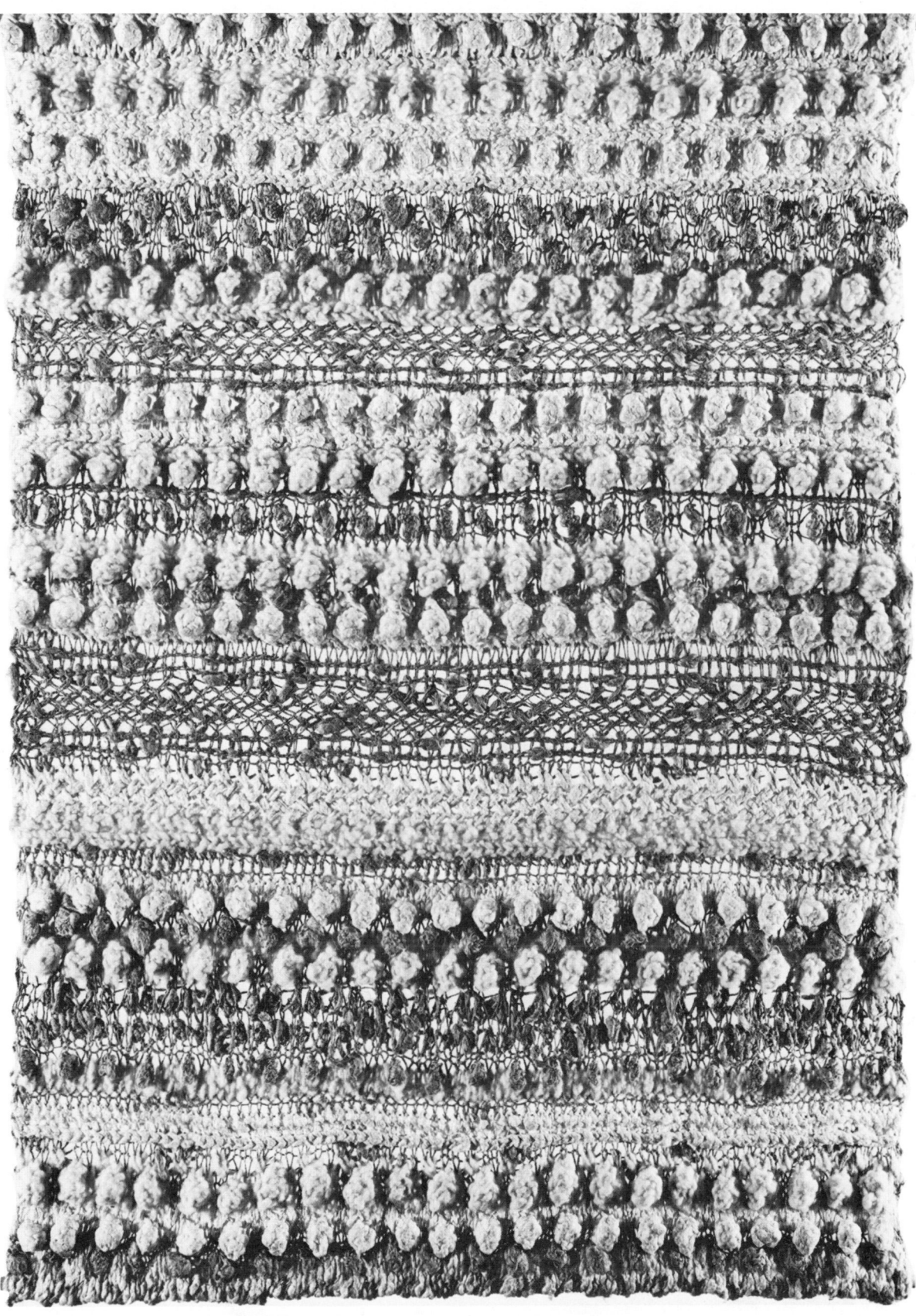

Illus. 27. "Popcorn," wall hanging, 28" × 36", (1967). Natural slub linen, white silk and natural, handspun wool. See detail on page 58. Shown at "Wall Hangings" travelling exhibit of the Museum of Modern Art, 1968.

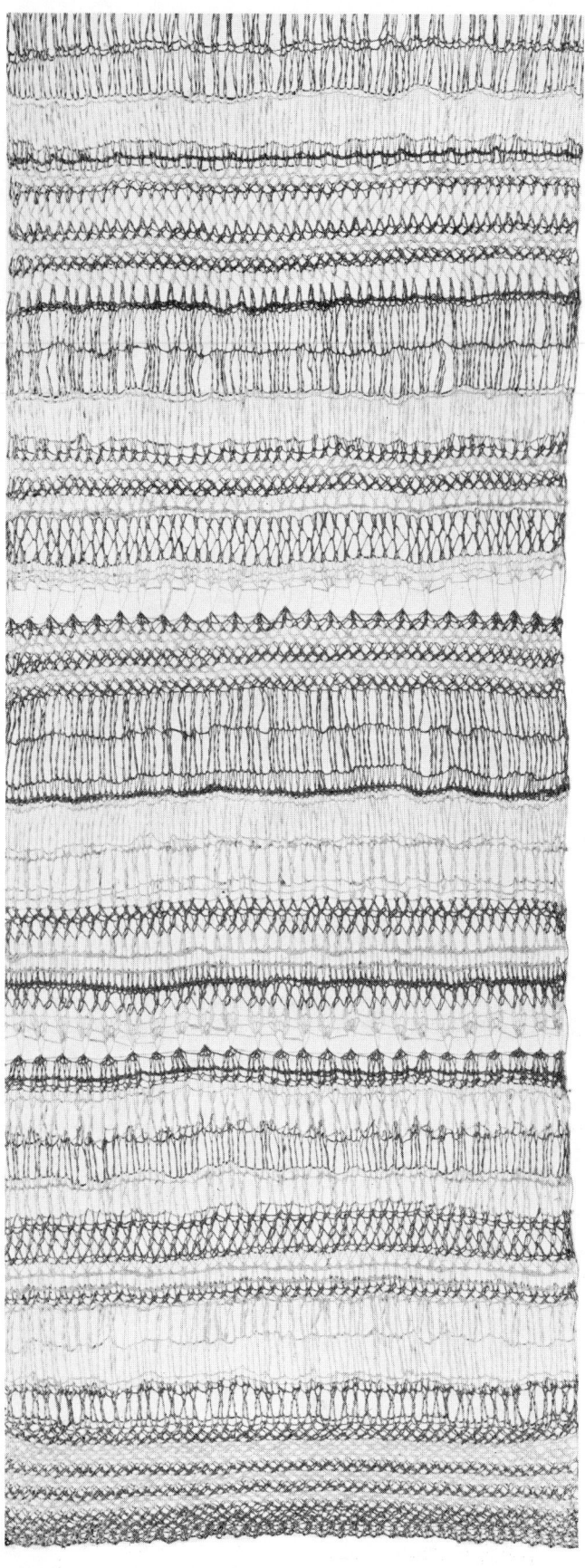

Illus. 28. "More Variations," wall hanging, approx. 20" × 50", (1967). Greek, handspun, natural silk and 5/1 natural linen. See detail on page 73.

Mohair, the long, silky hair of the Angora goat, is soft and smooth. It has a great luster and a spring to it not found in wool. If you want to use it for lacy constructions, it should be considered in combination with another yarn in order to add stability to the piece. It is combined with linen in Sample 3 (page 100) and in "Many Openings" (page 78). There is no problem when mohair is used alone in a closely knit fabric, such as in the pillow on page 107. One section of the pillow is worked in handspun mohair and the other in handspun wool. Many handspun yarns have a distinctive textural quality caused by unevenness in the spinning. This quality adds interest to even the simplest of stitches.

Yarns are also spun from metallic fibers. A fine metallic yarn, in gold or silver, adds a subtle sheen to the piece. There are several examples of its use in this book, but it can be most clearly seen in Sample 8 (page 105) and in "Middle Ages" (page 91). A sampling of the application of other materials such as Fiberglas, monofilament fibers, synthetic straw, and leather can be seen in Chapter 6, "Experiments."

Combining yarns for a more interesting mixture can be seen in various constructions throughout the book—in Sample 8, for example, metallic yarn was combined with synthetic straw. Yarn can also be doubled or tripled when a heavier weight is desired.

There are also novelty yarns. These are yarns which have been combined and then twisted together in such a manner as to give uneven and irregular surface characteristics. There are many varieties of these yarns and they can add to the textural interest of a piece once their use is understood. One such yarn is slub linen, which creates its own pattern when it is knit, as can be seen in "Popcorn." Another is linen bouclé. When this yarn is knit by itself it seems to lack character because it competes too much with the stitches. However, it is more successful when used together with a single-ply yarn and gives an interesting texture.

One of the many advantages for the traveling craftsman is the opportunity to gather unusual materials. It is difficult to resist the combination of fibers and textures and twists seen at yarn stores in foreign countries and at out-of-the-way native markets and bazaars; these materials seem so different or better or more exotic than anything found at home.

Many years ago, in Kalamata, Greece, I bought only a couple of pounds of handspun silk. The yardage must have been tremendous, because I have knit many pieces with it. It is used in "Circles" (page 47) and in "More Variations" (Illus. 28) as well as in other pieces. Handspun wool from Central America is used in "Popcorn."

4.   Blocking and Finishing

Proper blocking is important whether the knitting is conventional or creative, but it has a special importance in creative knitting. Rather than chance being disappointed with the end result, make and block a sample piece first. That will enable you to tell if the yarn is compatible with the stitches and patterns used. If the sample appears muddled looking, change the yarn to suit the design or change the needle size to create a more open effect. If the sample appears crisp and clear in its design, proceed with the larger piece. Experience in creative knitting is the best teacher.

In conventional knitting, the yarns used have a resiliency that results in an even stitch, but the yarns used in creative knitting have relatively no stretch factor so that there is apt to be more unevenness in the knitting. This unevenness will be taken care of by careful blocking in most cases. This is not to say that sloppy craftsmanship will be corrected by blocking; no amount of blocking will remedy this fault.

As mentioned in Chapter 3, an excellent blocking surface can be made from Celotex. It is lightweight and rigid, yet porous enough for pins to be easily inserted. If there is a storage or space problem, the regular 4' × 8' sheets can be cut to smaller, more convenient sizes and then, when needed for blocking, as many boards as necessary can be lined up next to one another. Boards cut to 2' × 4' are easy to handle and can be placed side by side until you have the necessary size blocking surface.

To prepare the board as a blocking surface, cover the top of it with wrapping paper, pull the paper tightly over the edges and tape it down. Mark off the paper top into 1-inch squares. These squares are meant as guides when the material is being stretched along its width and length. If more than one board is being used, place them side by side before covering them with paper that you have already marked off in squares. In that way the squares will be perfectly aligned. When more than one board is used, the marked paper may be pinned down rather than taped so that it can be taken off the board after blocking is completed, rolled up and stored to be used again. Small boards can be stored for reuse with the paper still in place.

By measuring the blocked sample, you will be able to tell to approximately what width and length to stretch the piece on the first pinning. Even if you do not make a sample for every piece, you can measure a sample that was made with the same yarn and the same number needle. For the most part, my knitting is not charted, and, if you have not charted yours, the best you can do is approximate the exact size of the finished piece. If 100 stitches have been cast on, and the gauge is 5 stitches to the inch, then the finished piece would be about 20 inches wide.

Only experience will give the complete answer to the blocking question. For example, when I first began to knit, I had a great tendency to stretch the pieces too wide, and after they had hung for a while they began to sag. This is especially true with linen, since it is very sensitive to changes in humidity. Pieces like "The Creature" (page 60) that have irregular edges present new considerations to the usual blocking method. There, repinning is done until the piece takes its natural shape.

If a piece has been knit with linen or a combination of linen and silk, dip it in a medium-strength solution of starch before blocking to insure that it will hold its shape. After dipping, squeeze out as much moisture as possible; the knitted work must be wet but not soppy. Then, holding the piece in your hands, stretch it along its length and width before putting it face up on the blocking board. While the piece may seem too stiff when it is removed from the blocking board, it will become less so after it has been hanging for a while. A stronger or weaker starch solution can be used depending on the effect you wish to achieve.

If a piece has been knit with wool or mohair and is loosely constructed, it will require careful handling to keep it from stretching. Fold the piece to a size that is easy to handle, then immerse it in water that has had fabric softener added. Remove the knitted piece and squeeze out as much water as possible. Roll in a terry cloth towel to remove any excess moisture before blocking. These directions apply particularly to stoles and blankets.

Rustproof 1½" T pins are recommended for blocking. They are put in at an angle, slanting away from the edge of the piece. For the first pinning, pin every 2 inches. The beginning edge is pinned first as this has the least amount of stretch along its width. The left edge is pinned next, since this has the least amount of stretch along its length. Pin for about 4 inches up the left side. Pinning is then done on alternate sides, and the piece is pulled along its length from time to time. When all sides are pinned, it is time to go back

and pin every ½ inch. The piece must be pulled taut but not so much as to distort it. It remains pinned until it is completely dry.

To finish the knitted construction as a wall hanging, after it is blocked and dried, sew in a hem and a heading. The heading is for the insertion of a bar or a rod from which the piece is hung. A small, lightweight rod may be inserted into the hem to stabilize the fabric and to keep the piece hanging straight. By studying the completed pieces in this book, you will see that some hems and headings are narrow while others are wide. This is usually a design factor that is dictated by the size of the piece. Some pieces that are long or heavy ask for a wide heading and the insertion of a large dowel.

Dowels can be sanded and either stained or painted to augment the design of the piece. If you have access to handsome pieces of wood, you can probably fashion some very interesting rods. Plastic rods can also be used, or those of wrought iron, or other metals. Rods can enhance a hanging, but proper balance between the two must be a consideration. Using an elaborate rod for a pattern that is also elaborate would be a mistake. On the whole, I have found that the simpler the bar, the better.

The actual hanging of the knitted work can be something of an event, so consider carefully where to hang it, keeping in mind that the beauty of the piece can be enhanced or detracted from by its surroundings and by the way in which it is displayed. Try hanging the piece against a wall that will complement it by lending some contrast in color. In some cases, hanging a piece slightly away from the wall creates shadow patterns that are easily observed through the openwork of the piece. Such patterns change according to variations in both the quality and the direction of the light, thus adding to the design details of the piece itself.

If you decide to store the wall hanging or plan to ship it, remove the rods and roll the knit piece carefully on a cardboard tube with tissues between the layers. Never fold knit pieces.

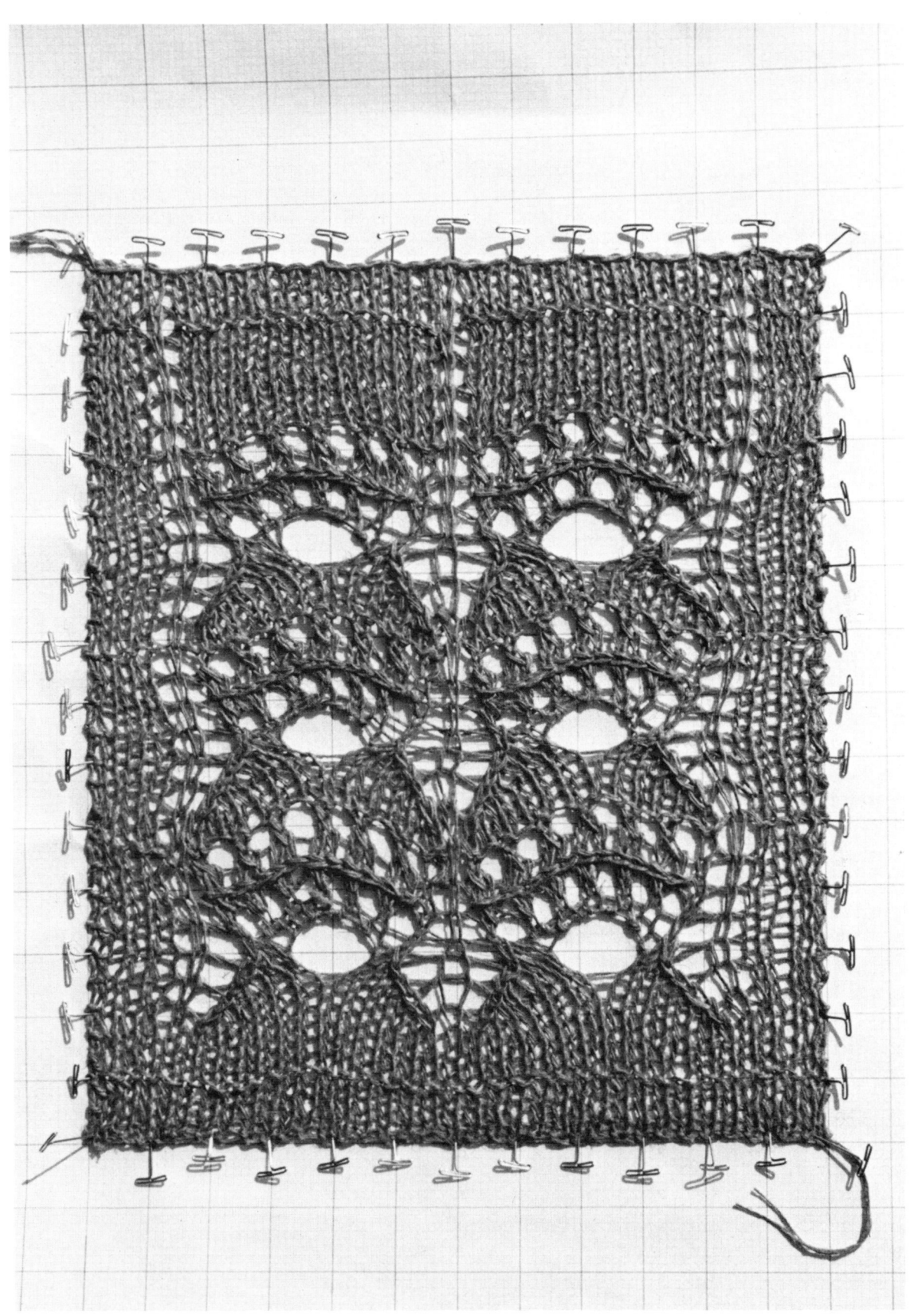

Blocking the sample. Sample is dipped into a medium starch solution, stretched gently until taut, and pinned to blocking board to dry. Lace Diadem Pattern, three repeats with variations.

Knitting Terms

K	knit
P	purl
st	stitch
sts	stitches
YO	yarn over
Sl	slip stitch
Sl pw	slip stitch purlwise
psso	pass slip stitch over
dec	decrease
KSB	knit into stitch below
tog	together
dp	double pointed needle
PR	purl reverse

5. Stitches and Patterns

All knitters are familiar with the dos and don'ts which are so rigid a part of knitting instruction—with the books that say, "Never knit into the back of the stitch" and "There is only one way to throw yarn." ("Throw" describes the motion of bringing yarn over or under the needle after the needle has been inserted into the stitch.) Such clamps on originality have not only inhibited the growth of knitting as a creative medium but have ignored the curiosity and imagination of the individual as well.

A creative knitter—or any creative person for that matter—is very apt to counter the statement "You can't do this and that" with "Why can't I?" and will go ahead and try. But those who are unsure of themselves will not do so and thus will compromise their abilities. It is unfortunate that the beginning knitter has been so restricted, for there is more than one way to insert the needle and to throw yarn, and they are included in this chapter.

Just as important as knowing that you can try anything is knowing what it is you are doing. From speaking to knitters at workshops I have held around the country and from reading their letters to me, I have learned that many of them do not understand the stitches in relation to their positions on the needle. *Stitch position on the left needle determines the direction the right needle takes in entering the stitch.* This enormously important point is that simple, and it will make all the difference in your knitting.

Once you have mastered the difference between uncrossed and crossed stitches and understand fully the directions of the stitches on the needle, you will no longer find yourself twisting them inadvertently, and your knitting will benefit by becoming more even and consistent.

The text and the detailed diagrams which follow show how the stitch movement varies according to how yarn is thrown on either the knit or purl rows. Each way is correct, but each places the stitch on the needle at a different angle. In all of this, one dictum does remain: yarn to the back for knit and yarn to the front for purl.

Uncrossed Eastern Stitch. To knit a stitch in the Uncrossed Eastern manner, the needle is inserted into the *back* of the stitch, and the yarn is thrown *over* the needle. See Diagram 1A.

By studying the diagram you will see that the stitches on the right needle and those remaining on the left needle are all facing in the same direction. Note also that the left side of the stitch faces towards the front of the needle.

To purl, the needle is again inserted into the *back* of the stitch, but the yarn is thrown *under* the needle. See Diagram 1B. Note the direction of the stitches in this diagram also and compare with your own knitting.

Crossed Eastern Stitch (*Left over Right*). The needle movements here are the reverse of the Uncrossed Eastern, but the yarn is thrown in the same manner.

To knit, the needle is inserted into the *front* of the stitch, and the yarn is thrown *over* the needle. See Diagram 2A. To purl, the needle is again inserted into the *front* of the stitch, but the yarn is thrown *under* the needle. See Diagram 2B. Notice that the stitches are now crossing left over right.

Cross knitting is historically thought to be the oldest form of knitting. Since this stitch results in a tight, firm fabric, it was most likely the one used to knit caps that were ultimately to be felted. It was also the stitch used for making the Greek bag which is shown in detail on page 23.

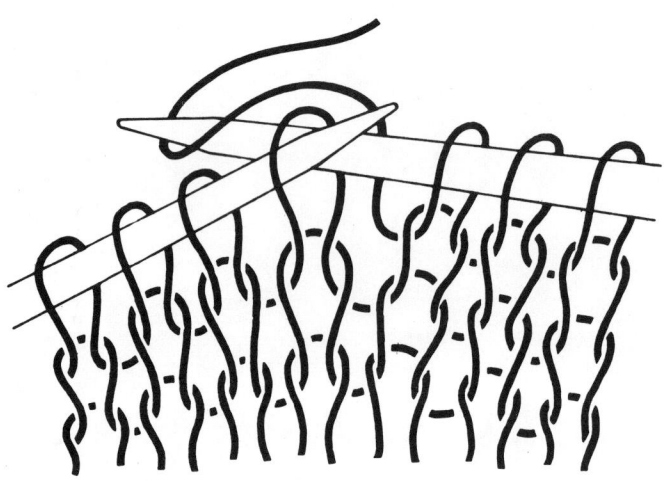

Diagram 1A. **Uncrossed Eastern Knit Stitch.** Needle inserted into *back* of stitch; yarn thrown *over* the needle.

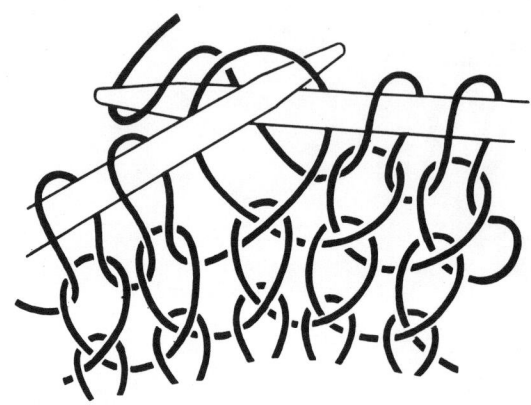

Diagram 2A. **Crossed Eastern Knit Stitch.** Needle inserted into *front* of stitch; yarn thrown *over* needle.

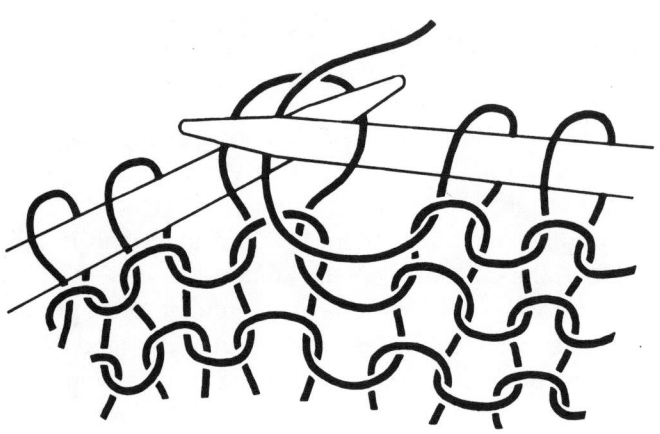

Diagram 1B. **Uncrossed Eastern Purl Stitch.** Needle inserted into *back* of stitch; yarn thrown *under* needle.

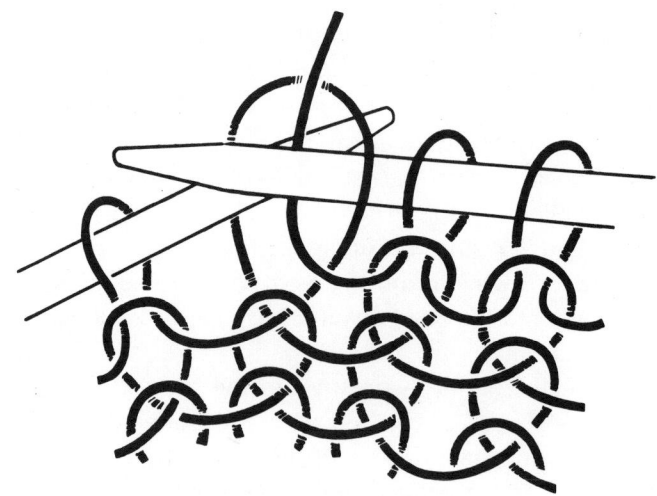

Diagram 2B. **Crossed Eastern Purl Stitch.** Needle inserted into *front* of stitch; yarn thrown *under* needle.

Uncrossed Western Stitch. This stitch is the one that all knitters are familiar with. Both knitting and purling are done into the *front* of the stitch. The yarn is brought *under* and *over* the needle to knit (see Diagram 3A), and *over* and *under* to purl (see Diagram 3B).

As you will notice in the diagrams, the stitches are on the needle with the left side of the stitch facing towards the back, instead of towards the front as in Uncrossed Eastern.

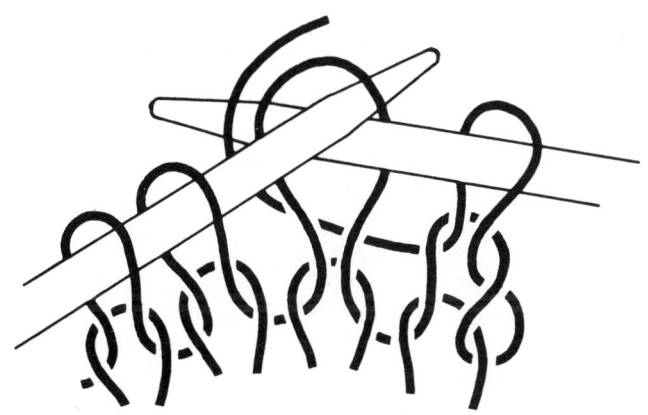

Diagram 3A. **Uncrossed Western Knit Stitch.** Needle inserted into *front* of stitch; yarn brought *under* and *over* needle.

Diagram 3B. **Uncrossed Western Purl Stitch.** Needle inserted into *front* of stitch; yarn brought *over* and *under* needle.

Crossed Western Stitch (*Right over Left*). The needle is inserted into the *back* of the stitch for both knit and purl. See Diagrams 4A and 4B. The yarn movements are the same as for the Uncrossed Stitch. The stitch will now be crossed right over left and can be compared with the Crossed Eastern Stitch, which is the left-over-right cross.

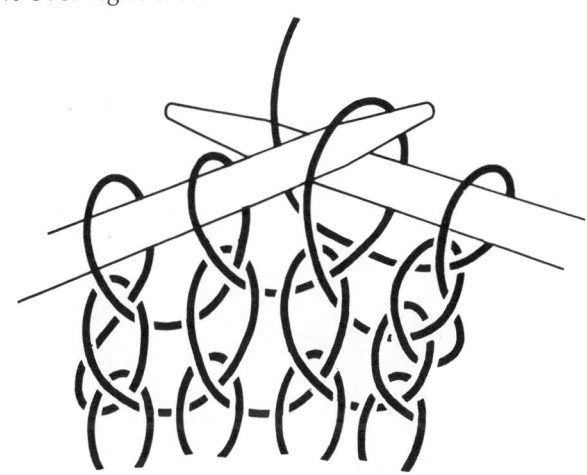

Diagram 4A. **Crossed Western Knit Stitch.** Needle inserted into *back* of stitch; yarn brought *under* and *over* needle.

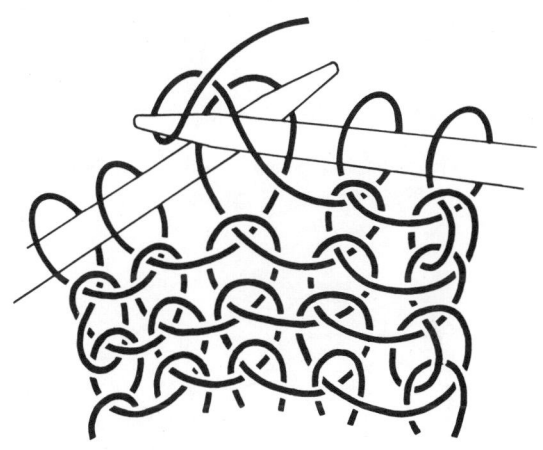

Diagram 4B. **Crossed Western Purl Stitch.** Needle inserted into *back* of stitch; yarn brought *over* and *under* needle.

To sum up the different methods of knitting, it can be seen that, in the Eastern manner, the needle is inserted into the front of the stitch to achieve a Crossed Stitch and into the back to achieve an Uncrossed Stitch. In the Western manner, the stitches are achieved by reversing these movements, the needle being inserted into the back of the stitch for a Crossed Stitch and into the front for an Uncrossed Stitch. Both Eastern methods have the same yarn movements, as do both Western methods.

The following stitches combine one yarn movement each from the Eastern and Western methods to form an Uncrossed and a Crossed Stitch.

Uncrossed Stitch (Combined Method). To knit, the needle is inserted into the *back* of the stitch, and the yarn is thrown *under* the needle, as shown in Diagram 5A.

Note that the stitches on the right needle slant in a direction opposite to those remaining on the left needle. The slant is caused by the yarn being thrown *under* the needle instead of *over* as in the Uncrossed Eastern Knit Stitch.

To purl, the needle is inserted into the *front* of the stitch, and the yarn is again thrown *under* the needle, as shown in Diagram 5B.

Crossed Stitch (Combined Method). The needle movements of the Uncrossed Combined Method are reversed to form a Combined Crossed Stitch.

To knit, the needle is inserted into the *front* of the stitch, as shown in Diagram 6A. To purl, the needle is inserted into the *back* of the stitch, as shown in Diagram 6B. The yarn movements are the same as in the Uncrossed Combined.

This is a very interesting stitch, and, if you are knitting it while reading the instructions, you can see that it produces a plaited fabric. Its crossings, right over left and left over right, can also be clearly seen in Diagram 6A. The plait thus formed becomes even more obvious when the resulting fabric is blocked.

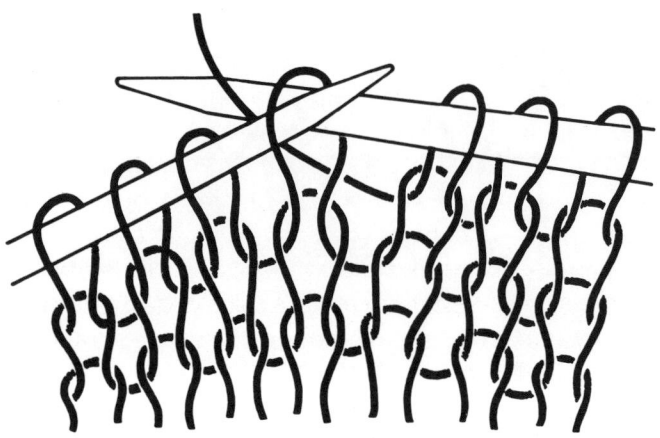

Diagram 5A. **Uncrossed Knit Stitch (Combined Method).** Needle inserted into *back* of stitch; yarn thrown *under* needle.

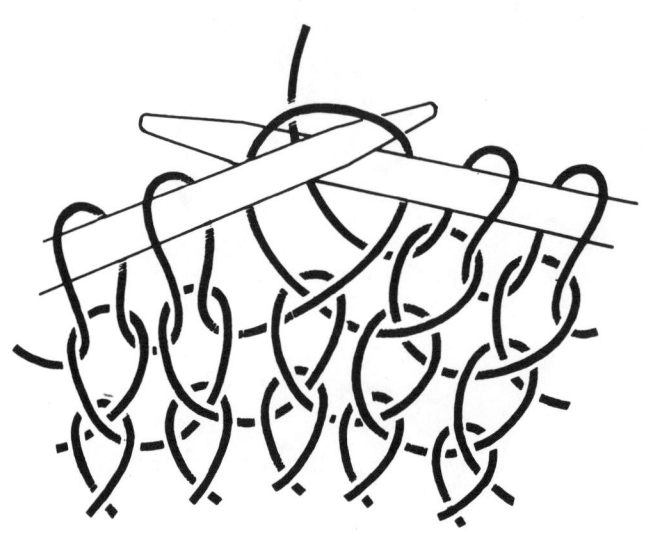

Diagram 6A. **Crossed Knit Stitch (Combined Method).** Needle inserted into *front* of stitch; yarn thrown *under* needle.

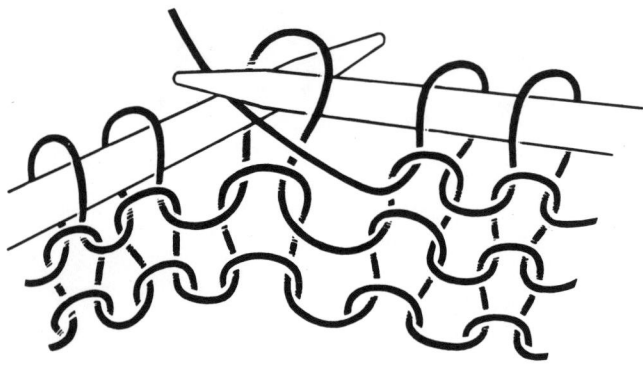

Diagram 5B. **Uncrossed Purl Stitch (Combined Method).** Needle inserted into *front* of stitch; yarn thrown *under* needle.

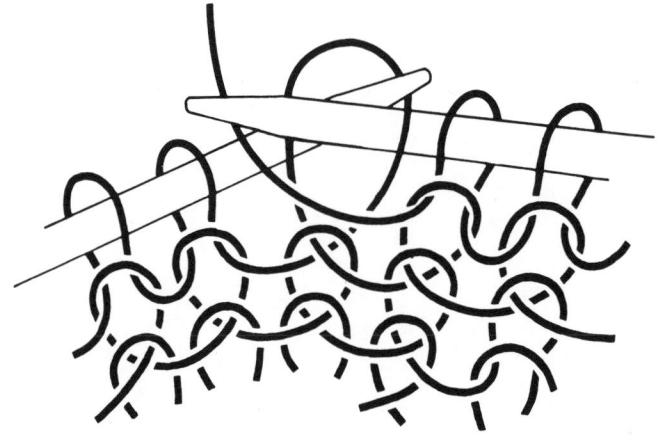

Diagram 6B. **Crossed Purl Stitch (Combined Method).** Needle inserted into *back* of stitch; yarn thrown *under* needle.

I prefer to use the Uncrossed Combined Method for the most part, and for good reason. The yarn is thrown under the needle for both knit and purl, which results in throws of the same length and produces a more even fabric. Such a method is considered the best one for making the Stockinette Stitch. Also, there are several stitches I use a great deal that are easier to do when the stitches are on the needle in the Uncrossed Combined Method—such stitches as the One Over One, the Horizontal, and the Plaited Basket. This means that most knitters must learn to adjust pattern directions when it comes to decreasing. How to do this is demonstrated on page 62.

Whether to knit in the English manner (holding the yarn in the right hand) or in the Continental manner (holding the yarn in the left hand) is a matter for personal preference. I prefer to knit in the Continental manner. If I am knitting two colors in the same row I use both the English and Continental methods, holding one color yarn in the right hand and the other color yarn in the left. This technique for using different colors in one row is known as stranded knitting and it was referred to in Chapter 2.

Regardless of whether you use the English or Continental manner, I highly recommend to each knitter that you try the different ways of throwing yarn. Your understanding of knitting will profit from this exercise. Once you know how the stitches are put onto the needle, there will not be a pattern or a knitting problem that you cannot cope with.

Before going on to the stitches, I must add a cautionary word about splicing. In the type of knitting described in this book, splicing becomes extremely visible when done in the middle of a row, particularly in openwork or lace patterns. So try to splice at the end of a row. I prefer not to splice at all. Instead, I leave the end of the yarn free after completing a row and I continue knitting with a new end of yarn at the beginning of the next row. Rather than knitting the yarns together, I weave the loose ends into the selvage after the piece is completed.

The stitches and patterns here are those that relate to my own work; some are not well known, and those that are better known are given with variations. After you have mastered them, I hope you will enlarge upon them. There can be great joy in inventing your own stitch. It may be based on a well-known one, but to the person who has developed it, it is a discovery nonetheless. By studying the photographs in the book, especially the details, you can plot the stitch construction and see for yourself how the stitches combine to form design patterns.

All diagrams which follow are shown in the Uncrossed Combined Method. If you are using a different method, be sure to watch the direction of the decrease stitches.

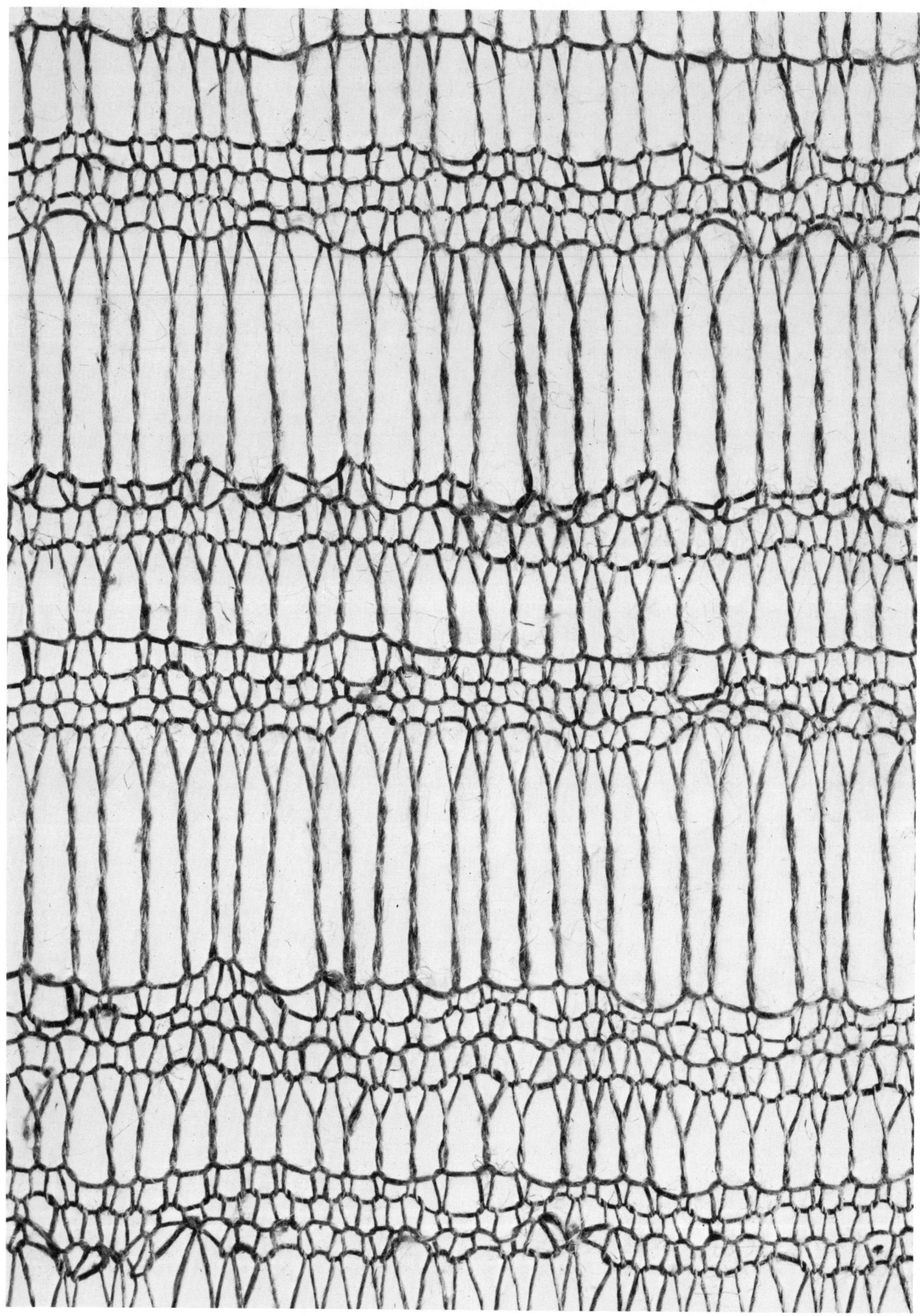

FANCY CROSSED THROW

This is actually an elongated Crossed Stitch and is made by throwing the yarn around both needles.

Insert right needle into stitch as if to knit. Throw yarn *under* and *over* right needle, *under* and *over* left needle, and *under* right needle. See Diagram 7A. Open needles slightly and draw a single stitch through (this will be the last throw that was put onto needle). See Diagram 7B. The extra throws will slip off needle.

When the row is completed, pull the fabric smartly to even the stitches on the needle. This stitch can be lengthened by throwing the yarn more times over the needles.

A detail of a linen hanging worked in Fancy Crossed Throw is shown in Illus. 29. Note that there are rows of both short and long stitches. In between some of the lengths are several rows of the Garter Stitch.

The detail in Illus. 30 is of a similar piece in mohair and linen. The effect in this finished piece is, as you can see, quite different from the other.

Illus. 30. Fancy Crossed Throw using mohair and linen.

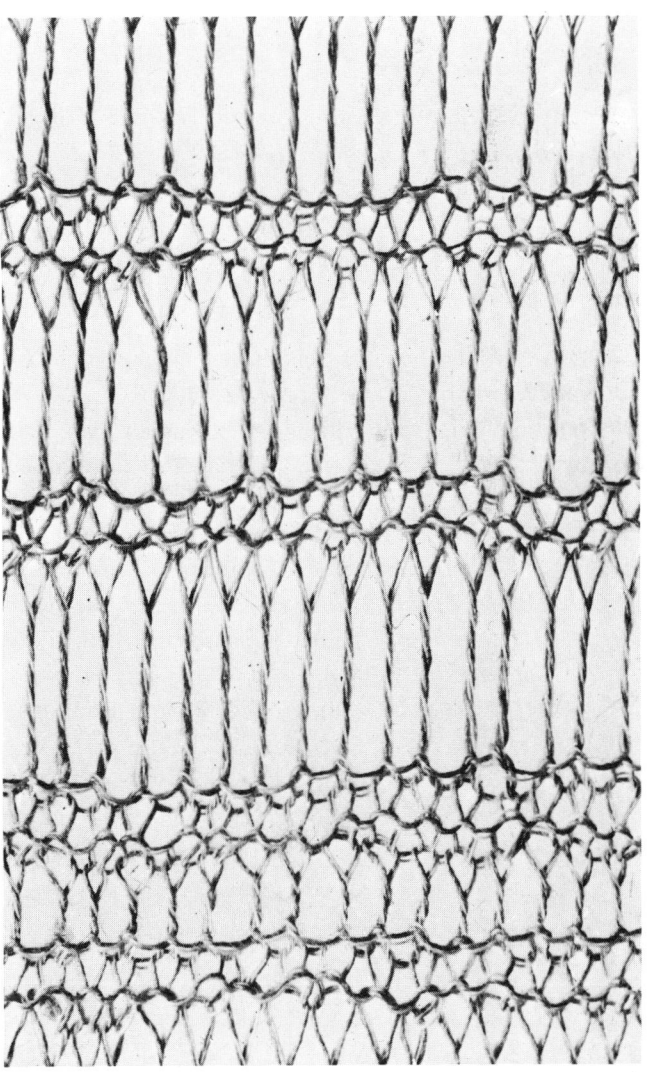

Diagram 7A. **Fancy Crossed Throw.**

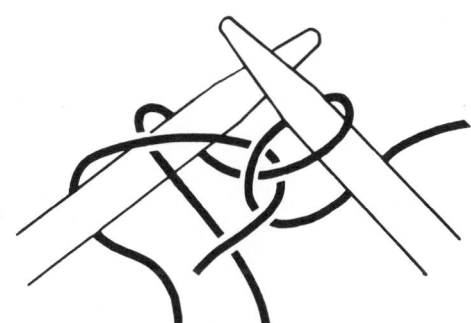

Diagram 7B. **Fancy Crossed Throw.** Drawing single stitch through.

Illus. 29. Detail of linen casement on page 13 shows both long and short stitches done with Fancy Crossed Throw. Rows of Garter Stitch are between some rows of Fancy Crossed Throw.

Still another version of the Fancy Crossed Throw in linen is shown in Illus. 31. The extra long stitches here are made by throwing the yarn several times over both needles. On the next row the pattern varies with a three into three stitch as follows:

Insert needle into three sts as if to purl, (P1, K1, P1) into sts as if one.

This pulls the stitches together and still maintains the correct stitch count. In this piece, several rows of the Garter Stitch were used between the Throw rows. See details of "More Variations" (page 73) and "Shells" (page 81) for the different interpretations of the Fancy Crossed Throw.

The needle can also be inserted knitwise into the three stitches to (K1, P1, K1) into them as if they were one. If this is done into the *back* of the three stitches, they will slant from right to left; if into the *front*, they will slant from left to right. See detail of "Shells" for these. Different variations and slants can be done on succeeding rows.

A pattern based on the Fancy Crossed Throw is worked as follows:

Multiple of 10 sts.

Row 1. Knit.

Row 2. *P1, K1, K5 Fancy Crossed Throws, K1, P2*, repeat * to *.

Row 3. Knit.

Row 4. *K3 Fancy Crossed Throws, K1, P3, K1, K2 Fancy Crossed Throws*, repeat* to *.

This pattern, when done in linen, makes an excellent casement fabric. There are tight areas and long areas that counteract each other beautifully. The stretch factor would be minimal.

Aside from providing an overall pattern, the Fancy Crossed Throw (similar to other stitches throughout the book) can be used as a pattern insertion as in Illus. 69 on page 88 or in isolated rows as in Illus. 70 (page 89). Further uses can be seen in still other constructions.

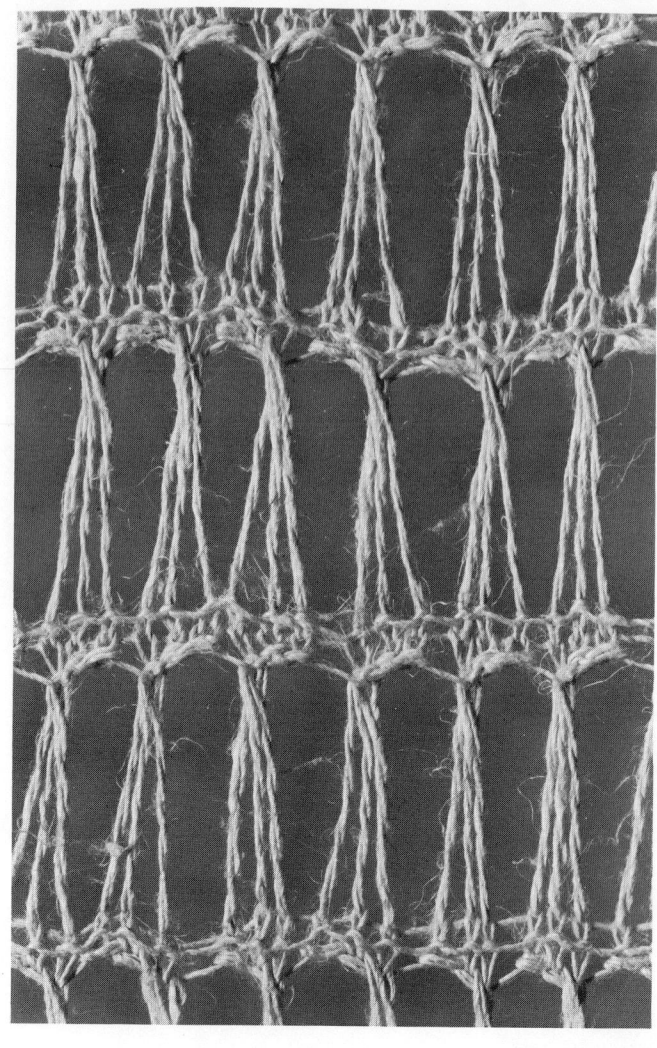

Illus. 31. Detail of a casement. Bleached white 5/1 linen. Fancy Crossed Throw with a three into three stitch on the next row.

DOUBLE KNIT

This stitch has many uses and advantages, and its possibilities are unlimited. For instance, it creates areas of tension next to areas that have a lot of stretch. The detail of "Circles" (Illus. 32) fits this example. It uses single-ply linen for the Double Knit sections and single-ply handspun silk for the Stockinette Stitch sections. The shortening and narrowing of the linen areas and the lengthening and widening of the silk areas produce a strong pattern caused by the different stretch factors of the two yarns and the stitch construction used.

There are many other pieces where Double Knit has been used to obtain a point of tension against lacy sections, such as "The Kings" (Illus. 33) and the works in Illus. 57, 63, 64, 71 and 72. Blankets made with alternating areas of single Knit Stitch and Double Knit are very lightweight, yet warm.

Illus. 32. Detail of wall hanging, "Circles," (1964). 5/1 natural linen and single-ply handspun silk. Double Knit creates short, narrow areas next to wider, longer areas of Stockinette Stitch.

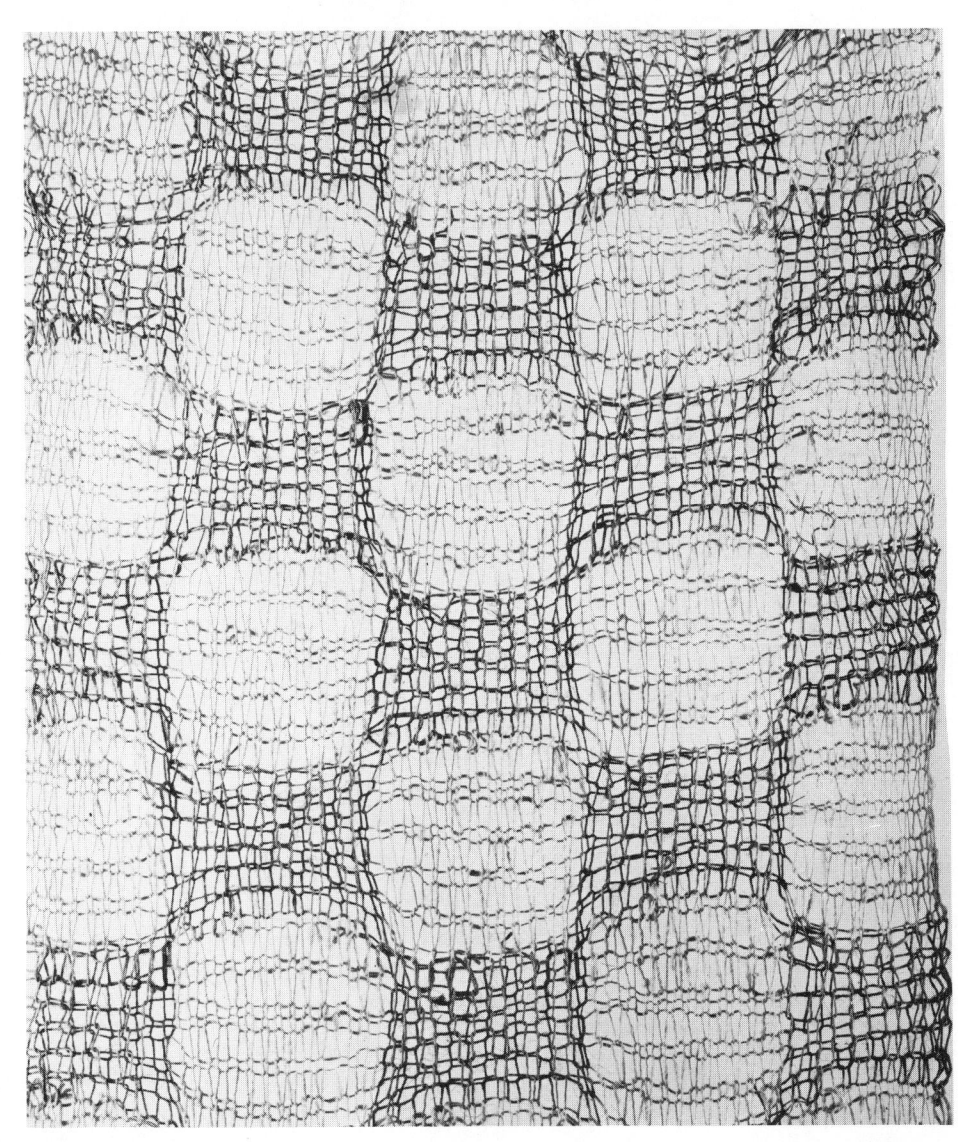

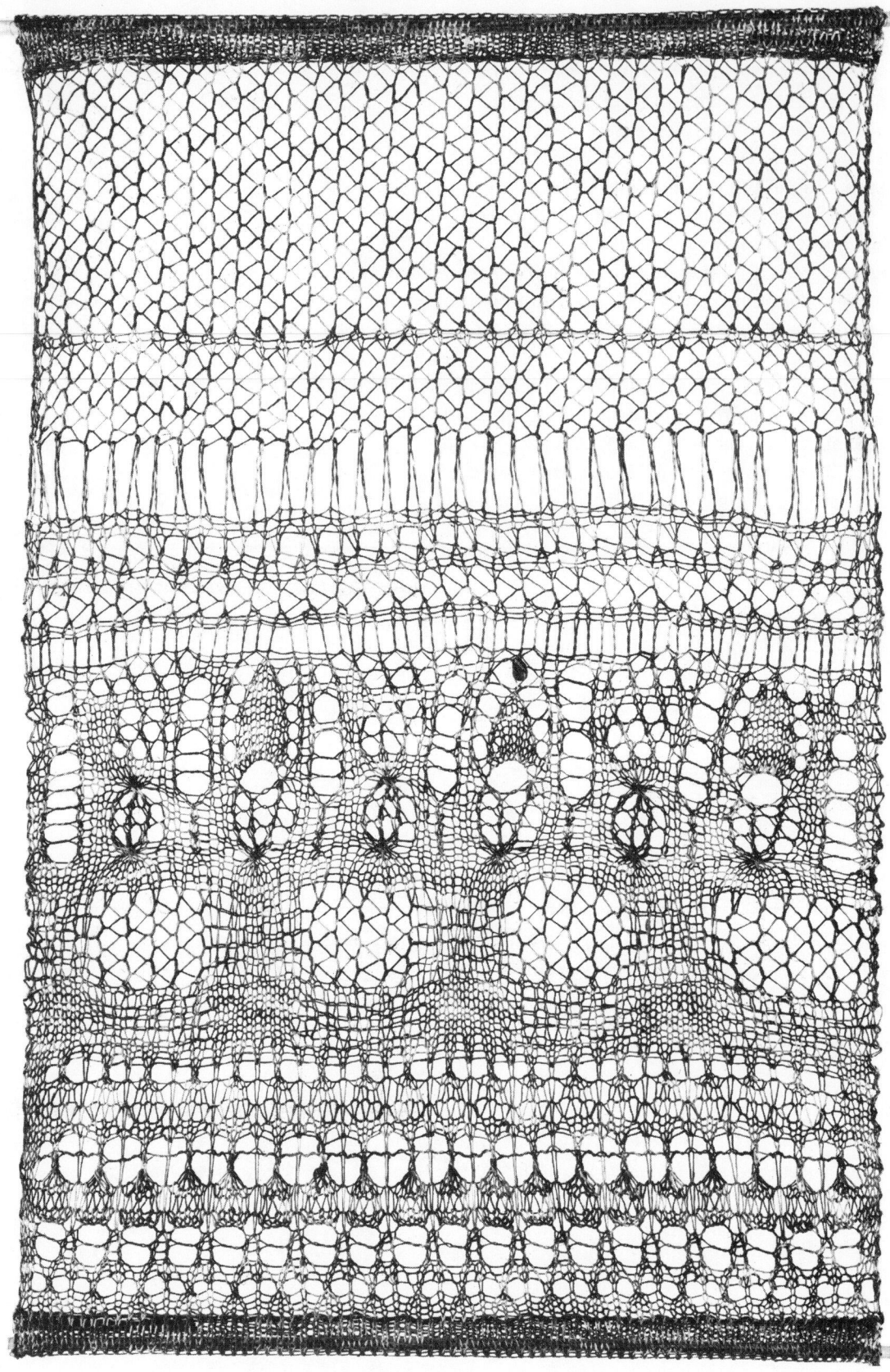

Illus. 33. "The Kings," wall hanging, 19¼" × 29", (1966). 5/1 natural linen and ikat-dyed red and black linen. Areas of Double Knit complement areas of openwork done in Lace Faggot Stitch. Other areas are in Bell-like Pattern, Fancy Crossed Throw, Ladder, One Over One, and variations of Lace Stitches. (Merit Award, Craftsmen U.S.A., 1966. Collection of Roger Dunham.)

Double Knit can also be used to define a pattern. An example of this is on page 69, where the Cross is formed by a Double Knit section of silk, linen, and metallic yarn. This stitch also provides two layers of fabric that can be used as pockets to hold stones, mica, plastic, and other found objects. In "Peruvian Seeds" (Illus. 34 and 35) seed pods from Peru have been inserted; in "Rocks and Rills" (page 65), beach pebbles; in Illus. 56 (page 77), mica from North Carolina; and in Illus. 65 (page 85), pearl rings.

This stitch is made as follows:
    Even number of sts.
    * K1, yarn forward, Sl 1 pw *, repeat * to *.
    Repeat row for required length.

For a variation:
    Even number of sts.
    * insert needle into st, make a Double Throw (see Diagram 8A) and pull through a double loop, yarn forward, Sl 1 pw *, repeat * to *.
    Repeat row for required length.

Either of these methods can be used for making pockets. The first method results in a more compact pocket, and the second in a more open one. After the desired length for a pocket has been completed, proceed as follows:
    Slip every other stitch onto a third needle in order to open the pocket. Found objects may now be inserted. Return stitches to their proper needle.
Whatever pattern you were doing can now be continued. The next row will close the pocket.

Also when making a pocket, an odd number of stitches can be used instead of an even number. For this variation:
    * Sl 1, K1 *, repeat * to *, ending Sl 1.
Or:
    * K1, Sl 1 *, repeat * to *, ending K1.

Either of these variations is done until the desired number of stitches is on the needle for the pocket.

Illus. 34. This detail of "Peruvian Seeds" shows Double Knit areas with seed pods, Stockinette Stitch with beads, Horizontal and One Over One Stitches, twisted stitches, and areas of Lace with Bobbles.

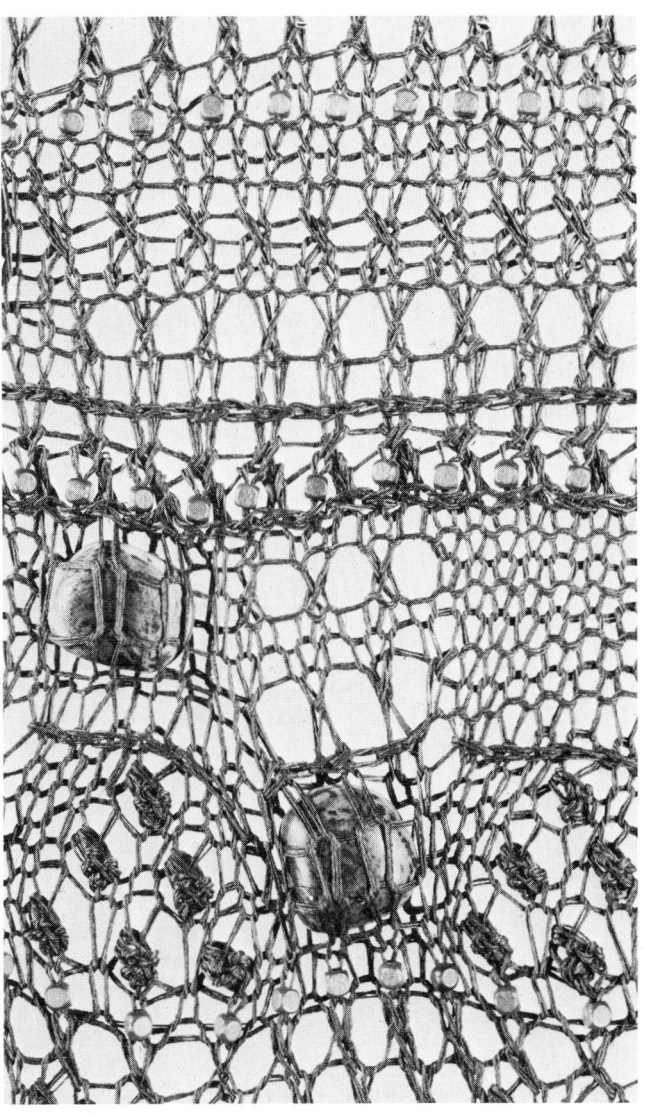

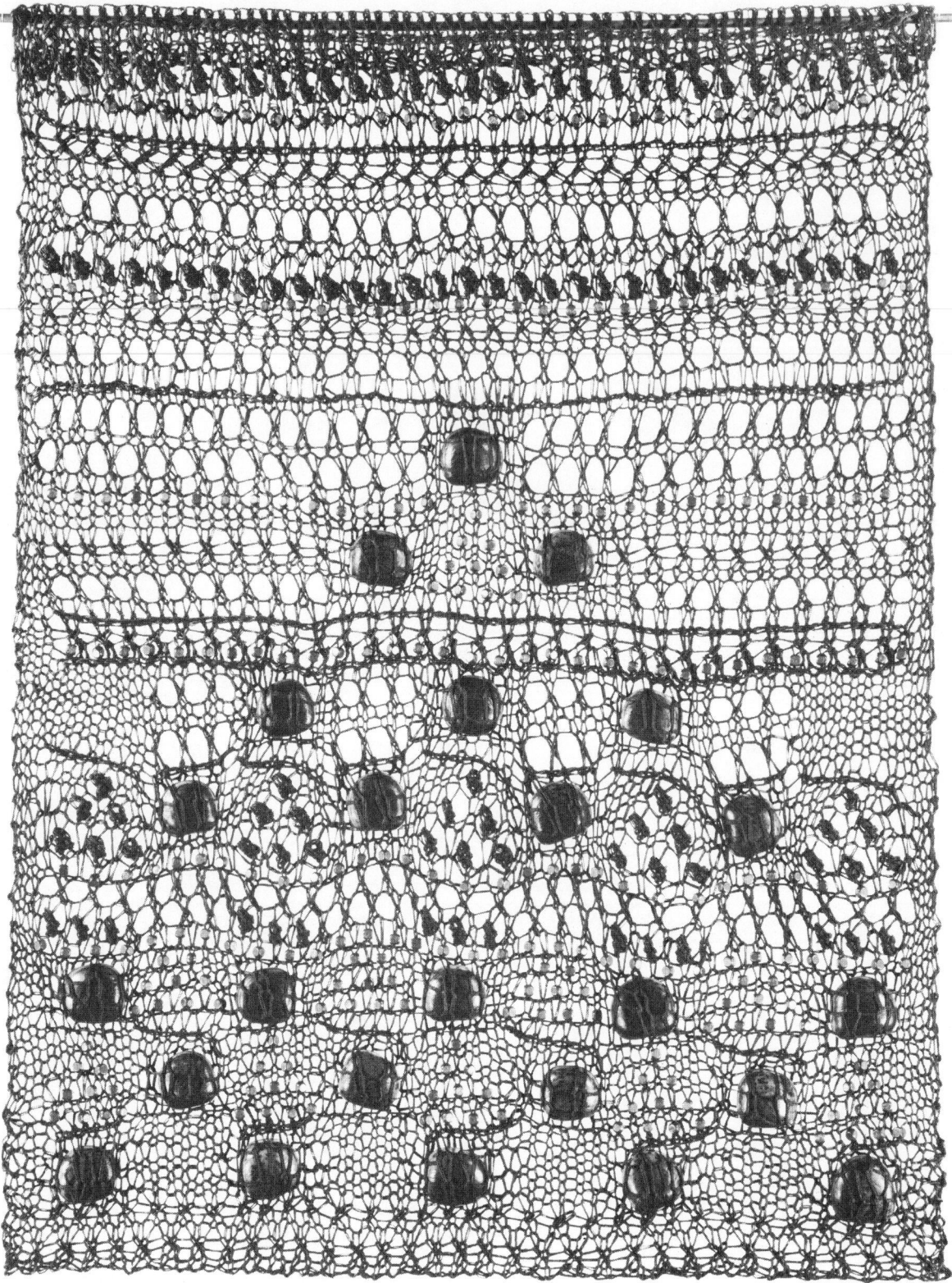

Illus. 35. "Peruvian Seeds," wall hanging, 18" × 22", (1969). Black linen used double, seed pods from Peru, and brown wooden beads. The seed pods are inserted in pockets of Double Knit. Other features of the design are as follows: the square beads are added on in alternate areas with the Stockinette Stitch; and Bobbles are used with a Lace Stitch. Short rows of Horizontal Stitch separate the different areas.

MAKING A DOUBLE THROW

Stitches can be lengthened by taking an extra throw around one needle, as shown in Diagram 8A. To make the stitch:

> Insert needle knitwise into stitch and throw yarn twice over right needle. See Diagram 8A. Drop second throw on the next row, which can be purl, as in Diagram 8B. A Double Throw may be done on purl rows also.

The throw is dropped to make a longer stitch. The stitch can be made to any required length by adding still more throws.

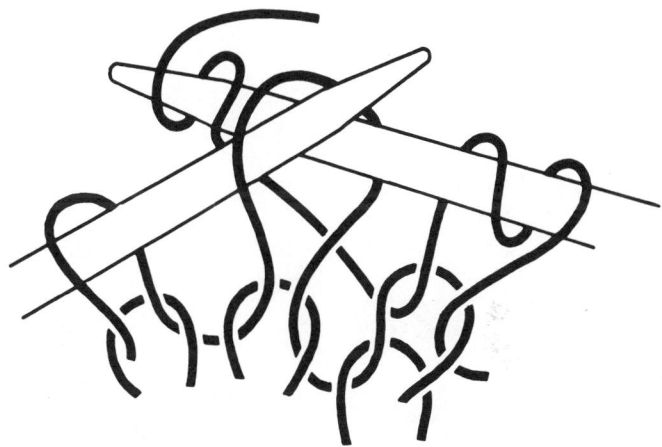

Diagram 8A. **Making a Double Throw.** Needle inserted knitwise; yarn thrown twice over right needle.

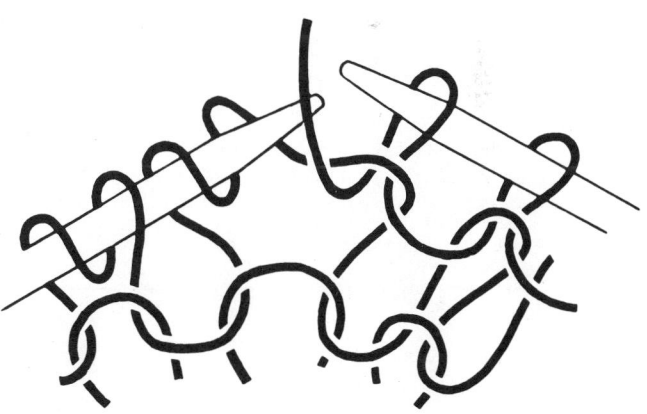

Diagram 8B. Dropping the Second Throw on the Purl Row.

KNIT INTO STITCH BELOW

Another stitch of great importance is this well-known one. Those who are not familiar with it can see how it is done by following Diagram 9. Note that the top stitch is dropped as the stitch below is knit. The stitch is presented here with variations.

One variation is done by making one or more additional throws over the needle when knitting into the stitch below. This gives a vertical effect. To make this effect even more definitive, purl a stitch on either side of knitting into the stitch below.

Another variation is:

* K2 tog, YO, KSB, YO, K2 tog *, repeat * to *.

Purl next row.

This principle is shown to great advantage in Illus. 36 and 37, in Illus. 39 and 40. Additional examples are in Illus. 51, 59, 72 and 78.

Illus. 36. Wall hanging, 14" × 36", (1968). Yellow slub linen and yellow wooden beads. Knit into Stitch Below leads into vertical lines of beads. Other sections are knit in Bobble (variation of the common Popcorn), Lace Stitches, and a variation on the Bell motif.

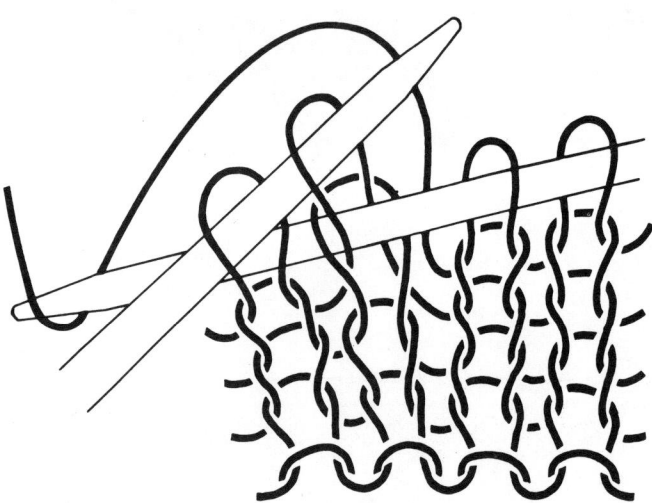

Diagram 9. **Knit into Stitch Below.**

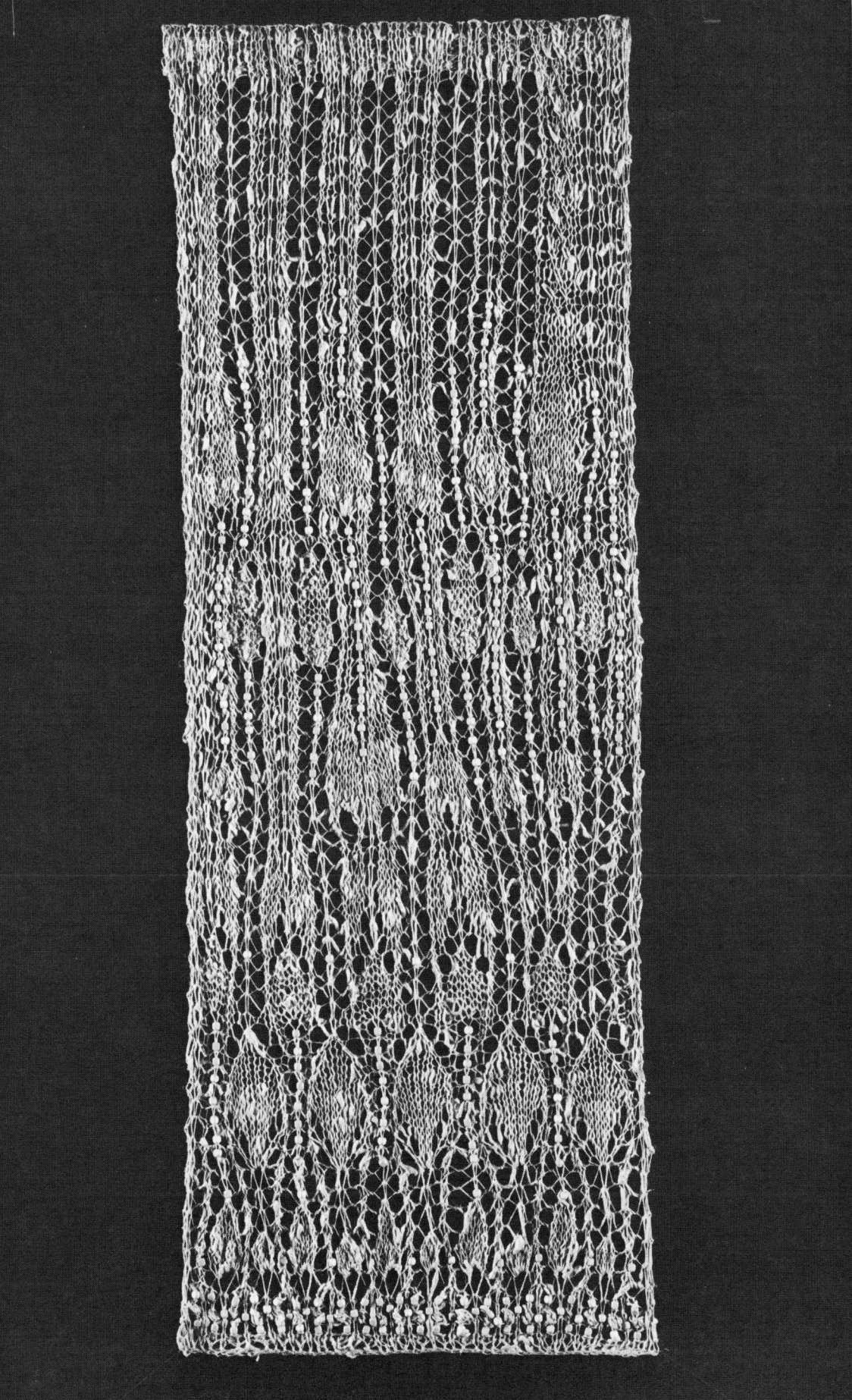

Illus. 37. Detail of previous picture shows square, yellow beads interspersed with the Knit into Stitch Below and with the Bobbles at the bottom. The lozenge-shaped areas were achieved by adding YO onto each side of the center and by decreasing back to the original amount of stitches.

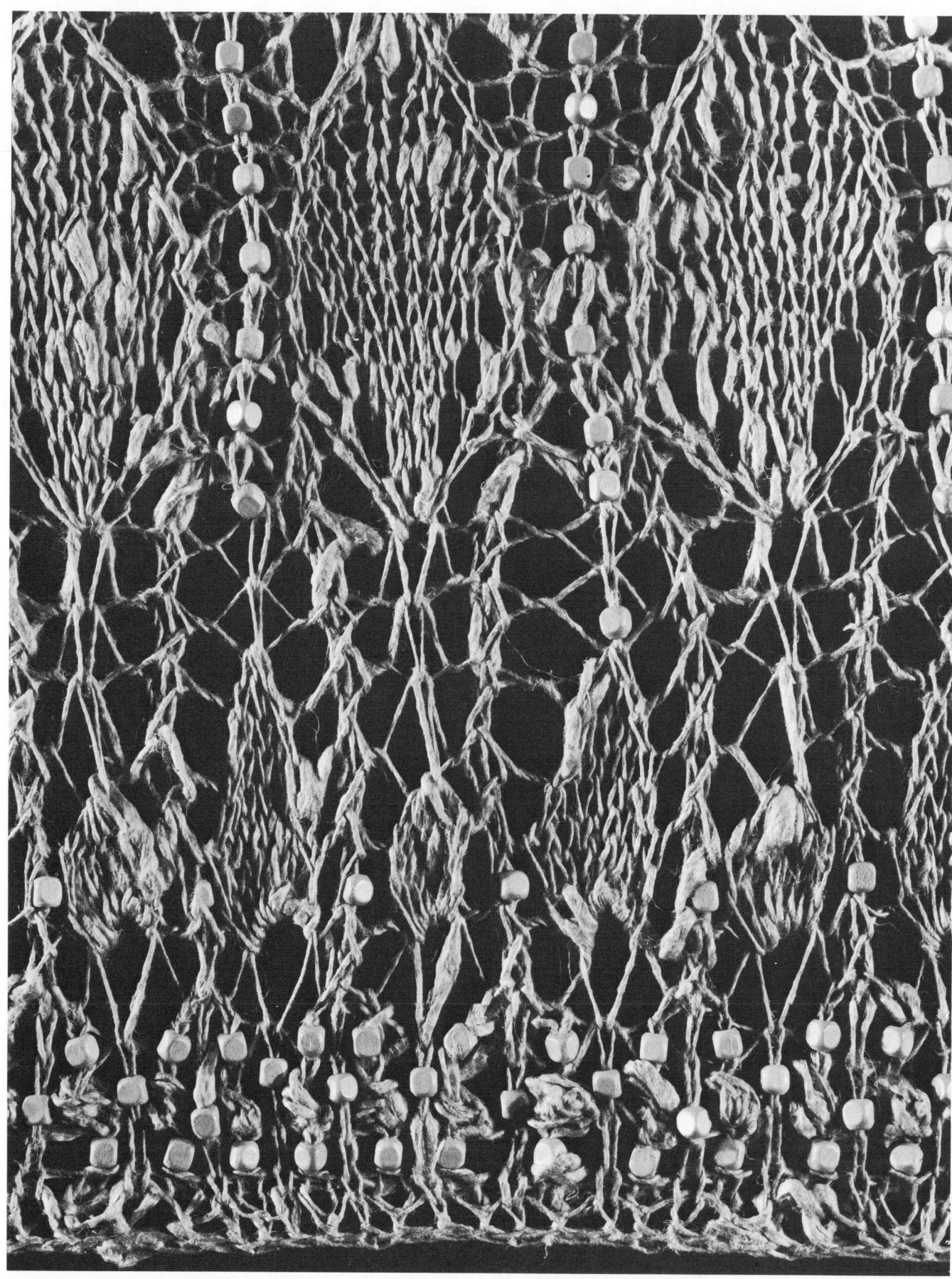

SURFACE ENRICHMENT—EMBOSSED MOTIFS

There are many varieties of embossed motifs; some are made by casting on stitches, others from increasing within a single stitch, and still others from gathering together a group of stitches. All can be arranged into almost any sort of design: vertical, horizontal, and diagonal. They can also be grouped into geometric shapes. Three examples of stitches used for emboss-ment follow.

1. Clustering

Clustering gives an effect unlike any other stitch. It is a wrapping technnique and requires a third needle to make.

SI 3 or more sts off left needle and put onto dp. Wrap yarn around sts three or more times (Diagram 10). Transfer sts from dp to right needle.

Another way is to knit the stitches before putting them onto the double pointed needle. After clustering, return them to the right needle. Different yarn, or perhaps even yarn of a different color, can be used for the wrapping to add a new dimension to the piece.

In Illus. 38, Clustering is done with contrasting mate-rials. In Illus. 39 and 40, and in "Vertical Trails" (page 59), Clustering is done with the same material used in knitting the piece. "Vertical Trails" also shows Cluster-ing used on either side of the Bobble (pages 58–9) in some areas to accentuate the surface enrichment.

Illus. 38. Detail of a wall hanging in natural linen and white silk shows Clustering done with contrasting yarns. Full view of piece (Illus. 68) on page 88.

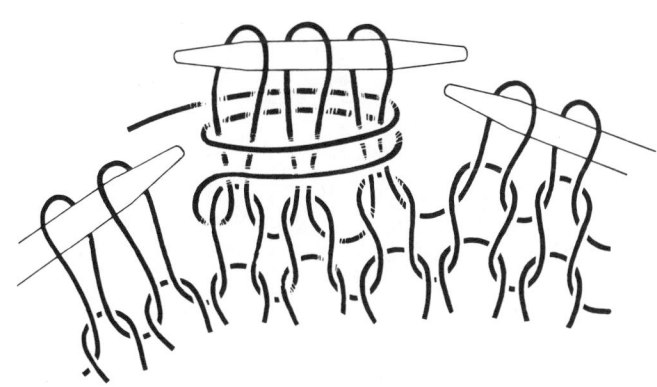

Diagram 10. **Clustering** Stitches.

Illus. 39. Wall hanging, 29" × 42", (1968). Black 1½ lea linen, #9 needle. Diamond Pattern with variations, Knit into Stitch Below, Bobble, and Clustering Stitches. This piece is based on the Diamond Pattern, which is one of the most elementary found in knitting books. Very careful attention was paid to decreasing. The first repeat has no variation to it, but the third diamond area has the variation of Knit into Stitch Below. Bobbles are also included in this area. The following diamond area is varied and elongated by repeating the directions for the middle row of the pattern several times. Bobbles are included here also, together with Knit into Stitch Below. In the center section of the piece, Clustering is used in the middle of the Diamond Pattern.

Illus. 40. Detail of previous picture. At the bottom of the detail, Knit into Stitch Below is shown intersecting the Diamond. Just above are three Clustering Stitches within the elongated diamond shape. YO, K2 tog can be seen at the very top of the photograph.

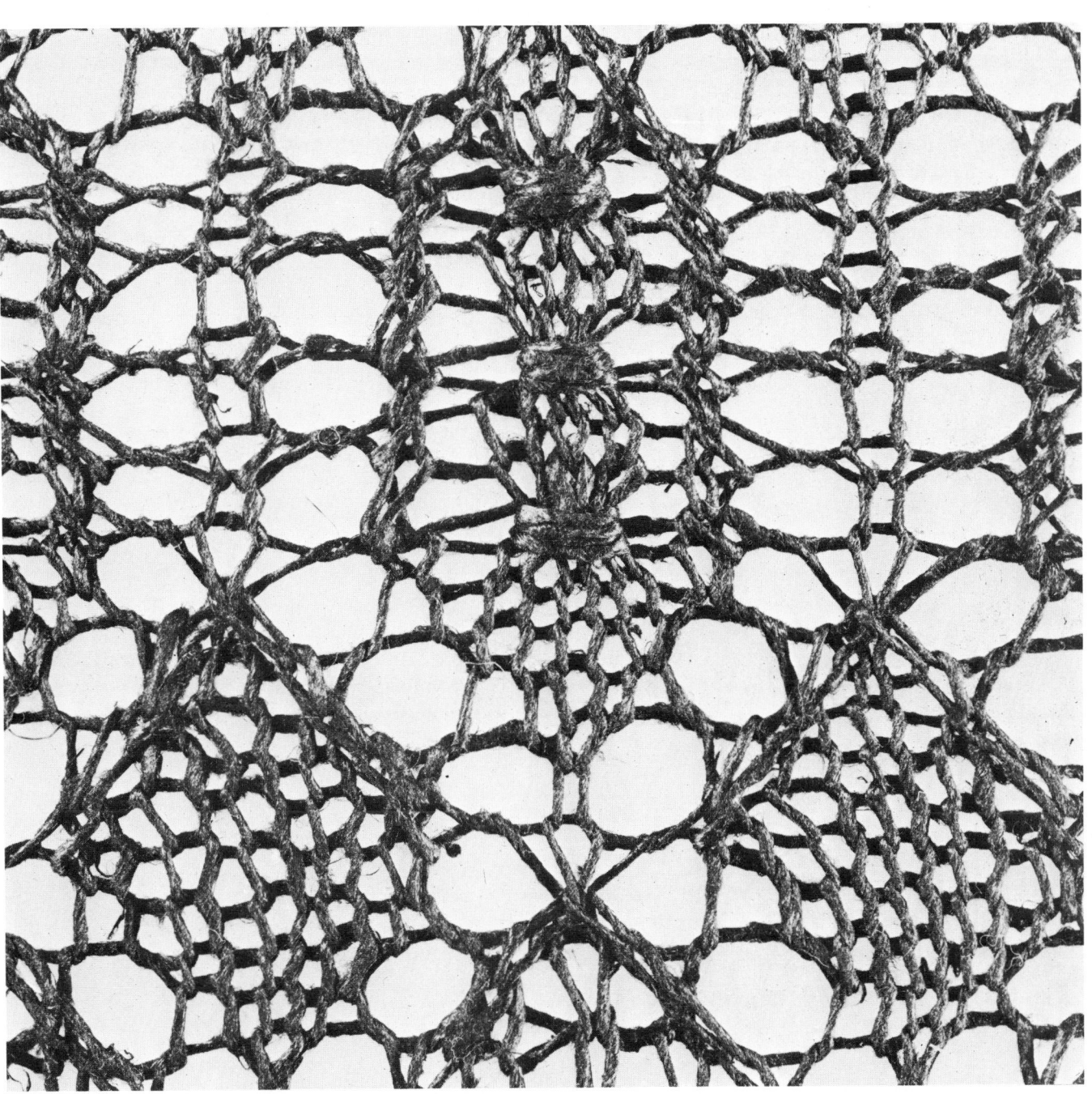

2. Popcorn

This well-known motif is done by making three stitches into one stitch as the following directions indicate. A variation is presented here and, with imagination, you can probably think of others to make.

(K1, YO, K1) into a st, turn work and K3, turn work and P3, turn work and K3, turn work and K3 tog. This completes the Popcorn.

For a larger Popcorn, add more stitches at the beginning. "Popcorn" (page 33 and Illus. 41) uses the Popcorn Stitch in alternating bands of wool and silk. The areas in linen are made with the Bobble Stitch.

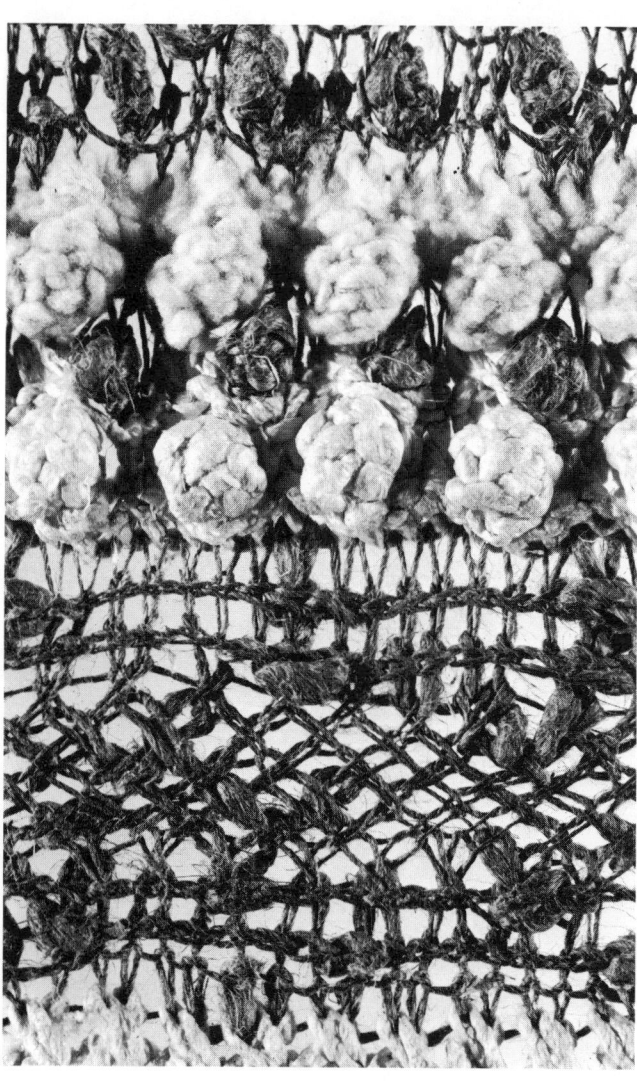

Illus. 41. Progressing upward in this detail of "Popcorn," the Plaited Basket and Horizontal Stitches lead into an area of Popcorns and Bobbles. The Popcorn Stitch is done in silk and wool, and the Bobble in linen.

3. Bobble

Similar in appearance to the Popcorn, it is also made by knitting several times into the same stitch.

K1 and return to left needle (Diagram 11A). K1 and allow st to remain on right needle. Insert needle into original st and K1, and return to left needle. K this st transferring it to right needle as before. Repeat until four sts in all have been made in this manner (Diagram 11B). Drop original st off needle. With left needle lift sts #1, #2, #3, over #4 (Diagram 11 C). This leaves the fourth stitch on the right needle and completes the Bobble.

Here, also, with a little imagination you can vary this stitch a great deal. For example, a greater number of stitches could be cast on for a larger Bobble.

A variation for a fatter Bobble is as follows:
Cast on 4 sts as before. Turn work and K4, turn work and P4, lift sts #1, #2, #3, over #4.

Or:
Cast on 4 sts as before. Turn work and K4, turn work and P4, turn work and K4, turn work and P4 tog.

Or:
Cast on 4 sts as before. Turn work and (K1, P1, K1, P1) into the 4 sts as if they were one, turn work and K4 tog.

Bobbles are used in Illus. 39, Illus. 42, Illus. 72 and Illus. 75. I usually choose the Bobble over the Popcorn when working with linen since the latter does not hold its shape as well in that yarn.

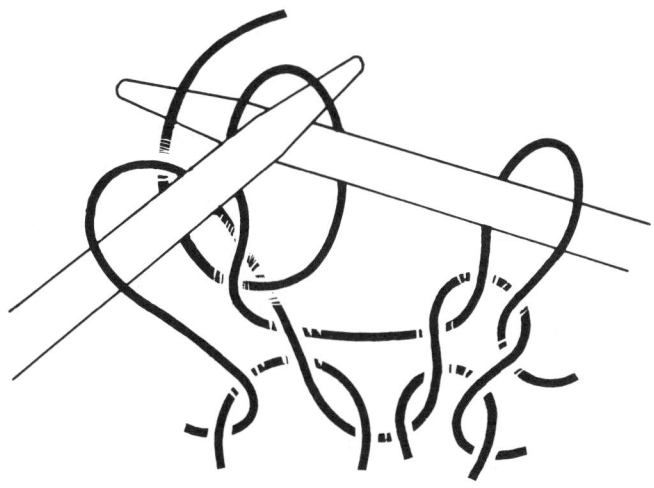

Diagram 11A. **Bobble.** First stitch returned to left needle.

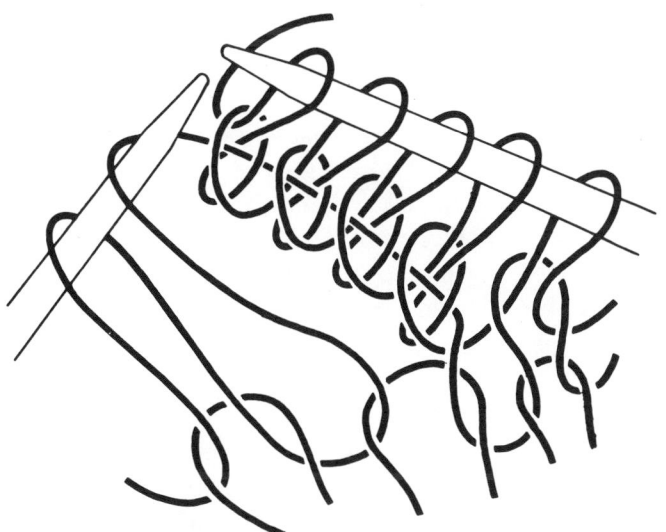

Diagram 11B. **Bobble.** Four stitches completed from one.

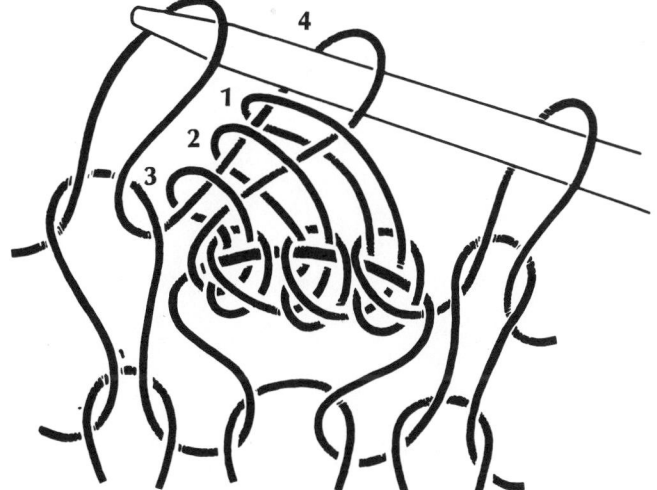

Diagram 11C. **Bobble.** Three stitches lifted off needle, leaving one on.

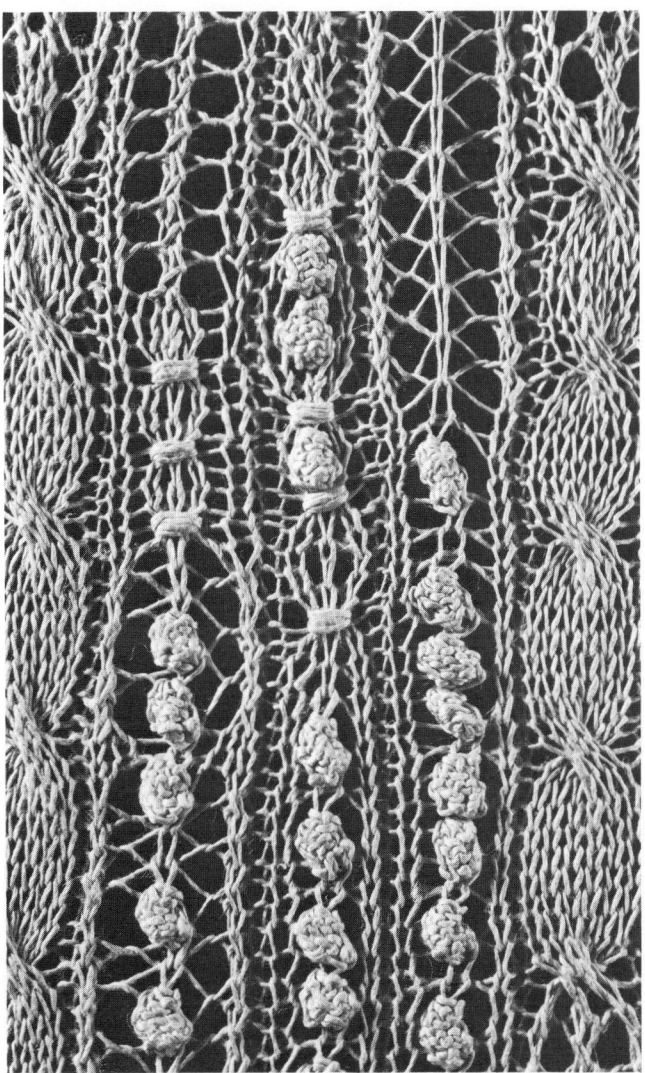

Illus. 42. This detail of "Vertical Trails" (full view on page 95) shows the Bobble in a variation, Cable, Knit into Stitch Below, and Clustering Stitches.

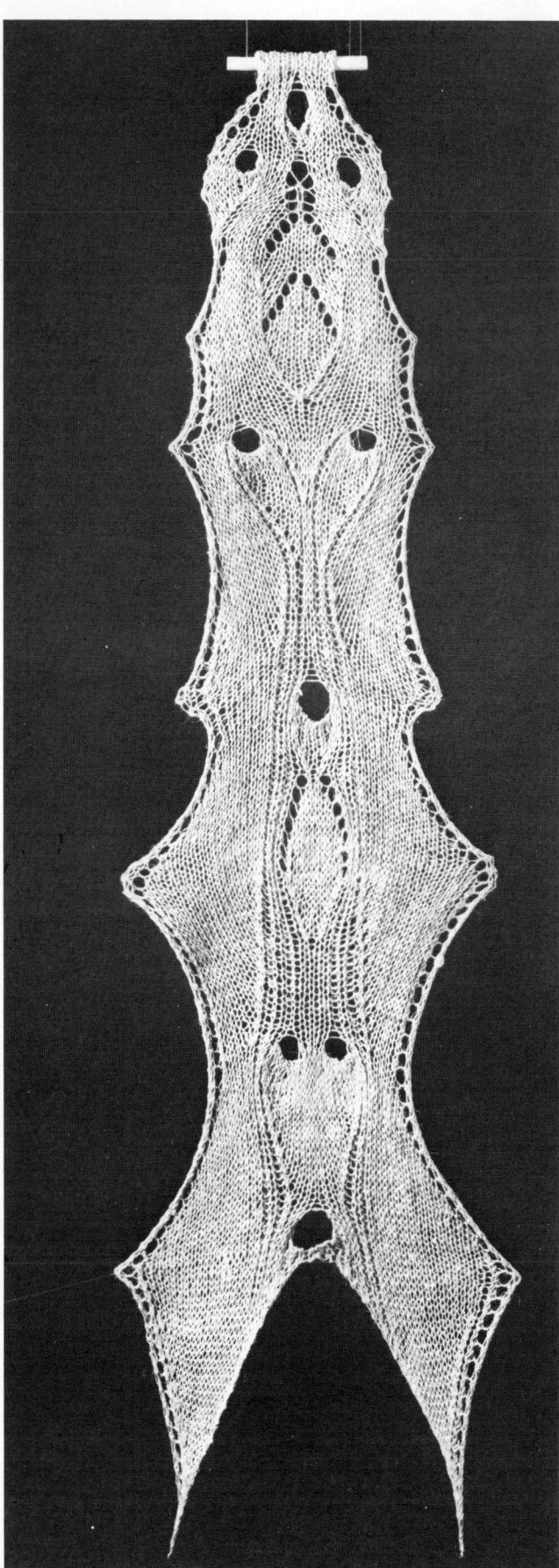

Illus. 43. "The Creature," wall hanging, 14" × 21", (1964). 5/1 natural linen. Pattern is a free expression of increasing and decreasing. Piece was turned upside down for hanging.

INCREASING

Increasing the stitches forms the basis of many pleasing variations. There are several ways of handling increases so that they will be either invisible or visible. An invisible increase will leave no open space in the fabric, whereas a visible increase will leave an open, lacelike space and can be used as a design element.

The invisible increase may be done in any of the following ways:

1. Knit into the stitch as usual, then knit into the front of the same stitch, making two stitches out of one. Drop original stitch from left needle.
2. Make a yarn over. On the next row, purl into the back of the Over.
3. Pick up the running thread between two stitches with the left needle, inserting it from front to back. On the next row, knit into this stitch from the back.

The visible increase is used in a number of lace patterns, including the Lace Diadem and the Diamond. It may be done in any of the following ways:

1. Make a yarn over. On the next row either knit or purl into the Over, but do not twist the stitch.
2. Pick up the running thread between two stitches with the left needle, inserting it from back to front. On the next row either knit or purl the running stitch, but do not twist it.

When increasing a number of stitches, use one of the methods indicated for such patterns as the Bell Pattern (page 76) or the Lace Diadem Eyelet Pattern (page 78).

Illus. 44. Detail of center section shows effective use of the visible increase of YO for an ornamental result.

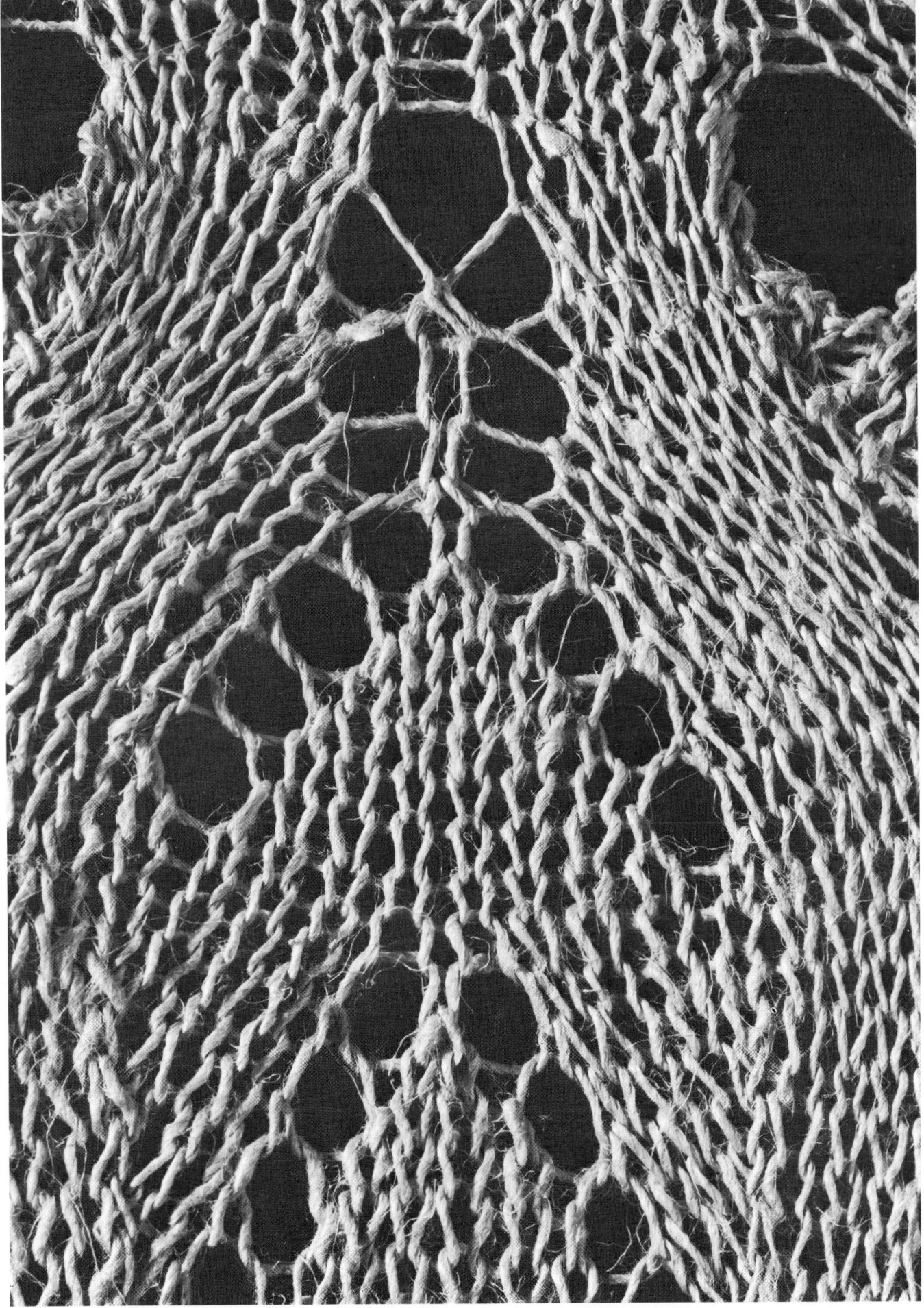

DECREASING

In some cases, decreasing is used to create an ornamental pattern after an increase of stitches. Attention must be given to the directional slant of the decrease, which can be from right to left or from left to right. The direction of decreasing will be determined by the individual pattern. Notice the importance of decreasing in the Bell Pattern.

For a Knit Decrease

If stitches are on left needle in the *Western Method*, decreasing is done as follows:

For a left over right decrease, K2 tog.
For a right over left decrease, Sl 1 pw, K1, psso.
These decreases will slant away from each other.

If you want the decreases to face each other, pyramid fashion, reverse order of decreasing:

First Sl 1, K1, psso.
Then K2 tog.

If you want a strong diagonal slant, decrease on one side only. An example of a left over right decrease can be seen in Illus. 46.

If stitches are on needle in the *Uncrossed Combined Method,* decreasing is done as follows:

For a left over right decrease, the position of the two decrease stitches are reversed so that they sit on the needle in the Western way. Then K2 tog.
For a right over left decrease, it is only necessary to K2 tog or Sl 1, K1, psso.

For a Purl Decrease

If stitches are on needle in the *Uncrossed Combined Method,* decreasing is done as follows:

For a left over right decrease, on reverse side of fabric, P2 tog.
For a right over left decrease, the Purl Reverse Method is used. The two decrease stitches must be placed on needle in the Uncrossed Eastern Method. Purl first stitch and transfer it to left needle (Diagram 12A) so that it is on needle in Uncrossed Eastern Method. Slip second stitch over first stitch (Diagram 12B).

Two definite directional slants can be seen in Illus. 45. The detail of this piece (Illus. 46) shows the left to right diagonal. The decrease was done on one side of the increased area only. The detail in Illus. 77 on page **94** plainly shows a strong right over left decrease on the right side and a left over right decrease on the

left side. Also notice the strong directional decreases in "Vertical Trails" (pages 59 and 95).

After adding on a number of stitches to knit a Hole, try decreasing in the following manner until you arrive at the original number of stitches. On the right side, decrease left over right. On the left side, decrease right over left. This will create a fan effect instead of the bell effect that was created in Illus. 47 and all the other pieces that used the Bell-like Pattern.

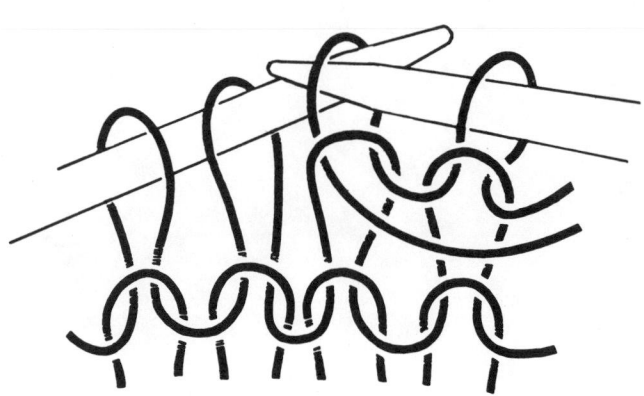

Diagram 12A. **Purl Reverse Decrease.** First stitch purled and transferred to left needle.

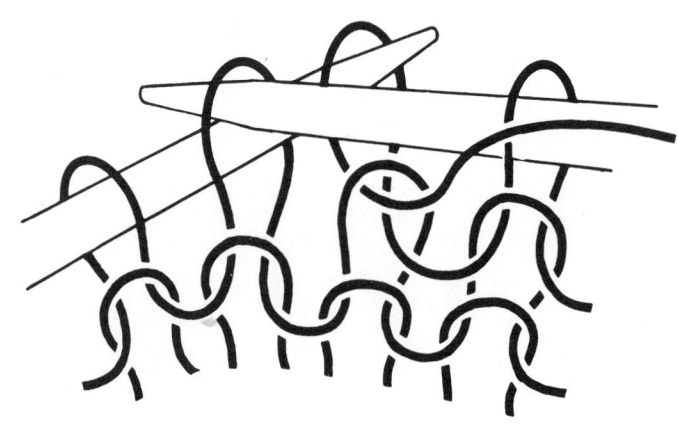

Diagram 12B. **Purl Reverse Decrease.** Second stitch slipped over first stitch.

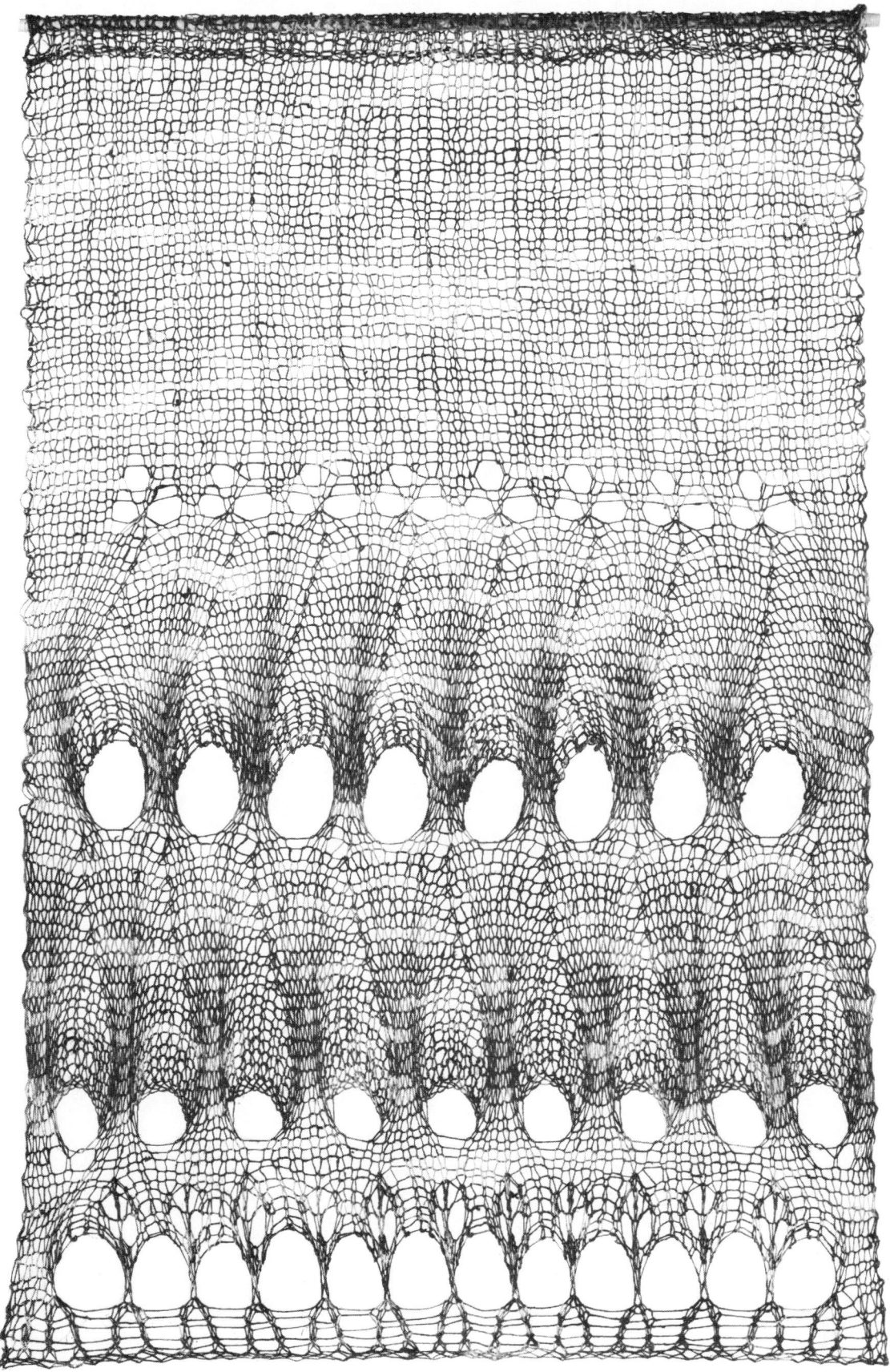

Illus. 45. Wall hanging, 20″ × 30″, (1964). 5/1 natural and ikat-dyed dark green, natural, and bronze linen. Bell-like motif with two definite directional slants obtained by decreasing on only one side of increased area.

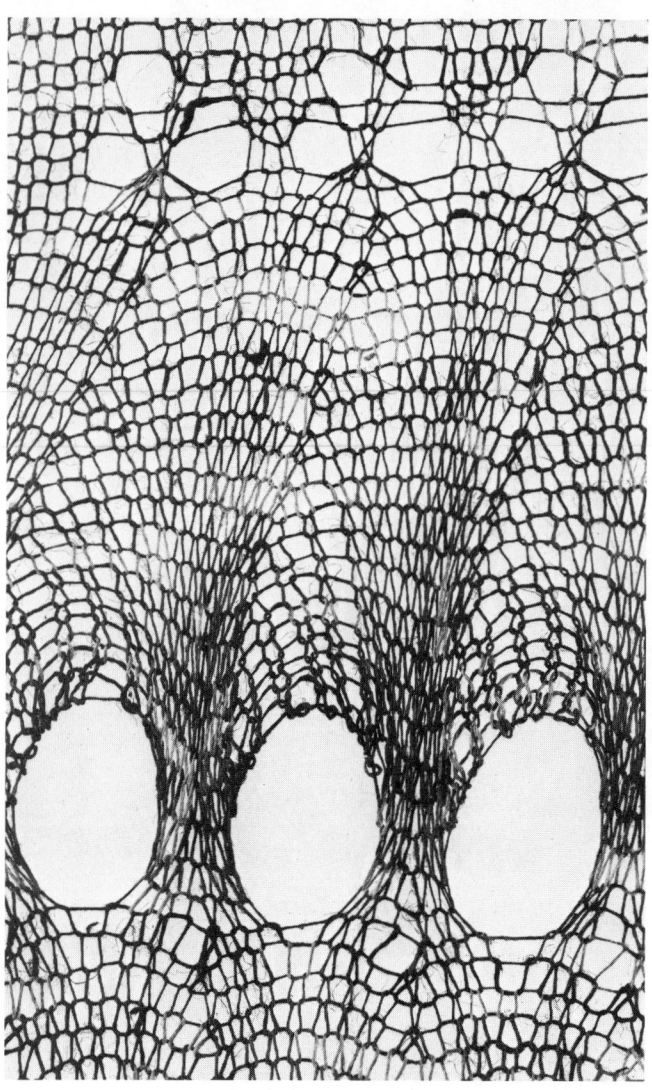

Illus. 46. Detail shows Bell-like motif with left over right decreasing.

Pillows

Thus far I have favored working in a single color, or with colors that are closely related, so as not to obscure the loveliness of the stitches. The three pillow covers show how variation can be achieved using only related shades of yellow silk in various spins and with varied degrees of sheen. (Photographs by the author.)

1. The different shades of silk effectively emphasize the diagonals. Knitting began at one corner; increasing was done at both ends of every other row until desired corner-to-corner size was achieved; then decreasing was done. Garter and Stockinette Stitches. (Collection of Mr. and Mrs. W. David Phillips.)

2. The center section was done in one shade, then cast off. Stitches were picked up all around and worked in different shades, thus creating an interesting motif. Plaited Basket Stitch. (Collection of Mr. and Mrs. W. David Phillips.)

3. The tufted quality of the Popcorn Stitch accentuates the sheen in the material. Such variations add interest to the work. Popcorn, Horizontal, and Plaited Basket Stitches. (Collection of Miss Anne Stackhouse.)

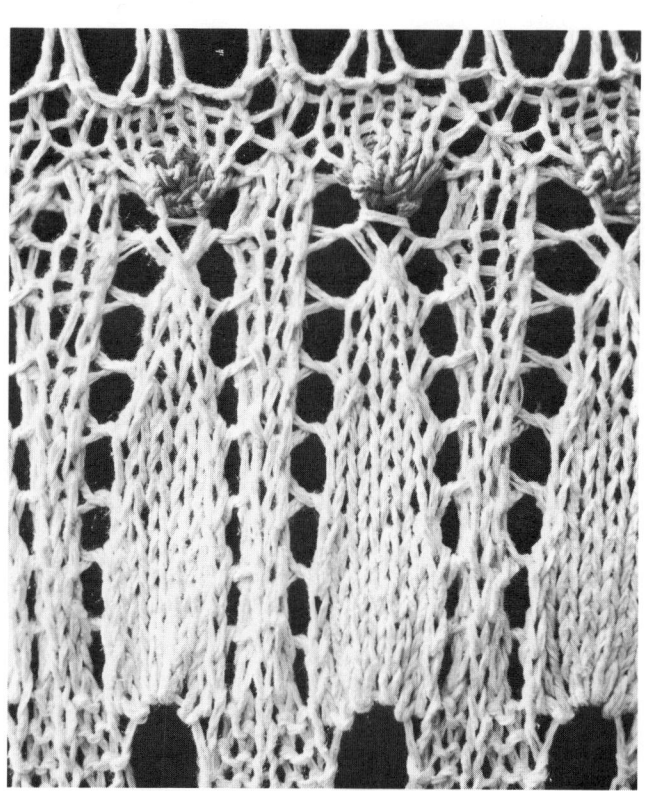

Illus. 47. Detail of wall hanging (full view Illus. 70, page 89) shows Bell-like Pattern. At the completion of the Bell, additional stitches were added in yellow silk to give a fan-like effect. (Photograph by the author.)

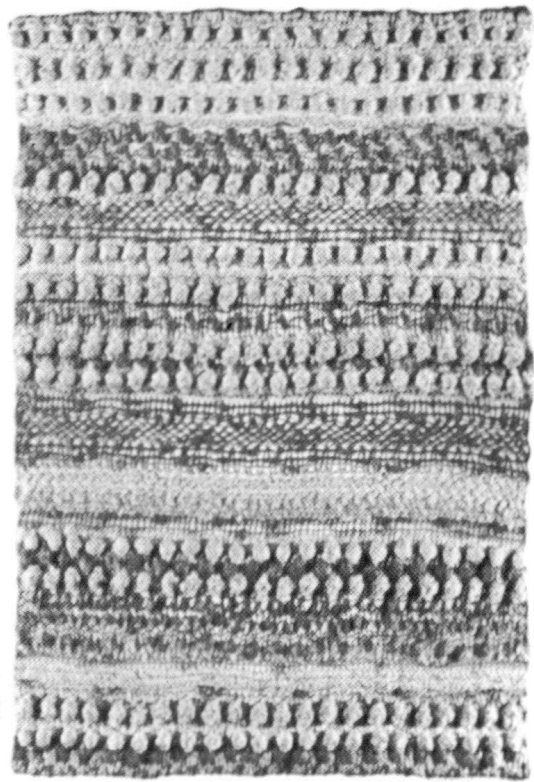

"Popcorn," wall hanging, 28" × 36". Popcorn Stitch is done in white silk and natural, handspun wool. Bobbles are done in natural slub linen. (Collection of Mrs. J.P. Phillips.)

"Rocks and Rills," wall hanging, 14" × 20". Knit in dark green linen with beach pebbles, using Double Knit, Bobbles, Horizontal, and Ladder Stitches. (Collection of Mrs. John P. Phillips. Photograph by Mary Walker Phillips.)

VARIATIONS ON INCREASING AND DECREASING

There are many ways to knit Eyelet or Hole motifs as part of the design. The Eyelet construction is based upon the addition and subtraction of stitches, and once you understand the principle involved, you will soon develop your own variations. Such motifs provide an ornamental addition to the fabric and can be used for occasional effect or can be grouped to form a pattern. Arrange them in almost any order—vertical, horizontal, and diagonal—and to form circular, diamond, floral and other patterns.

Casting on additional stitches by knitting is one way of forming a base for a Hole motif.

K1, as shown in Diagram 13A and return st to left needle, K1 into this st and return to left needle as before (Diagram 13B). Continue in this manner until the desired number of sts are on left needle.

Casting on in this manner creates a braided edge to upper part of Hole.

In "Near East" (Illus. 48), additional stitches were cast on by knitting in order to begin the Bell Pattern. They were cast on with a difference, however. Before casting on for this pattern the work is turned. After the stitches are cast on, the work is turned again, and the pattern is continued. The next row in "Near East" was knit into the back of the stitch, as shown in Diagram 14. Decreasing was done every other row on both sides of the additional stitches.

In "Many Openings" (page 79), the increase for the Lace Diadem Eyelet Pattern was made as follows:

YO3 between two sts. On the next row the YOs served as a base for (K1, P1, K1, P1, K1), making 5 sts into the Over.

A variation on this is:

* K1, YO * into the Over. Repeat * to * for desired number of sts, ending K1.

This treatment gives a looped edge to Hole area. Still another method of knitting Holes is diagrammed in 11A and 11B, the first two steps of the Bobble Stitch.

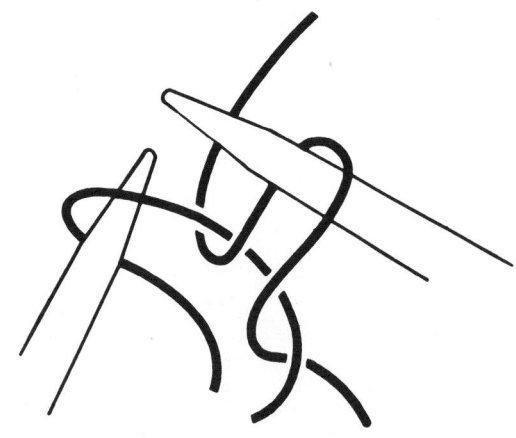

Diagram 13A. **Increasing** by Knitting on Additional Stitches. Knitting second stitch.

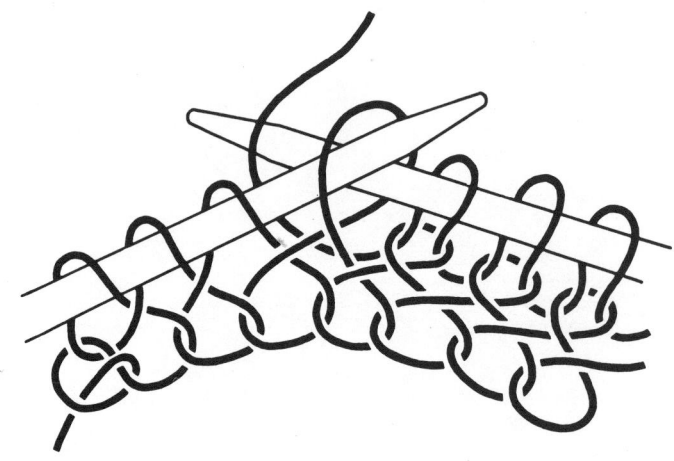

Diagram 14. Knitting into Back of Stitch. Technique used in "Near East."

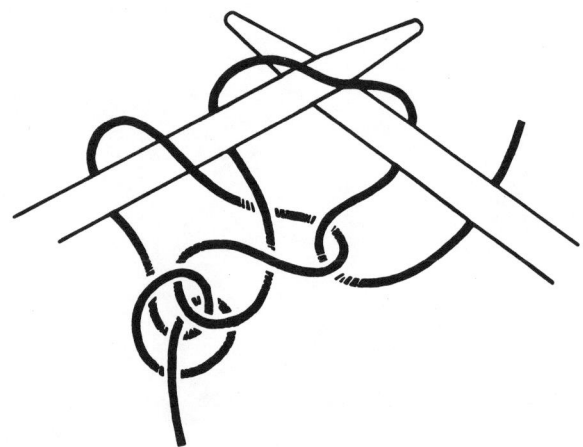

Diagram 13B. **Increasing** by Knitting on Additional Stitches. Transferring second stitch to left needle.

Illus. 48. "Near East," wall hanging, 4' × 9', (1964). 5/1 natural linen. Bell Pattern on a ground of uneven ribbing. Increasing and decreasing for this piece is described in the text. Finished work was shown at "Wall Hangings" exhibit, Museum of Modern Art, 1969. Photograph shows it exhibited at the Thirteenth Milan Triennale, 1964. (Collection of the Museum of Modern Art. Photograph by Ancillotti Fotografie, Milan.)

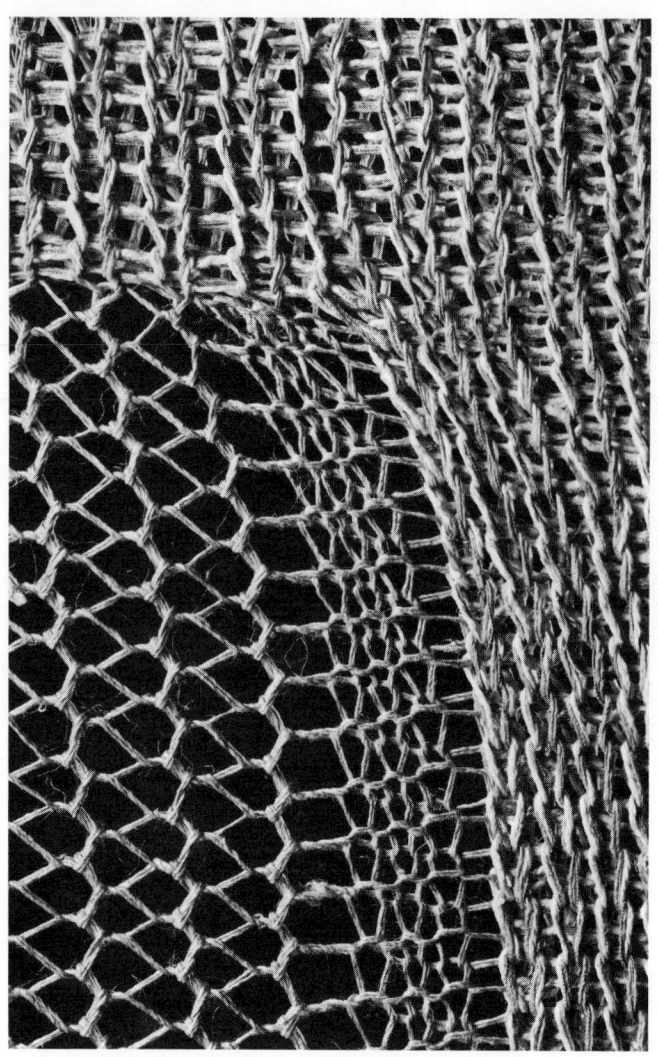

LACE FAGGOT STITCH

This simple Lace Stitch has great versatility. It is based on an even number of stitches and, like all lace patterns, is created by yarn overs and decreases.

The pattern is as follows:
  * YO, P2 tog *, repeat * to * for every row.

This stitch is used for the top section of "The Kings" (page 48). In Illus. 49 and 50, its use is shown in the open areas surrounding the Cross. In the knitted piece of red linen shown on page 84 beads are added after P2 tog is done. The Over stitch is pulled through the bead before the next P2 tog. In the detail of "Onward and Upward" (page 83), the beads are added onto the stitch that results from P2 tog.

A variation on this stitch is:
  * YO, K2 tog *, repeat * to * for every row.
For a further variation, purl the second row.

Illus. 49. This detail of "Cross" shows an area of Lace Faggot next to an area of Double Knit. Since the lacy area had so much stretch, it helped to compensate for the narrowing of the area that is a characteristic of Double Knit. An extra throw was done on every stitch of the Double Knit.

Illus. 50. "Cross," dossel, 34" × 70", (1967). 5/1 natural linen used double, white silk, and gold metallic yarn. Double Knit, Lace Faggot, Stockinette, and Garter Stitches.

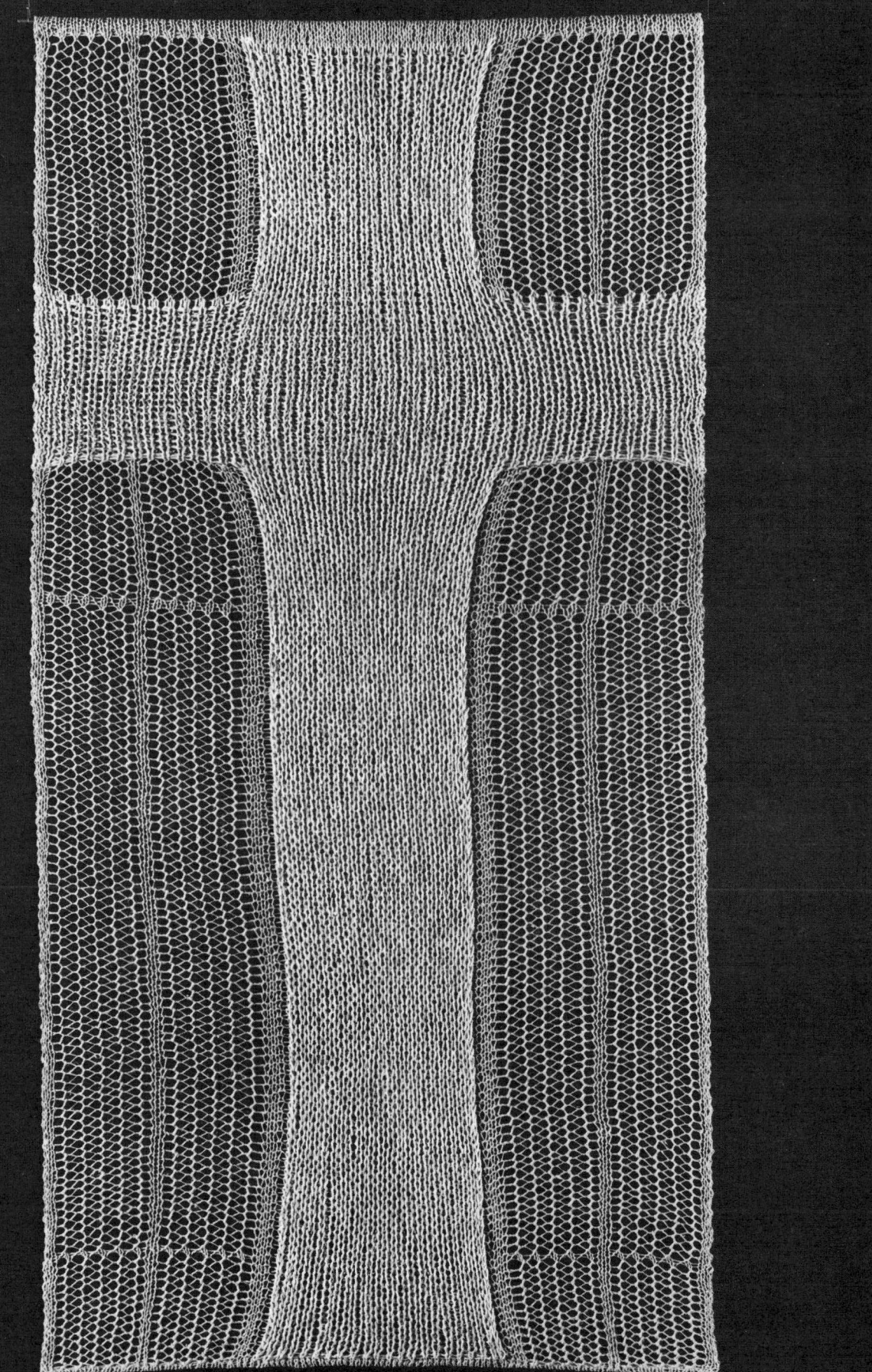

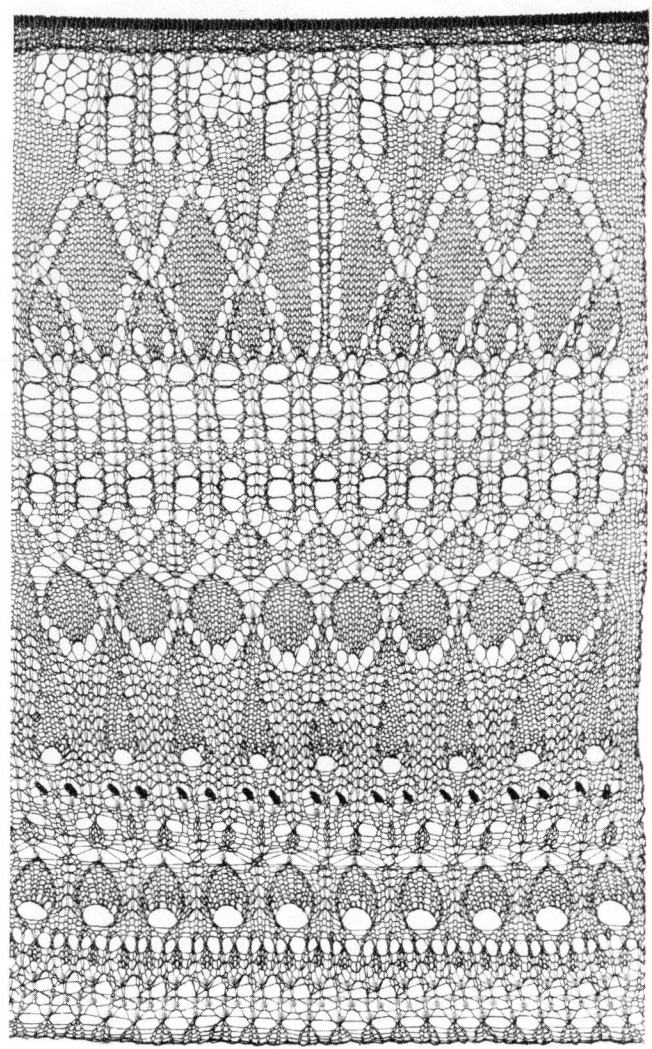

Illus. 51. "Peacocks," wall hanging, 19" × 28", (1967). Dark green linen used double and blue, glass beads. Top half has a great deal of Ladder Stitch separated by rows of Knit into Stitch Below with beads. Bell Pattern was used in lower half. Note a row of Bobbles towards the bottom and the great play of increasing and decreasing above the Bobbles. Decreasing for the Bell Pattern was done on one side only in some cases. (Collection of Frank B. Laury.)

THE LADDER STITCH

This stitch can be used to advantage when a lacelike effect is desired. It is a basic stitch, and its directions are as follows:

    Row 1. * K2 tog, YO, K2 tog *, repeat * to *.

    Row 2. * K1, (K1, P1) into YO, K1 *, repeat * to *.

    Repeat rows for pattern.

Be sure to watch the slant of the decreases so that those on either side of the hole do not slant in the same direction.

If every pattern row is knit, then every decrease row is not as evident. The second row can be purl instead of knit which will make the decrease very evident. If you decide to purl the second row, then pay attention to the decreasing on the knit row, so that it travels either right to left/left to right or left to right/right to left.

To break up the Ladder pattern in areas, knit a row and then purl a row between two pattern rows. The detail of "Peacocks" (Illus. 52) shows the Ladder Stitch with an extra row between the pattern. Knit into Stitch Below and adding a bead onto the stitch gives still another dimension to the piece. The top of Illus. 71 has a great deal of the Ladder Stitch.

SPIRAL RIB STITCH

This stitch is based on the increase/decrease principle and will give a bias fabric. It is also an example of knitting on three needles.

The pattern is as follows:

    Multiple of 12 sts arranged on three needles.

    Row 1. * Sl 1, K1, psso, K6, (K1, P1) into next st, K3 *, repeat * to *.

    Row 2. Knit.

A variation on this stitch is to do YO, K2 tog three times in place of K6 in the pattern row above. Purl the second row. For examples of this stitch, see the knitted hat on page **113** and the chair cover on page **115**. An entirely different effect is achieved by this pattern when it is done on two needles; a diagonal is formed rather than a spiral.

Illus. 52. Detail of "Peacocks" shows the Ladder Stitch, Knit into Stitch Below, and glass beads. There is also decreasing and visible increasing.

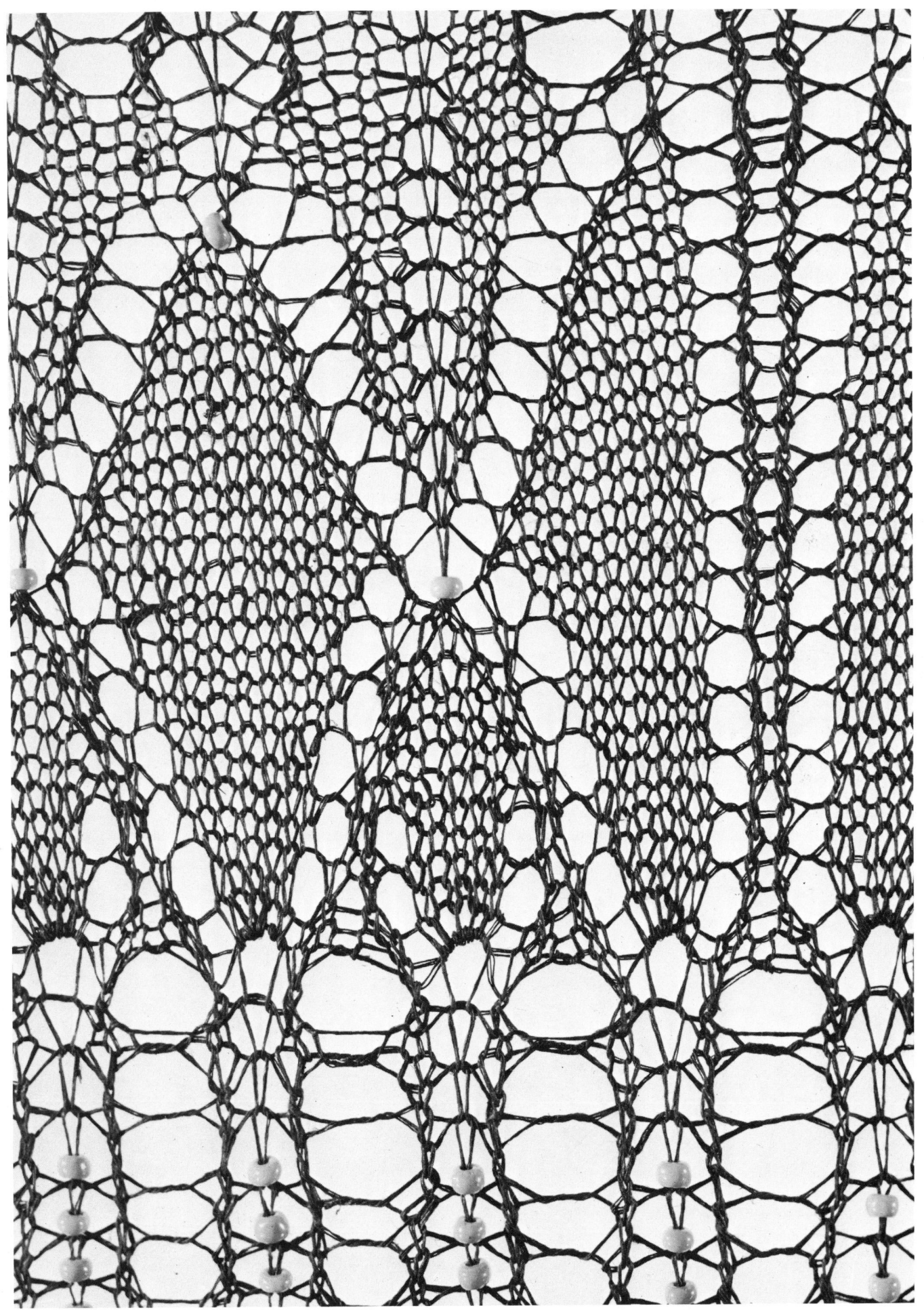

ONE OVER ONE STITCH

A stitch that is a must for every creative knitter is the One Over One motif with its variations. It is really a two-stitch Cable and can cross right over left or left over right. At the beginning of the chapter, I mentioned that I knit and purl using the Uncrossed Combined Method; it is because of the One Over One and its many variations that I mention this method once again and recommend it.

To do the stitch:

Take the needle behind the first st and insert it into the second st, as shown in Diagram 15A. K1, leaving it on the needle, then knit the first st, as shown in Diagram 15B. SI both sts off needle. Continue in same way across row. Purl second row, as shown in Diagram 15C.

The following two stitches (Plaited Basket and Horizontal) are based on the One Over One Stitch.

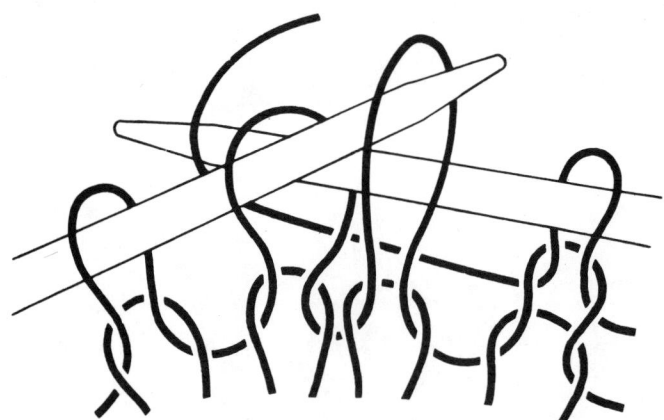

Diagram 15A. **One Over One Stitch.** Knitting into second stitch.

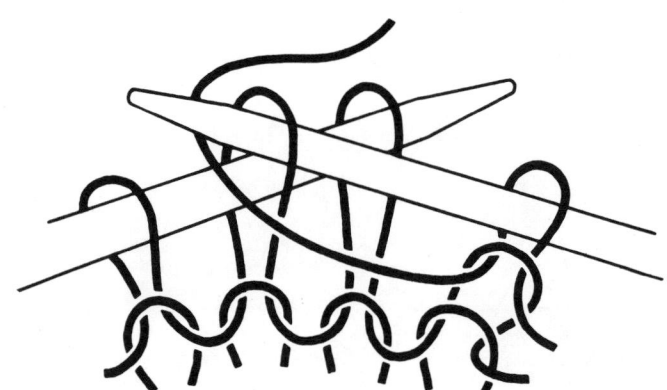

Diagram 15C. **One Over One Stitch.** Purling the second row.

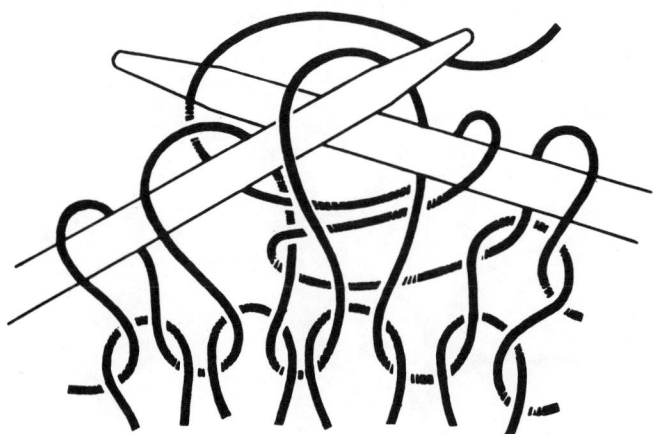

Diagram 15B. **One Over One Stitch.** Knitting into first stitch.

PLAITED BASKET STITCH

This variation of the One Over One is done as follows:

An odd number of sts.

Row 1. K2, * K1 over 1 *, repeat * to *, ending K1.

Row 2. P2, * P1 over 1 *, repeat * to *, ending P1.

Repeat rows for pattern.

Once you understand the principle of this stitch, it can also be done with an even number of stitches.

To make a variation on this stitch, do a Double Throw over the needle. This will give a much more lacy effect. You may want to use this method when doing Plaited Basket Stitch for several rows between other areas to keep the piece from narrowing.

For another variation the following is done:

An odd number of sts.

Row 1. K2, * K1 over 1 *, repeat * to *, ending K1.

Row 2. Purl.

Row 3. K1, * K1 over 1 *, repeat * to *, ending K2.

Row 4. Purl.

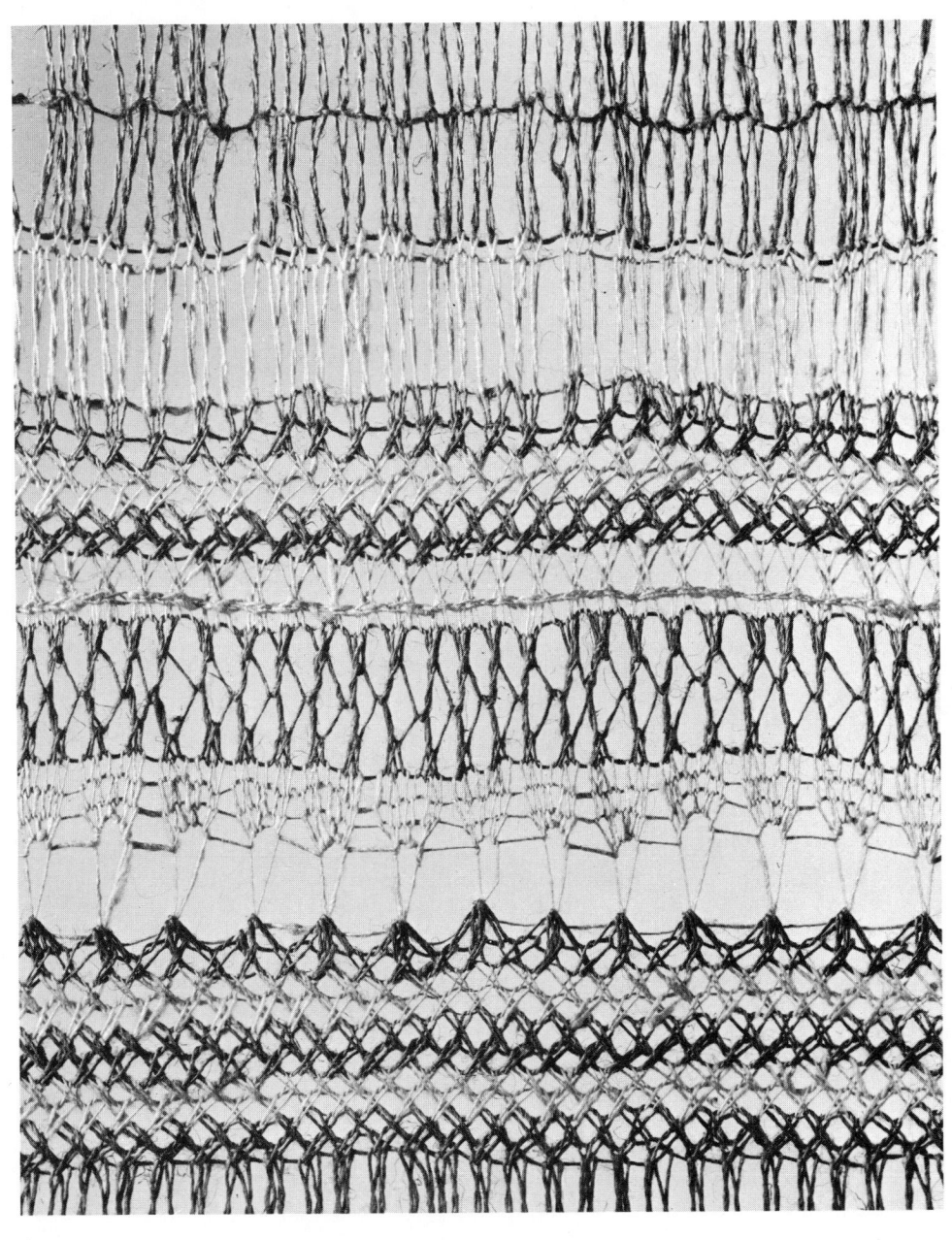

Illus. 53. Detail of "More Variations" (full view on page 34) shows Plaited Basket Stitch along with Fancy Crossed Throw. A row of Horizontal Stitch is in the center. Note the manner of increasing from a single stitch to make many stitches.

HORIZONTAL STITCH

This is still another variation on the One Over One principle. To do the stitch:

Into the first st knit two sts, transfer one st back to left needle (Diagram 16A). * K1 over 1, transfer stitch from right to left needle* and repeat* to *across row until third from last st has been transferred back to left needle, knit last two sts tog, then with third from last st K1 over 1.

The Purl row is shown in Diagram 16B.

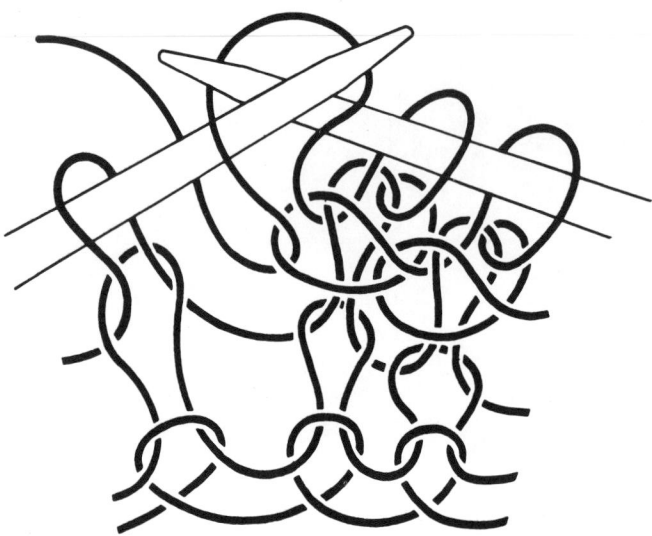

Diagram 16A. **Horizontal Stitch.** Transferring stitch back to left needle.

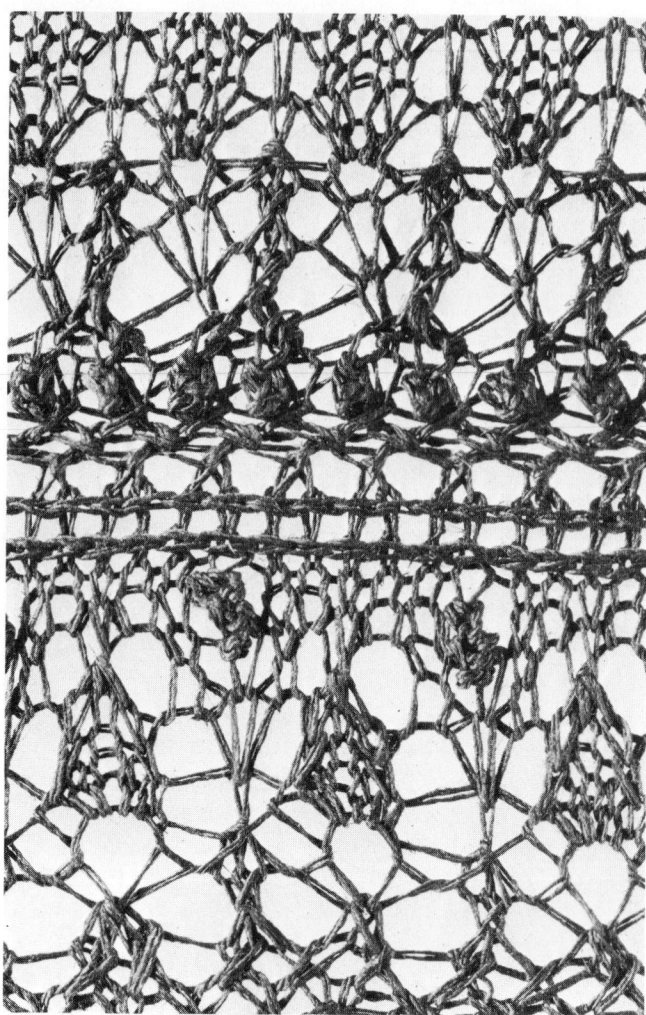

Illus. 54. Detail of wall hanging shows use of many different stitches including Horizontal, Bobble, and Knit into Stitch Below.

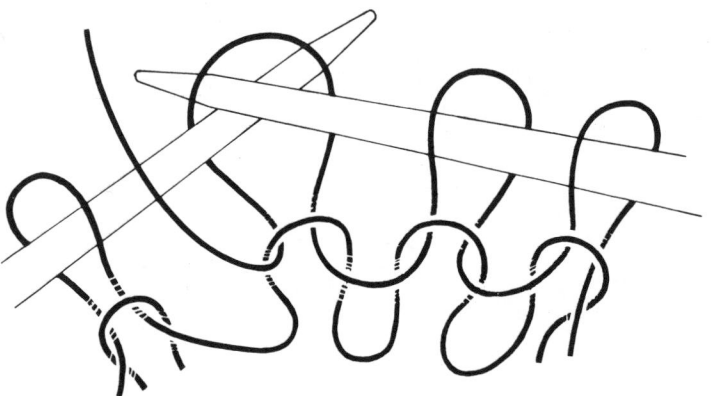

Diagram 16B. **Horizontal Stitch.** Purl row.

By increasing on the first stitch and by knitting the last two stitches together, the piece is kept from going on the bias. If the next row is to be Horizontal Stitch also, you do not have to increase at the beginning and decrease at the end because the two rows will compensate for each other.

This is the only truly horizontal stitch that I know of, and it gives great stability to what otherwise might be a droopy piece. The late Trude Guermonprez, well-known weaver and textile designer, innovated this variation of the One Over One when she was in a class of mine several years ago. It is used in a number of pieces throughout this book. Two examples are Illus. 55 and Illus. 56. I have also used it at the beginning and end of some areas of Double Knit and occasionally for only part of a row as seen in details of "Onward and Upward" (page **83**) and "Peruvian Seeds" (page 49).

The following patterns are also used for knitted constructions in this book. All are patterns that give marvelous effects and that combine well with others. *These are also written for the Uncrossed Combined Method* and use decreases appropriate to that method. When using another method, watch carefully the slants in the decreases.

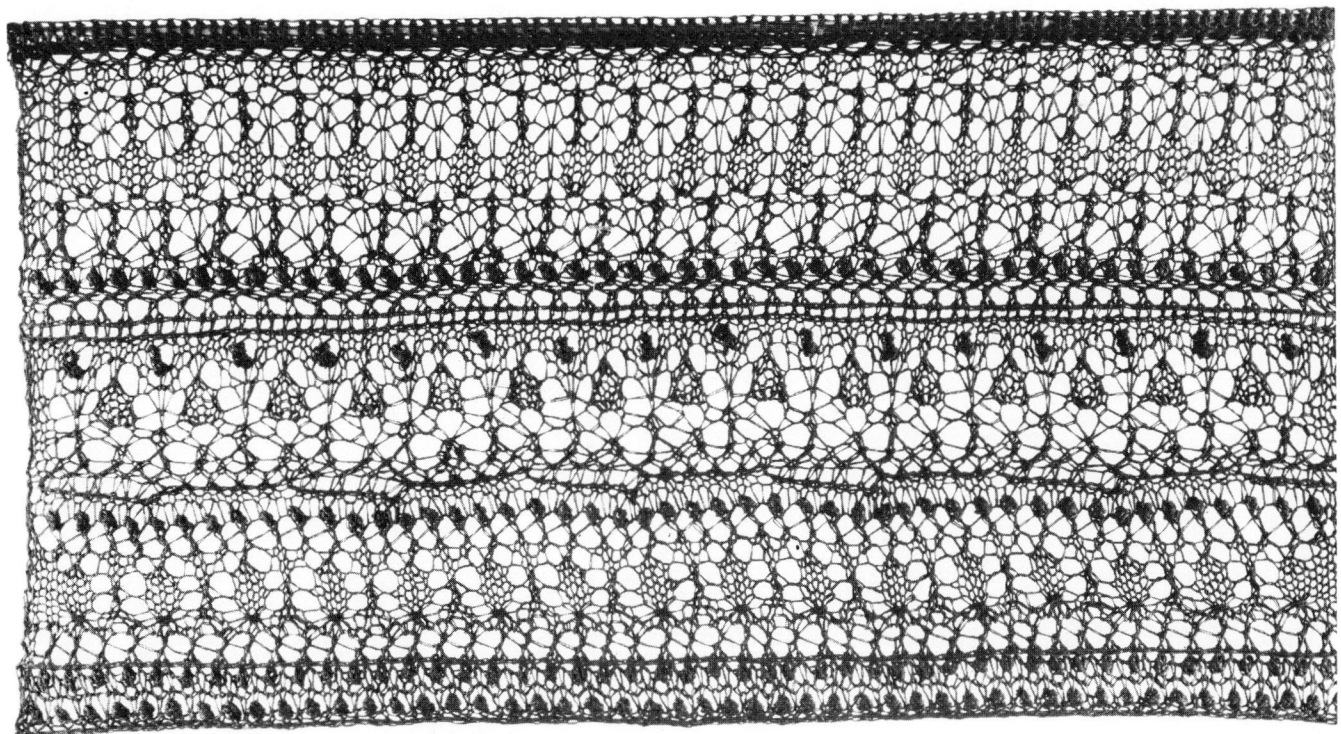

Illus. 55. Wall hanging, 29" x 15", (1968). Collection of Mr. and Mrs. John Cleave. Black 5/1 linen used double. Full view of detail on previous page. Shows effect of Horizontal Stitch used in conjunction with other stitches.

BELL PATTERN

This is an exciting pattern to create and can be used as an overall repeat, or to alternate, or as a pattern insertion. Similar to other motifs that have been described, it can also be grouped to form geometric shapes. *Since these instructions are for the Uncrossed Combined Method, reverse position of the two stitches that are to be decreased.* The variation of the Bell Pattern given here is used in "Near East" (page 67).

The pattern is as follows (for the left over right decrease, see page 62):

Multiple of 4 sts, plus 4.

Row 1. K2, * P4 *, repeat * to *, ending K2.

Row 2. P2, * K4 *, repeat * to *, ending P2.

Row 3. K2, * P4 *, repeat * to *, ending K2.

Row 4. P2, * K2, turn work and cast on 9 sts by knitting (see Diagrams 13A and 13B, page 66), turn work and K2 *, repeat * to *, ending P2.

Row 5. K2, * P2, K9 into back of sts (see Diagram 14, page 66), P2 *, repeat * to *, ending K2.

Row 6. P2, * K2, P9, K2 *, repeat * to *, ending P2.

Row 7. K2, * P2, K2 tog, K5, left over right dec, P2 *, repeat * to *, ending K2.

Row 8. P2, * K2, P7, K2 *, repeat * to *, ending P2.

Row 9. K2, * P2, K2 tog, K3, left over right dec, P2 *, repeat * to *, ending K2.

Row 10. P2, * K2, P5, K2 *, repeat * to *, ending P2.

Row 11. K2, * P2, K2 tog, K1, left over right dec, P2 *, repeat * to *, ending K2.

Row 12. P2, * K2, P3, K2 *, repeat * to *, ending P2.

Row 13. K2, * P2, Sl 1, left over right dec, psso, P2 *, repeat * to *, ending K2.

Row 14. * K1, K2 tog (this will eliminate the extra st that would be added if there were no dec at this point), K2 *, repeat * to *, ending P2.

This pattern may be varied by the number of stitches that are cast on for the increase.

BELL FRILLING PATTERN

Little bell shapes that stand out from the fabric are formed by this pattern. It can be seen in Illus. 56 and can be compared there with the Bell Pattern which is also used. To do Bell Frilling:

Multiple of 9 sts, plus 8.

Row 1. * P8, K1 *, repeat * to *, ending P8.

Row 2. * K8, P1 *, repeat * to *, ending K8.

Row 3. * P8, YO, K1, YO *, repeat * to *, ending P8.

Row 4. * K8, P3 *, repeat * to *, ending K8.

Row 5. * P8, YO, K3, YO *, repeat * to *, ending P8.

Row 6. * K8, P5 *, repeat * to *, ending K8.

Row 7. * P8, YO, K5, YO *, repeat * to *, ending P8.

Row 8. * K8, P7 *, repeat * to *, ending K8.

Row 9. * P8, YO, K7, YO *, repeat * to *, ending P8.

Row 10. * K8, P9 *, repeat * to *, ending K8.

Row 11. * P8, YO, K9, YO *, repeat * to *, ending P8.

Row 12. * K8, P11 *, repeat * to *, ending K8.

Row 13. * P8, YO, K11, YO *, repeat * to *, ending P8.

Row 14. * K8, P13 *, repeat * to *, ending K8.

Row 15. * P8, YO, K13, YO *, repeat * to *, ending P8.

Row 16. * K8, P15 *, repeat * to *, ending K8.

Row 17. * P8, YO, K15, YO *, repeat * to *, ending P8.

Row 18. * K8, P17 *, repeat * to *, ending K8.

Row 19. * P8, YO, K17, YO *, repeat * to *, ending P8.

Row 20. * K8, P19 *, repeat * to *, ending K8.

This pattern can be continued or cast off. If the 18 increased stitches are cast off at this point, then the next rows would repeat Rows 1 and 2 as many times as desired.

Illus. 56. Wall hanging, 24" × 48", (1968). 5/1 natural linen used double, natural silk, and mica from North Carolina. Rows of Horizontal Stitches separate areas done in variations on Bell and Bell Frilling Patterns, Double Knit, Clustering, Bobble, Knit into Stitch Below, and the YO, K2 tog variation of the Lace Faggot.

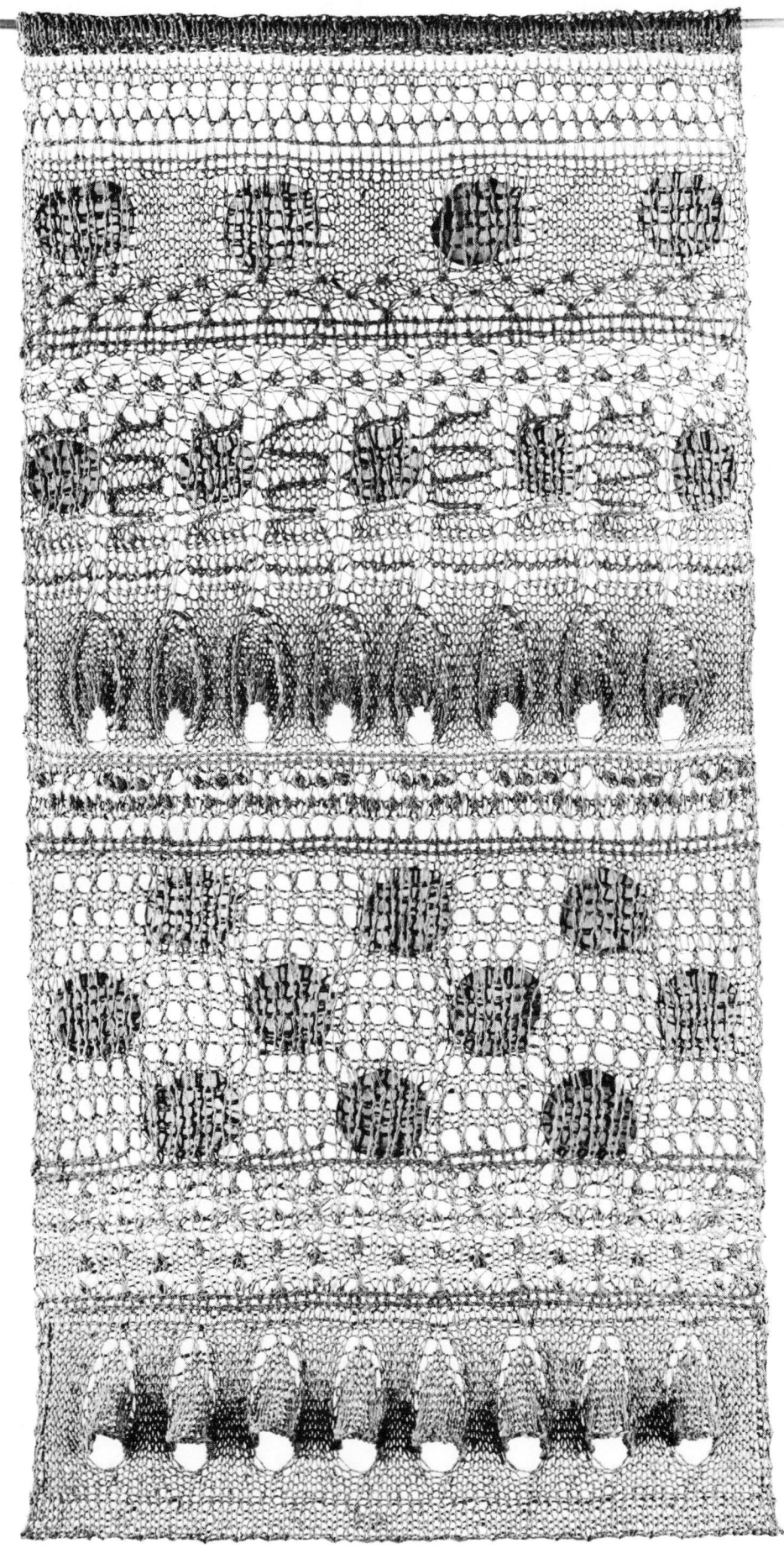

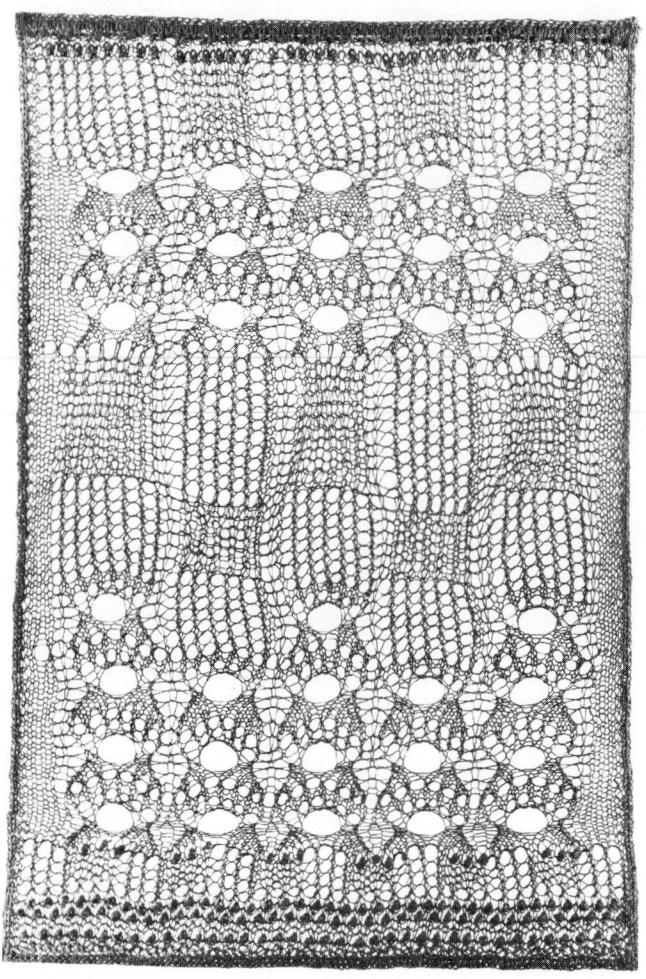

LACE DIADEM EYELET PATTERN

This pattern has several names and variations. "Many Openings" (Illus. 57 and 58) shows a variation of Lace Diadem. In Illus. 59, it is varied and is used as part of the design. One form of the pattern is done according to the following directions. (For left over right decrease see page 62. For Purl Reverse decrease see page 62.)

Multiple of 14 sts, plus 5.

Row 1. K3, *K2 tog,   K9, left over right dec, K1 *, repeat * to *, ending K2.

Row 2. P2, * P1, P2 tog, P7, Purl Reverse dec *, repeat * to *, ending P3.

Row 3. K3, *K2 tog, K2, YO3, K3, left over right dec, K1 *, repeat * to *, ending K2.

Row 4. P2, * P1, P2 tog, P2, (K1, P1, K1, P1, K1) making 5 into Over, P1, Purl Reverse dec *, repeat * to *, ending P3.

Row 5. K3, *K2 tog, K6, left over right dec K1 *, repeat * to *, ending K2.

Row 6. P2, * P1, P2 tog, P6 *, repeat * to *, ending P3.

Row 7. K3, * K1, (YO, K1) 6 times, K1 *, ending K2.

Row 8. Purl.

Rows 9 and 10. Knit.

The pattern rows may end here or may continue as follows:

Row 11. K2, * (K2 tog, YO) 7 times *, repeat * to *, ending K3.

Row 12. Purl.

Illus. 57. "Many Openings," 28" × 40", (1967). Brown 5/1 linen and brown mohair. Lace Diadem Pattern, Bobble, Knit into Stitch Below, Lace Faggot, Double Knit, and Garter Stitches. At no time in this piece is the Lace Diadem used in its pure form. The use of Knit into Stitch Below between pattern repeats creates a strong vertical effect which separates the piece into five areas. At the end of each pattern repeat there is an alternate patterning of Double Knit areas and lacy areas. Bobbles begin and end the piece.

Illus. 58. A detail of "Many Openings" shows alternate areas of Double Knit (bottom left) and Lace Faggot (bottom right), as well as the Lace Diadem Pattern (upper half) and the division of these areas by Knit into Stitch Below. Notice how the decreasing provides very definite curves when worked from one area to another.

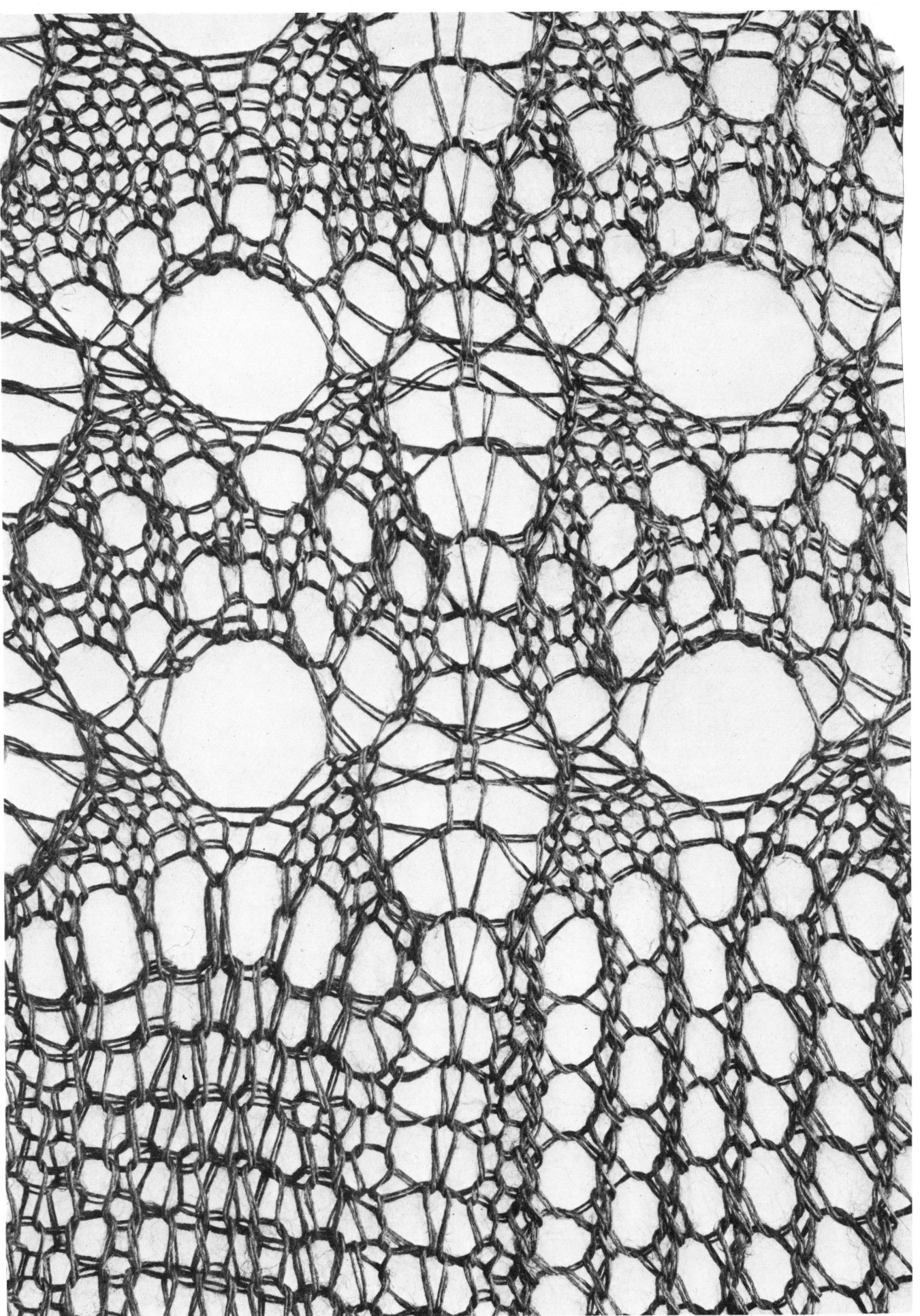

Illus. 60. "Shells," casement, 48″ × 82″, (1967). Collection of The Art Institute of Chicago. 5/1 natural linen used double, and natural silk. Shell Pattern, Fancy Crossed Throw, Knit into Stitch Below, and Ladder Stitches are used.

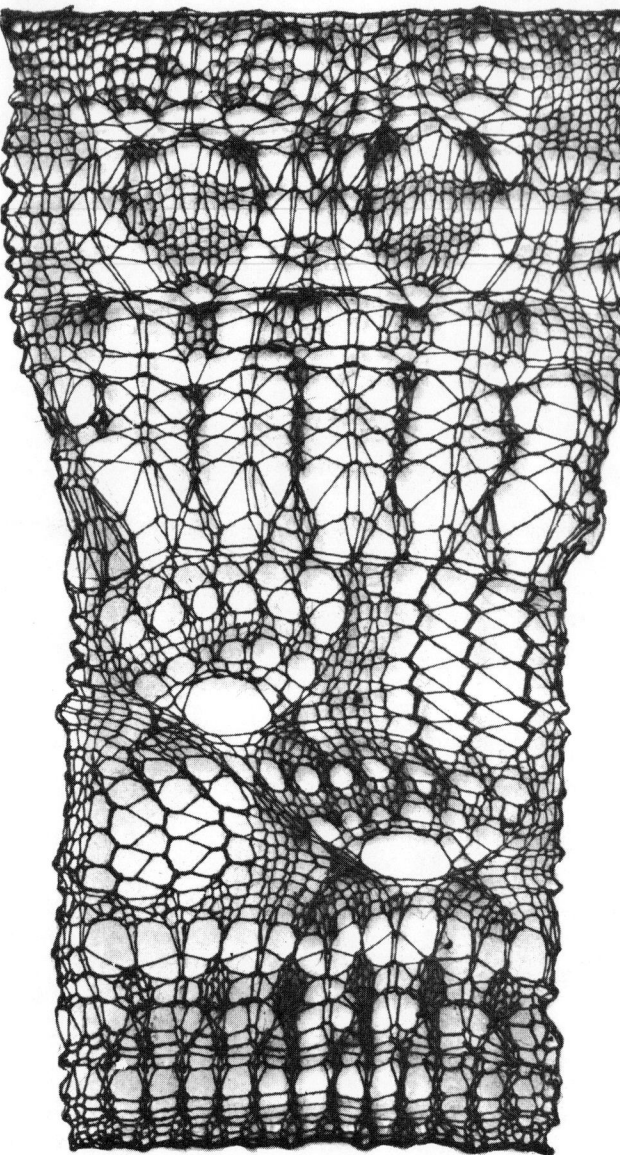

SHELL PATTERN

This pattern can be seen in "Shells" and the detail of it (Illus. 60 and 61).

> Multiple of 6 sts, plus 2.
>
> Rows 1 and 2. Knit.
>
> Row 3. K1, * insert needle into st and make three throws *, repeat * to *, ending K1.
>
> Row 4. K1, * K into first throw of each st and drop other throws (this will give long sts) *, repeat * to *, ending K1.
>
> Row 5. K1, * Sl 3, K2 tog, p3 sso, (K1, P1, K1, P1, K1) into next st *, repeat * to *, ending K1.
>
> Rows 6, 7, and 8. Knit.
>
> Row 9. Repeat Row 3.
>
> Row 10. Repeat Row 4.
>
> Row 11. K1, * (K1, P1, K1, P1, K1) into next st, Sl 3, K2 tog, p3 sso *, repeat * to *, ending K1.
>
> Row 12. Knit.

Illus. 60. "Shells," casement, 48″ × 82″, (1967). 5/1 natural linen used double and natural silk. Shell Pattern, Fancy Crossed Throw, Knit into Stitch Below, and Ladder Stitches.

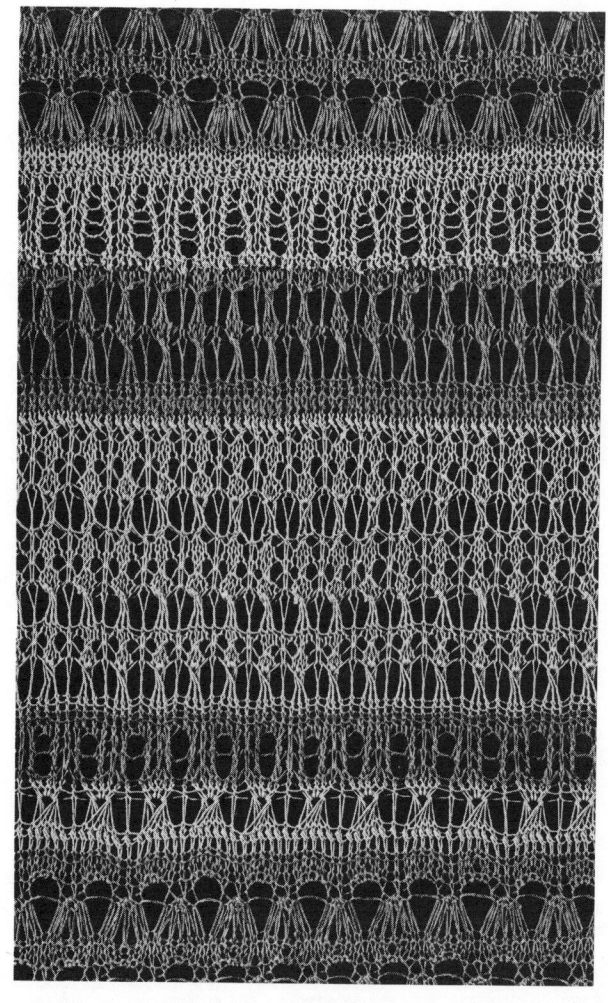

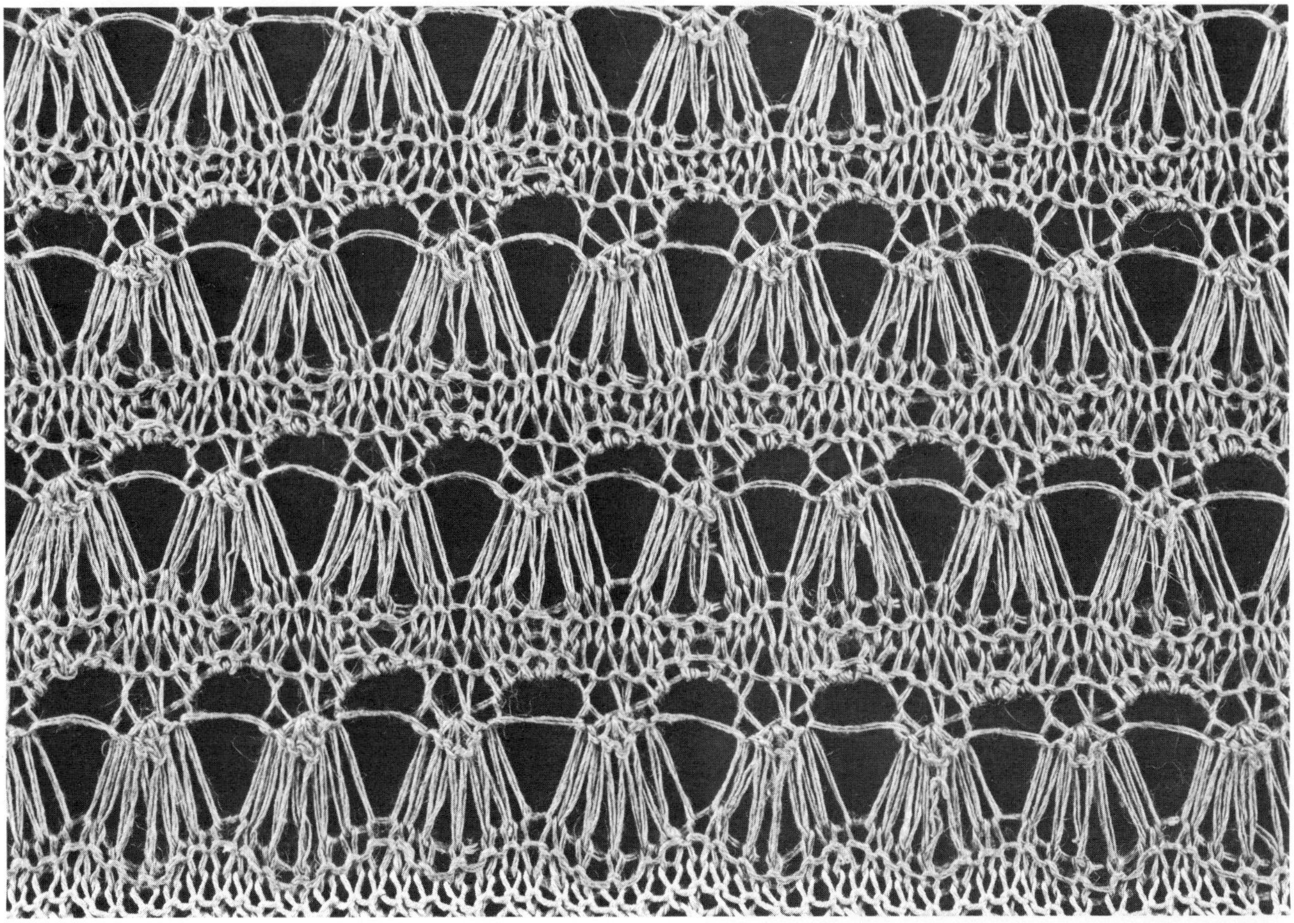

Illus. 61. Detail of "Shells" showing Shell Pattern (done in linen).

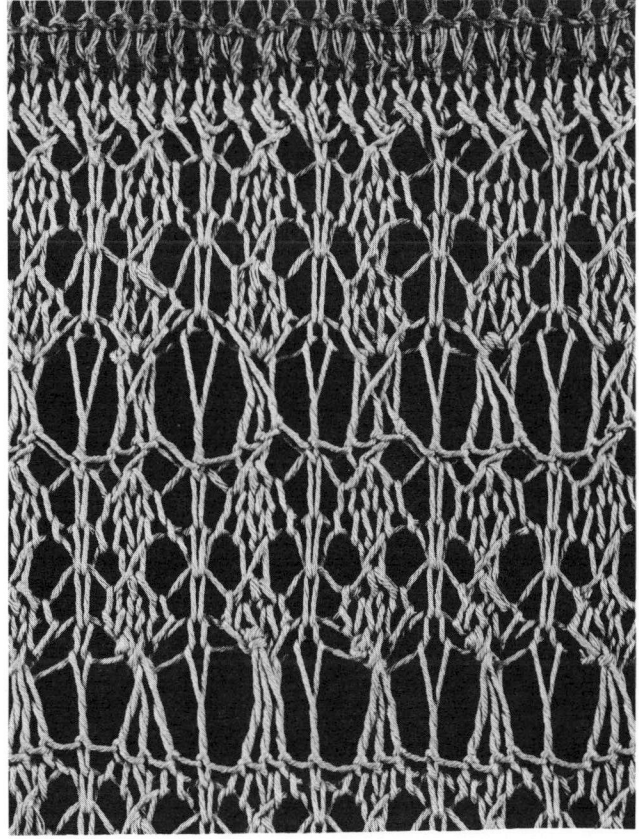

Illus. 62. Detail of "Shells" shows the area worked in silk with the use of Knit into Stitch Below and Fancy Crossed Throw. Note how the Fancy Crossed Throws are varied.

BOWKNOT OR BUTTERFLY PATTERN

This pattern may be seen in "Onward and Upward" (Illus. 63) and in its detail (Illus. 64).

Multiple of 10 sts, plus 4.

To make this pattern alternate, figure the number of sts as follows: 10 + 5 + 4 edge sts. This pattern is written on that multiple.

Rows 1, 3, 5, 7, and 9. K2, * yarn forward and Sl 5 and yarn back, K5 *, repeat * to *, ending Sl 5, K2.

Rows 2, 4, 6, and 8. Purl.

Row 10. The instructions within the brackets complete the Butterfly and are to be repeated where indicated on other rows to complete the pattern. P2, * [P2, turn piece to front, insert right needle under loose strands and into middle stitch corresponding to middle strand. Pull free end of yarn through and place loop on right needle. Turn work, P loop and next st tog—this pulls the loose stitches together to make the Butterfly, P2], P5 *, repeat * to *, ending [to], P2.

Rows 11, 13, 15, 17, and 19. K2, * K5, yarn forward and Sl 5 and yarn back *, repeat * to *, ending Sl 5, K7.

Rows 12, 14, 16, and 18. Purl.

Row 20. P7, * Butterfly and Purl as in Row 10 following instructions from bracket to bracket, P7 *, repeat * to *

A variation on making the Butterfly is as follows:

P4, * the next st is the middle of the loose strands, turn work, pick up strands with right needle, turn work and P middle st tog with loose strands, P9 *, repeat * to *, ending P4.

Another variation is to do the pattern without gathering the loose strands into a butterfly; then, when the pattern is finished, wrap the strands with a contrasting material.

Illus. 63. "Onward and Upward," wall hanging, 36" × 34", (1968). 5/1 natural and ikat-dyed green linen. Natural wooden beads. This piece has many things going on in it. Above the section shown and described in Illus. 64, there is a small Bell motif between areas of Garter Stitch; the Horizontal Stitch precedes and follows these areas. A section similar to the beginning is then put in with beads, and the Ladder Stitch is knit in areas that lead into the Bell Pattern. Alternating areas are Double Knit, and then the Ladder Stitch is done with beads added onto either side of pattern. The Bell Pattern is developed again with alternating areas done in Double Knit followed by the Butterfly Pattern going into a lacy area.

Illus. 64. Detail of "Onward and Upward" shows the Bowknot or Butterfly Pattern at the top of the photograph. To analyze the rest of the stitches, begin at the bottom of the photograph. The first section is in alternating areas of YO, P2 tog every row and Double Knit. At the end of the second section, which is the alternate of the first, there is use of the Horizontal Stitch. The Butterfly Pattern follows and a wooden bead is added where the floating stitches are pulled together. There are also areas of Stockinette Stitch and Lace Stitch with the Butterfly Pattern.

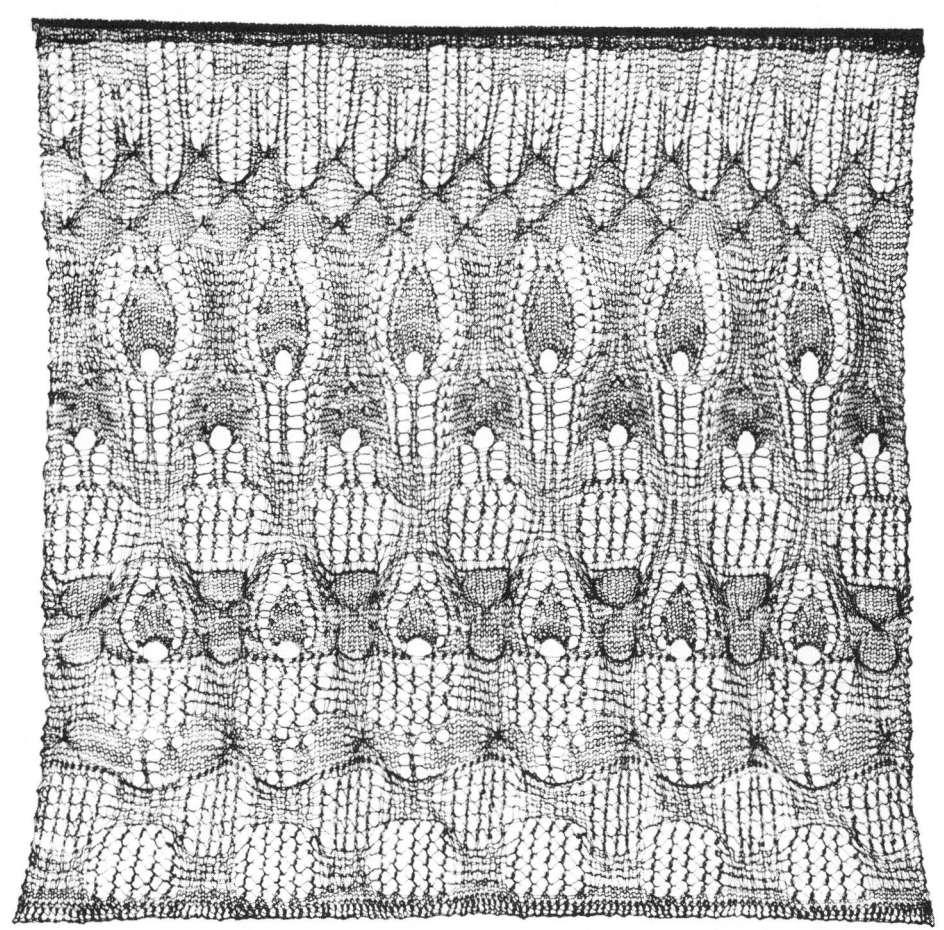

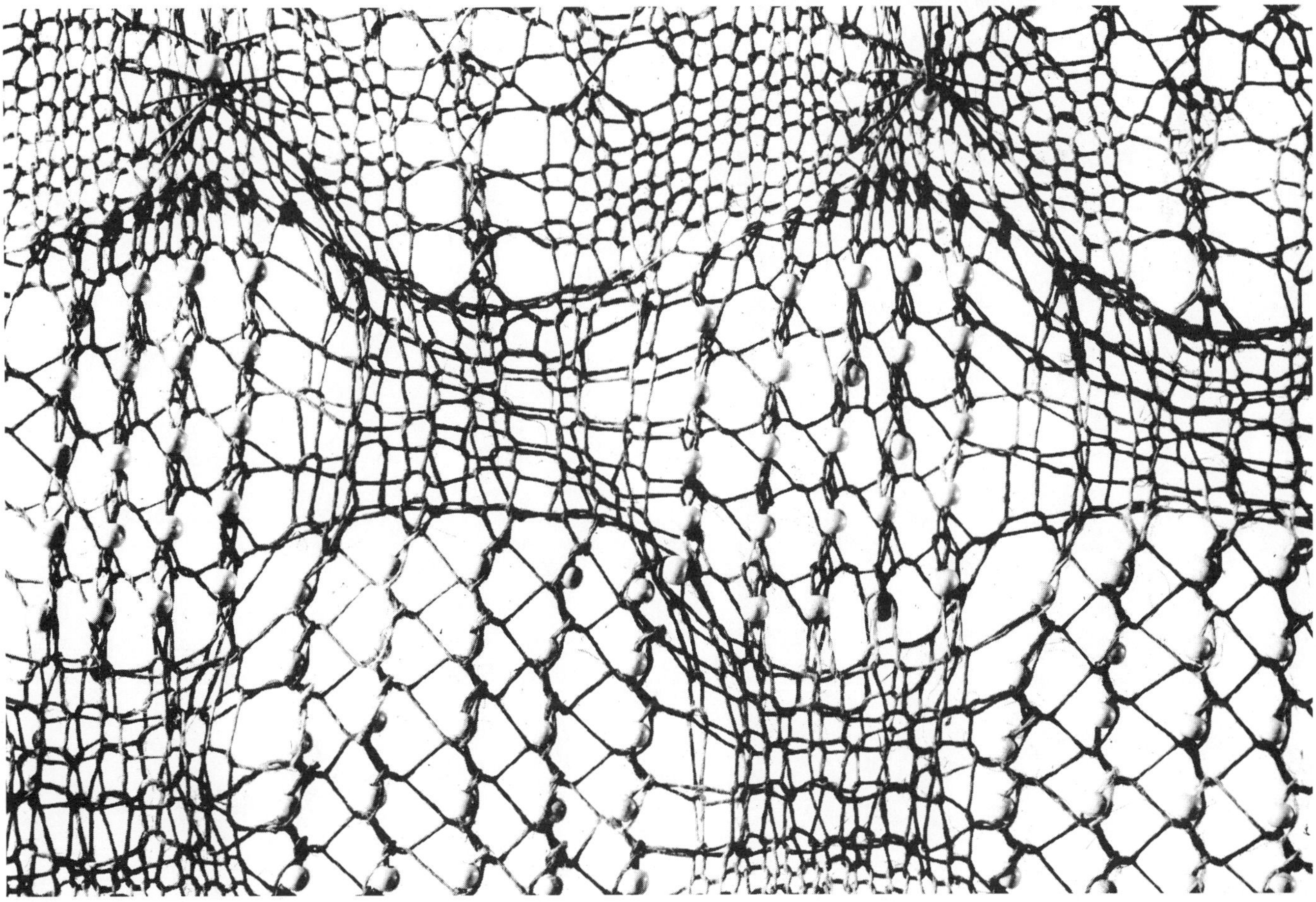

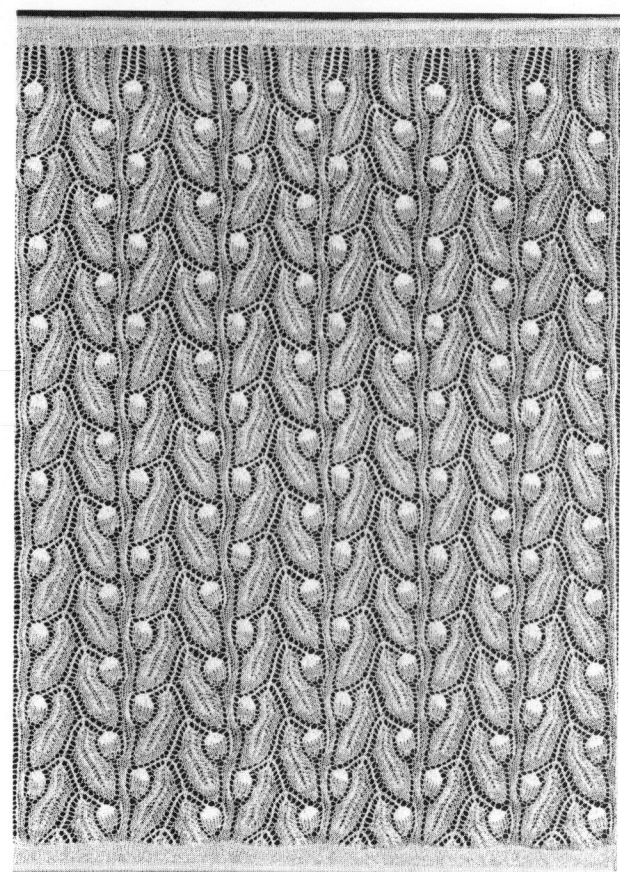
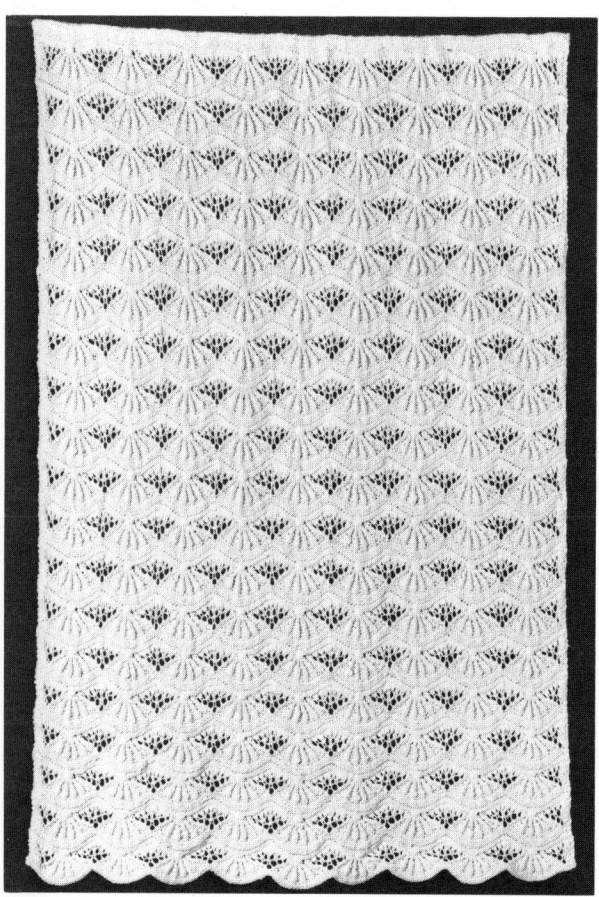

HONEYCOMB PATTERN

This stitch is shown in Illus. 65 and 66. It can also be seen in "Yellow Variations" (pages 92 and 93).

Multiple of 8 sts, plus 6.

Cast on 38 sts.

Rows 1 and 2. Knit.

Row 3. K2, * Sl 2 pw, K6 *, repeat * to *, ending Sl 2 pw, K2.

Row 4. P2, * Sl 2 pw, P6 *, repeat * to *, ending Sl 2 pw, P2.

Rows 5 and 7. Repeat Row 3.

Rows 6 and 8. Repeat Row 4.

Rows 9, 10, 11, and 12. Knit.

Row 13. K6, * Sl 2 pw, K6 *, repeat * to *.

Row 14. P6, * Sl 2 pw, P6 *, repeat * to *.

Rows 15 and 17. Repeat Row 13.

Rows 16 and 18. Repeat Row 14.

Rows 19, 20, 21, and 22. Knit.

I could continue for pages, but all the fun of discovery would be lost. Knitting is a constant adventure. There is always a new stitch to experiment with, or a new pattern to try, or even an old pattern friend that you can knit with different yarns thus giving it your own interpretation. So great is the diversity of patterns that no one pattern book includes them all. Each time you explore an unfamiliar book, you will discover a pattern you have not tried, and you will gain a bit of knowledge that you did not have before. This discovery and knowledge, and what you do with it, will stimulate you, the creative knitter, to still more exciting works of art.

Wall hanging, 24″ x 48″. (Collection of Gladys Peters.) Knit in 5/1 natural linen (used double) and natural silk, with mica inserted into pockets formed by Double Knit Stitch. Uses variations of the Bell and Bell Frilling Patterns. For further analysis, see page 77.

Wall hanging, 19″ × 40″. Knit in red Scandinavian linen using many different kinds of stitches.

Wall hanging, 20″ × 35″ Knit in 5/1 natural and ikat-dyed red linen, with red, wooden beads. Stitches include the Double Knit, Lace Faggot, Stockinette, Cable, Plaited Basket, and One Over One. Piece was turned upside down for hanging. (Collection of Harold D. Crosby.)

Wall hanging, 14″ × 36″. (Collection of Miss Anne Stackhouse.) Yellow slub linen and yellow, wooden beads. Vertical effect is achieved by use of extra throws over the needle when using Knit into Stitch Below. For further analysis, see page 54.

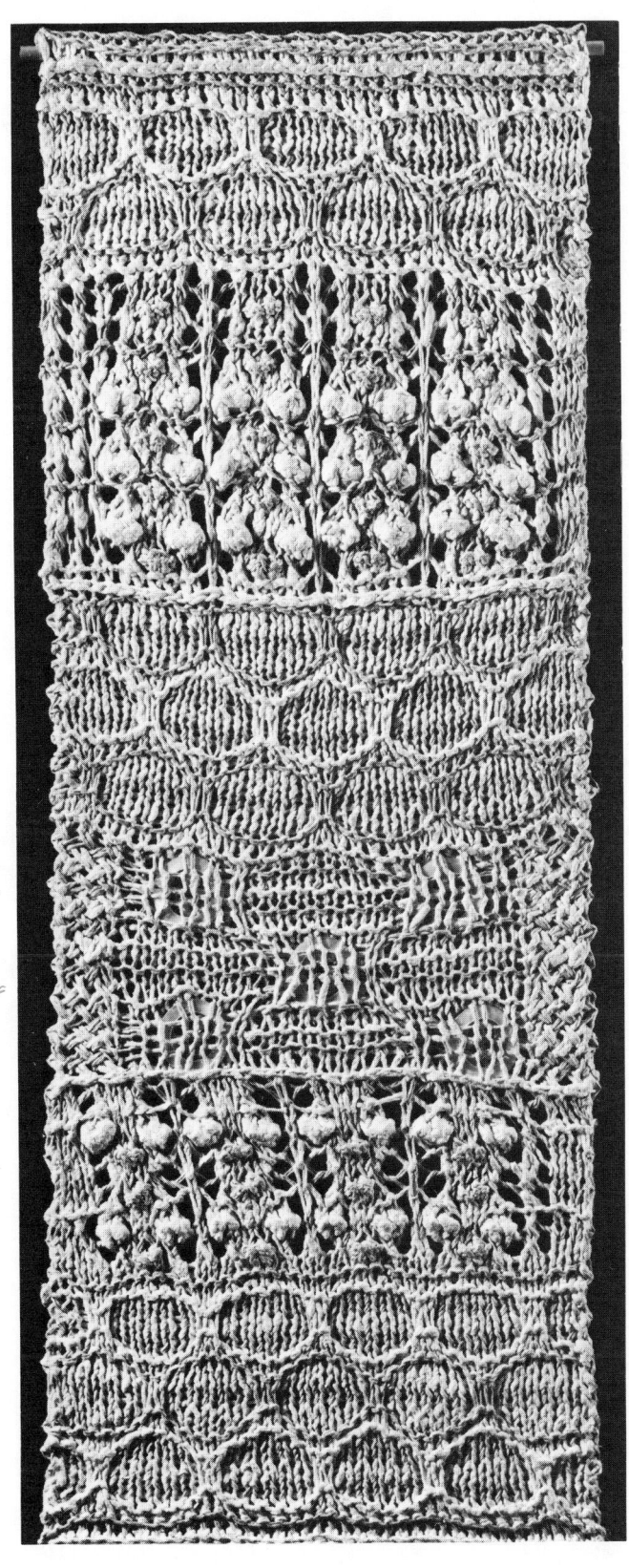

Illus. 65. Wall hanging, 13″ × 34″, (1967). 5/1 natural linen, white silk, and pearl rings. Honeycomb Pattern, Bobble, Plaited Basket, Knit into Stitch Below, Double Knit, and Garter Stitches. The pearl rings are used in the pockets of Double Knit. (Collection of Mrs. Bobby Copeland.)

Illus. 67. This is an interesting detail of "The Kings" (page 48) because of all the variations that are shown. Starting at the bottom there is a turned Cable leading into a lacy area. By doing YO three times a large hole is made, and is the base for adding on stitches for the Bell Pattern in the following row. One Over One is knit in alternating rows leading into the Ladder Stitch. A row of Fancy Crossed Throws is shown at the top.

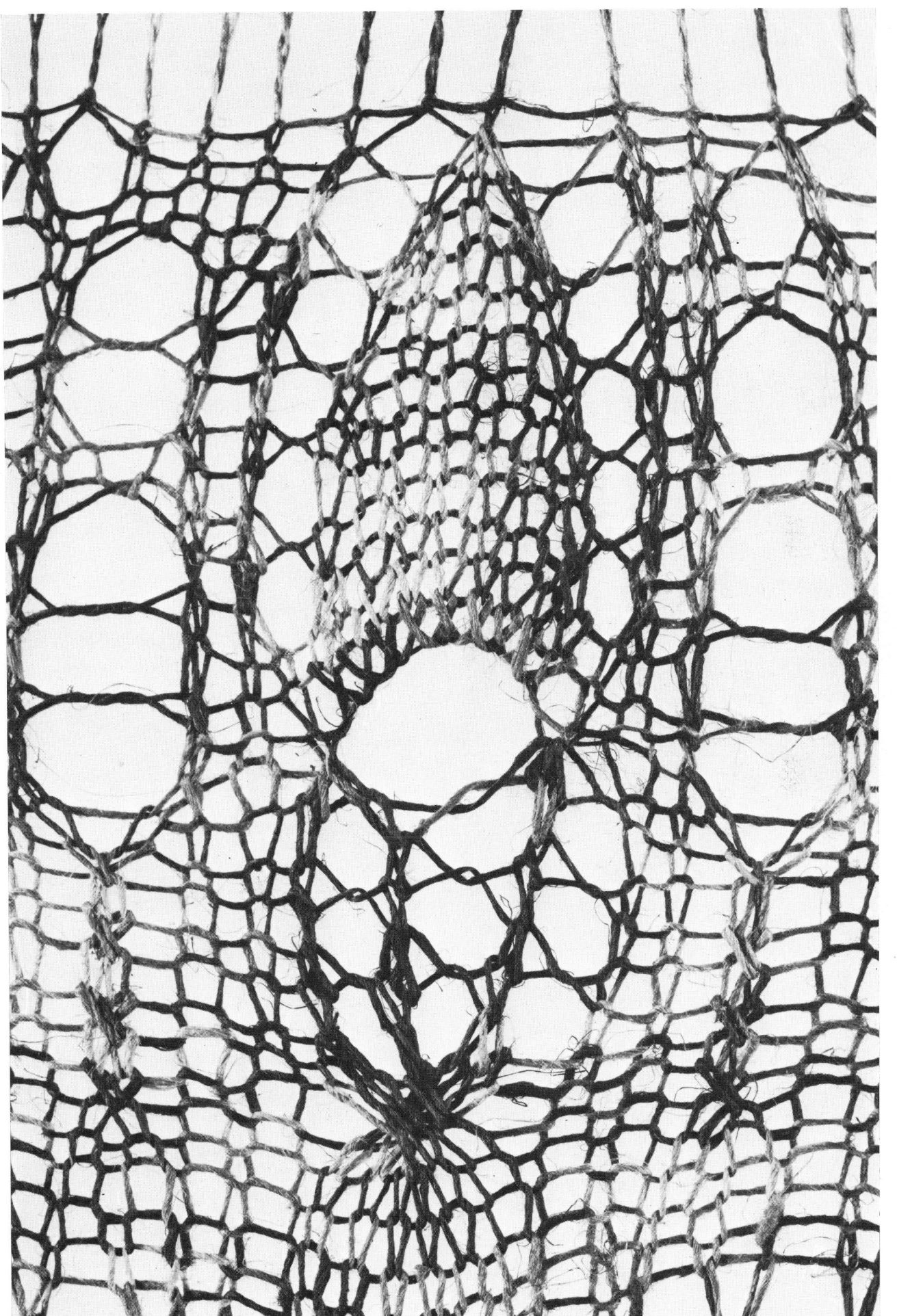

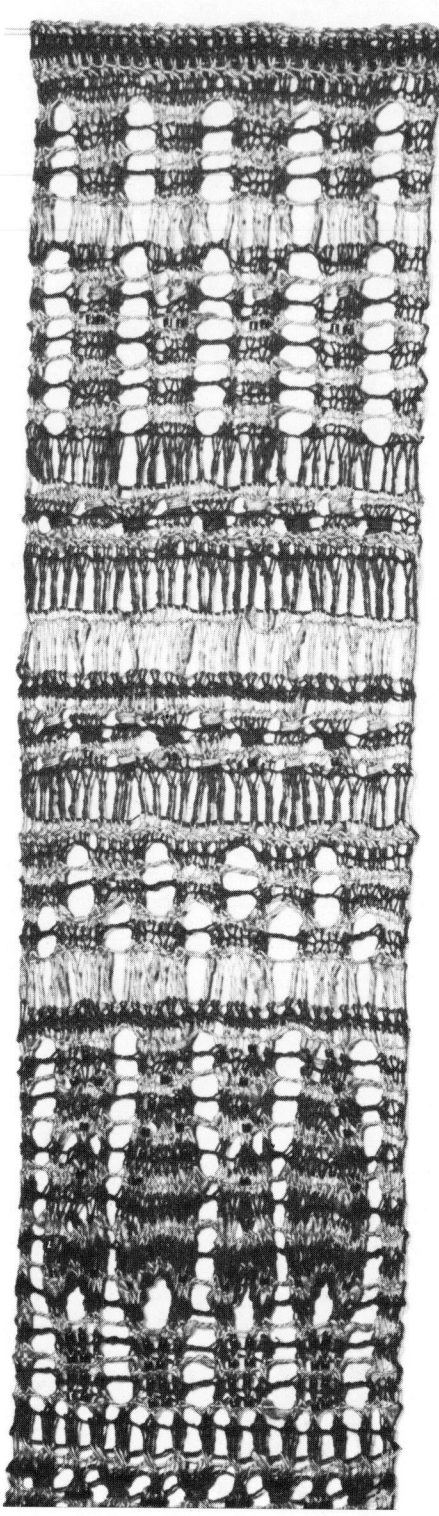

Illus. 69. Wall hanging, 14″ × 43″, (1965). Moss green and black slub linen with black glass beads. Fancy Crossed Throw, Clustering, and Ladder were a few of the many kinds of stitches used. The piece was originally knit in black and white. The combination, however, produced a disjointed piece, so I dyed it. (Collection of Marianne Harvey, Hants, England. Photograph by Gayle Smalley.)

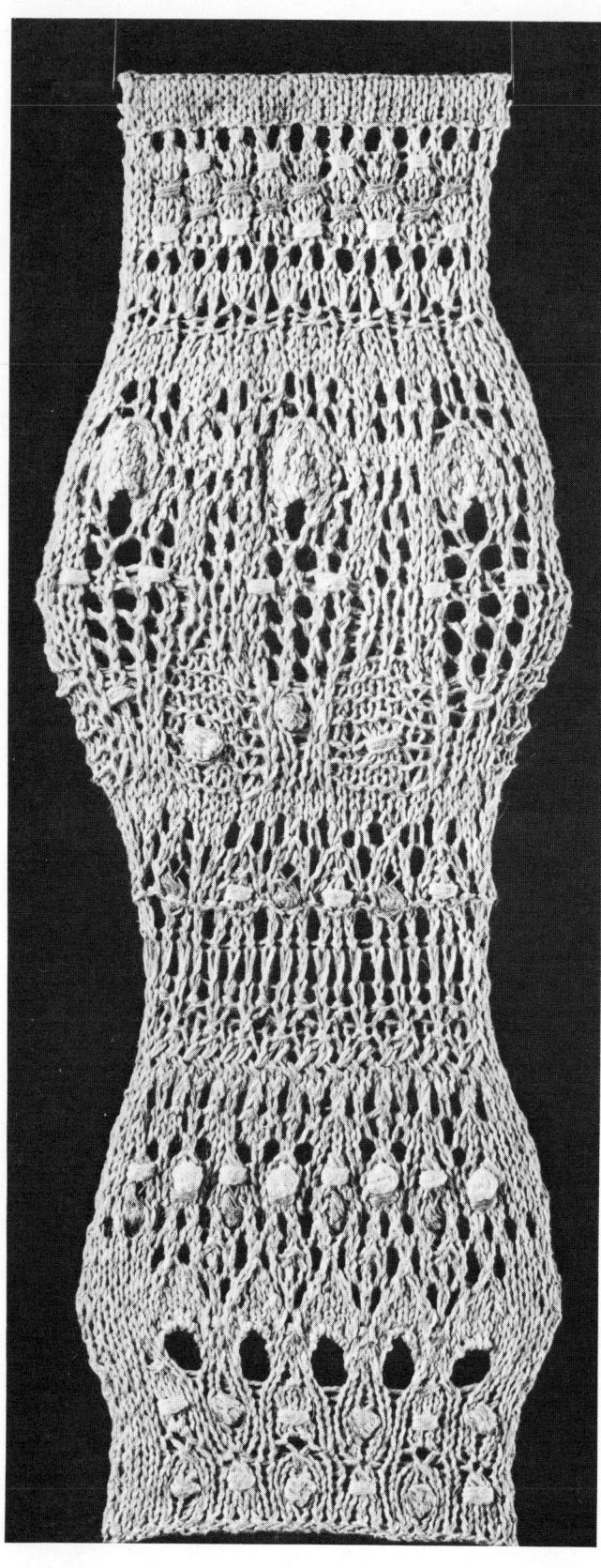

Illus. 68. Wall hanging, 10″ × 29″, (1965). 5/1 natural linen and white silk. This piece uses a large variety of stitches.

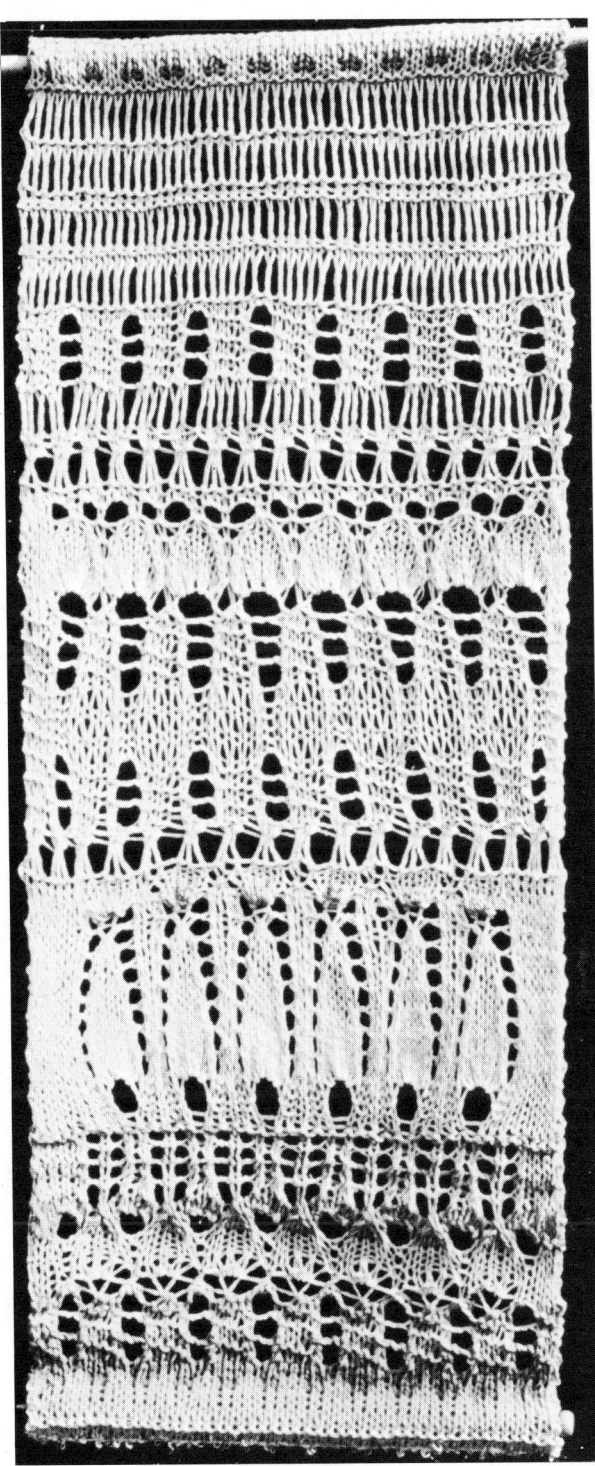

Illus. 71. Wall hanging, 21″ × 52″, (1966). Natural linen and silk. White silk is used for Clustering. This pattern uses many different stitches. (Collection of the Museum of Contemporary Crafts, gift of the author. Photograph by Gayle Smalley.)

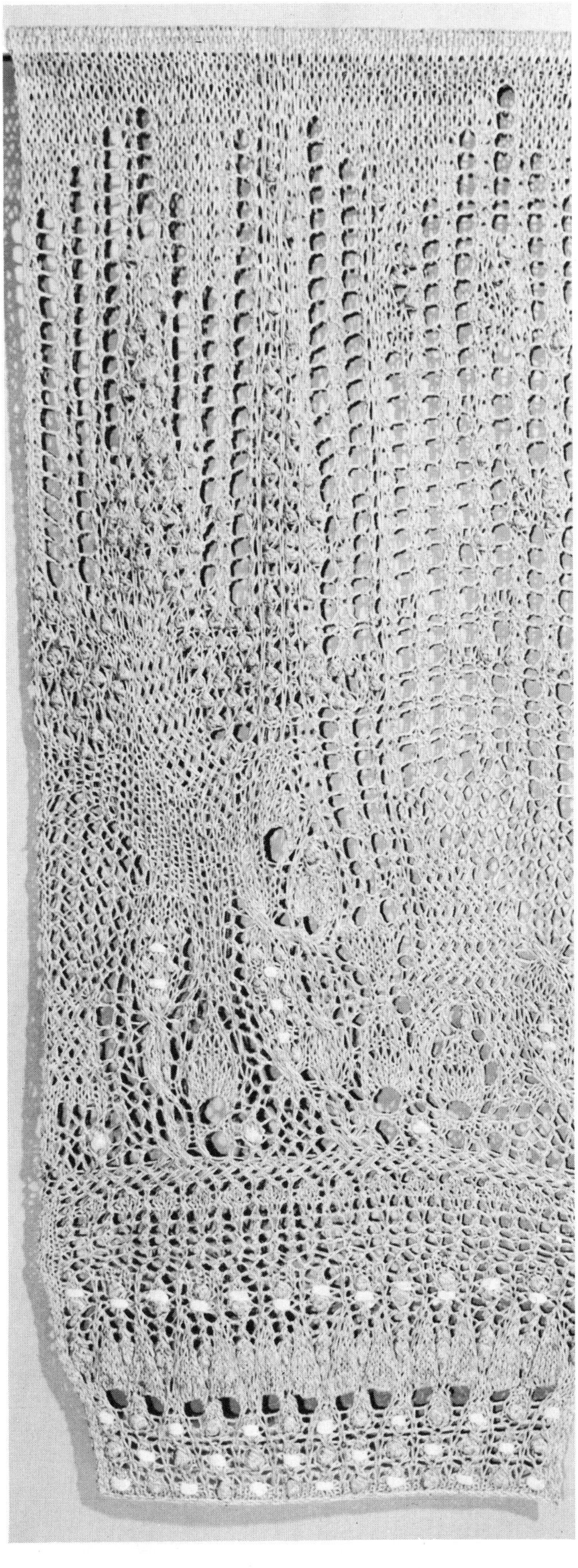

Illus. 70. Wall hanging, 14″ × 36″, (1965). White and yellow linen. White and yellow silk. Combination of the Bell Pattern, Fancy Crossed Throw and Ladder Stitches with their variations. (Photograph by Fred Albert.)

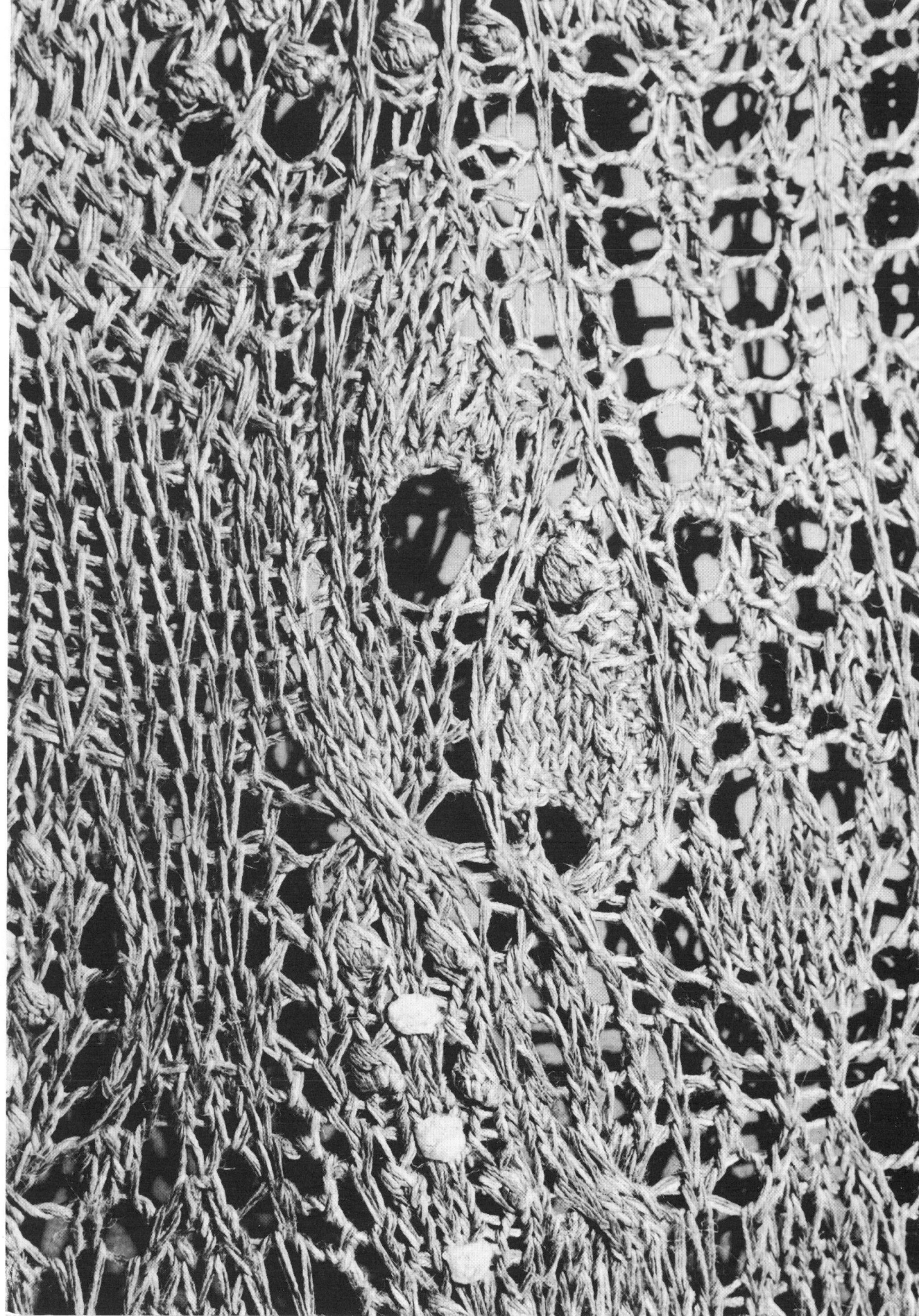

Illus. 73. "Middle Ages," wall hanging, 11" × 16", (1966). Gold 10/22 linen, gold silk, and gold metallic yarn. Bobble, Lace, Plaited Basket, and twisted Garter Stitches. From the very start, increasing was done on both sides of every row. Near the point at the beginning is an area of Bobble done in silk; linen and silk and several kinds of metallic yarn are also combined. This is followed by the Plaited Basket in silk and linen combined, and metallic yarn alternating. After more Bobbles of silk and linen, there are several rows of Lace Stitch in metallic yarn. Further on in the piece are several rows of twisted Garter Stitch. The Bell Pattern is in the upper half. Fine wire was incorporated into the first rows of increase for the Bell Pattern so that the bells could be pulled out during blocking to give surface dimension to the piece. When the piece was completed, it was finished off with a row of single crochet around the edge. (Photograph by Gayle Smalley.)

Illus. 72. Detail of previous photograph. The following stitches can be seen: Double Knit, Ladder, Cable, Bobble, Clustering, Knit into Stitch Below, and Plaited Basket. (Photograph by Gayle Smalley.)

Illus. 74. "Yellow Variations," 29" × 41", (1967). Yellow slub linen and yellow silk. Honeycomb Pattern, Bobble, Double Knit, Ladder, and Plaited Basket Stitches. There are also variations of the Lace Faggot and much use of increasing and decreasing. (Collection of Mr. and Mrs. W. David Phillips.)

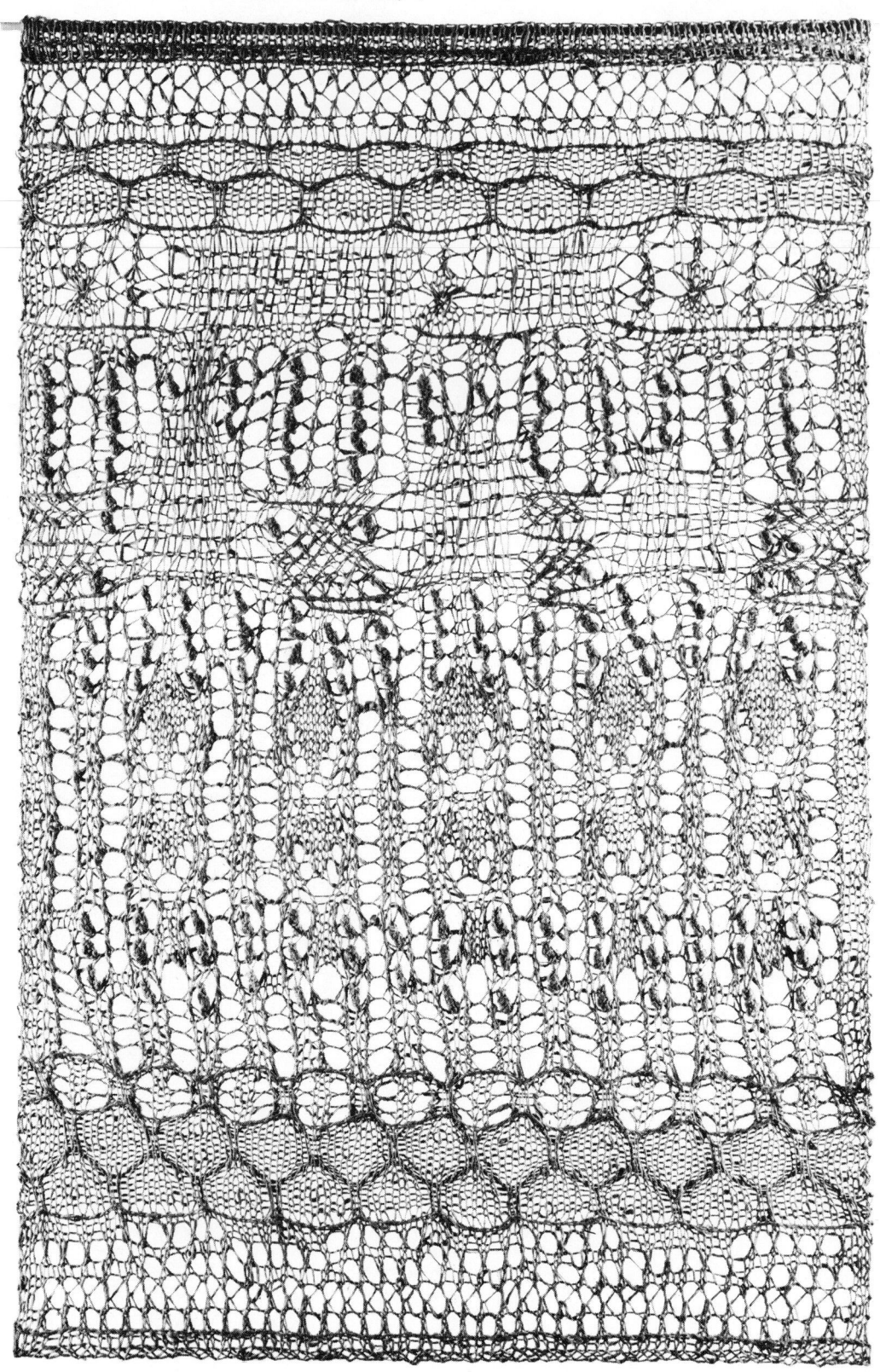

Illus. 75. Detail of "Yellow Variations" shows areas of Double Knit, Bobble, Ladder, and Plaited Basket Stitches.

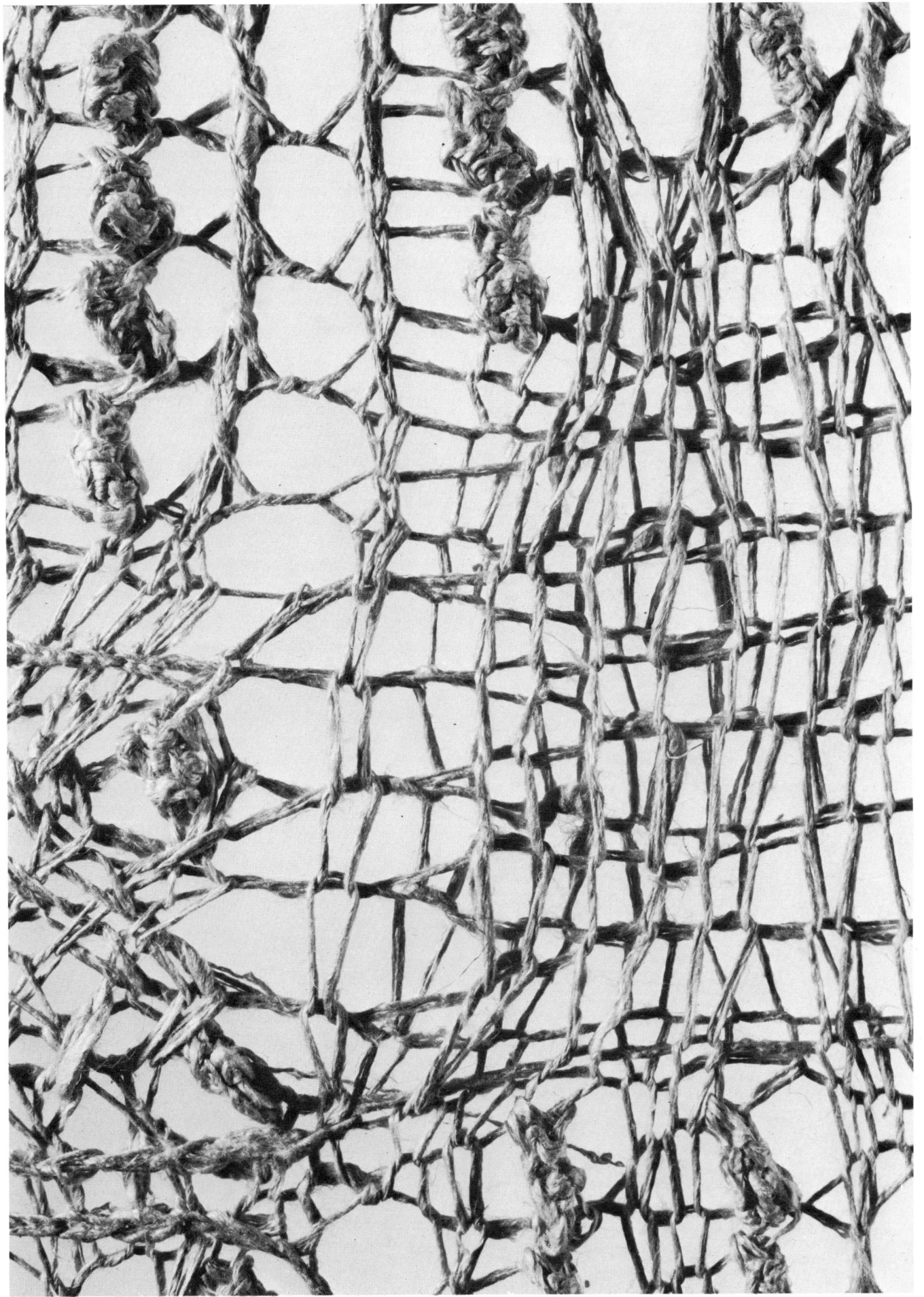

Illus. 76. Wall hanging, 12" × 29", (1967). 5/1 natural linen. (Collection of Mr. and Mrs. R. Lance Factor.) The piece was started with a row of YO, K2 tog. The second row was purled. Two rows of Plaited Basket follow and lead into the Ladder Stitch with Knit into Stitch Below in between. The Ladder Stitch is repeated twice, and it is varied on the second repeat by increasing to three stitches on the Over. On the next knit row, the three stitches are decreased by being knit together, resulting in an area that looks a little like a face with a wide smile and a pointed hat. By doing Knit into Stitch Below with a Double Throw a base is provided for the added-on stitches of the Bell Pattern.

Illus. 77. This detail of the previous picture shows the Bell Pattern in a variation. It is developed after the Ladder Stitch, and the two stitches that are the base for the Bell are also the center ones of the Ladder Stitch. The outside stitches, combined with Knit into Stitch Below, provide three stitches that are worked in the following manner: YO, P3 tog, YO. Purl on next row.

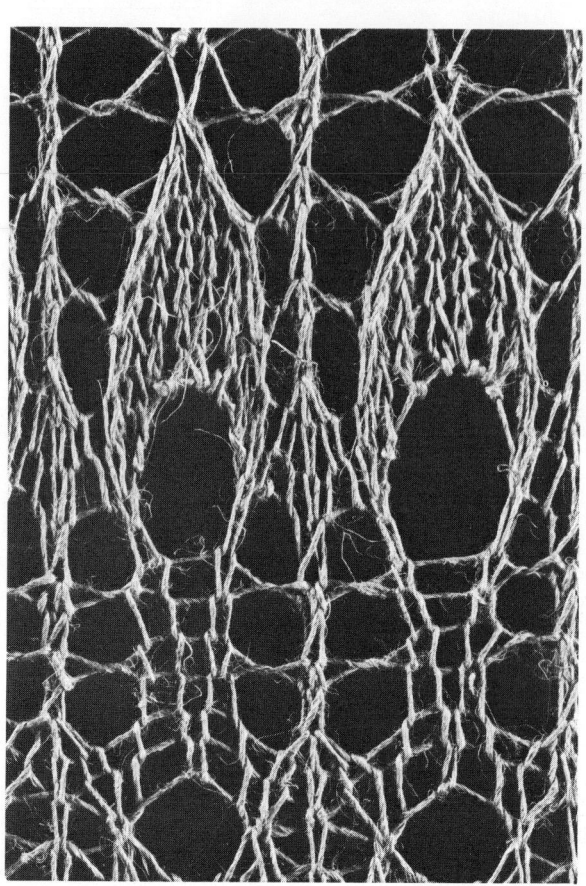

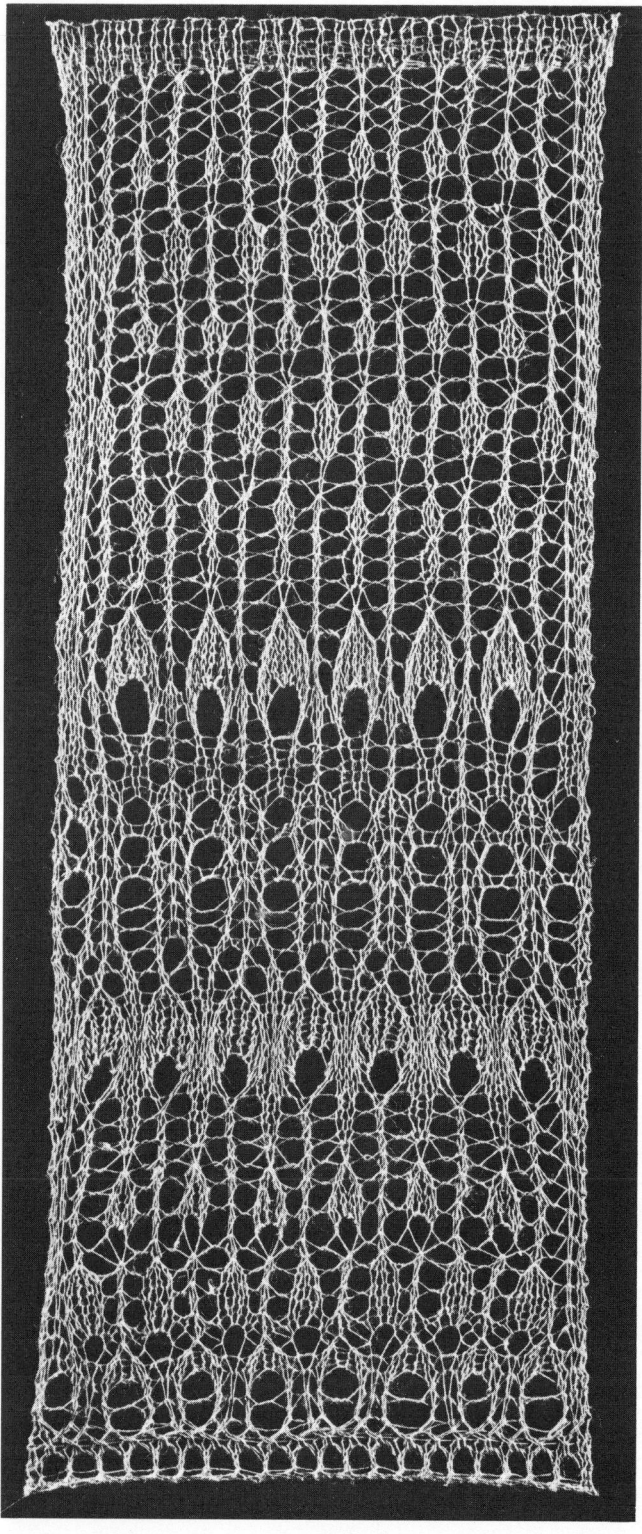

Illus. 78. "Vertical Trails," wall hanging, 53" × 69", (1968). Natural 1½ lea linen. Collection of Gennie Donald, Christchurch, New Zealand. Bell pattern, Knit Into Stitch Below, Clustering, Bobble, Cable and Lace Faggot, with variations of Ladder Stitch.

It might be interesting to analyze this piece on your own. You could begin with the Cable Stitch and count the different variations used. Notice that the Bell Pattern emerges as an extension of the Cable Stitch, as does the Ladder Stitch at the top of the photograph. Knit Into the Stitch Below is done before the Bobble in many cases. The Clustering Stitch is done before and after Bobbles. YO, knit 2 tog with its variation, K2 tog, YO, is used within a cable, also.

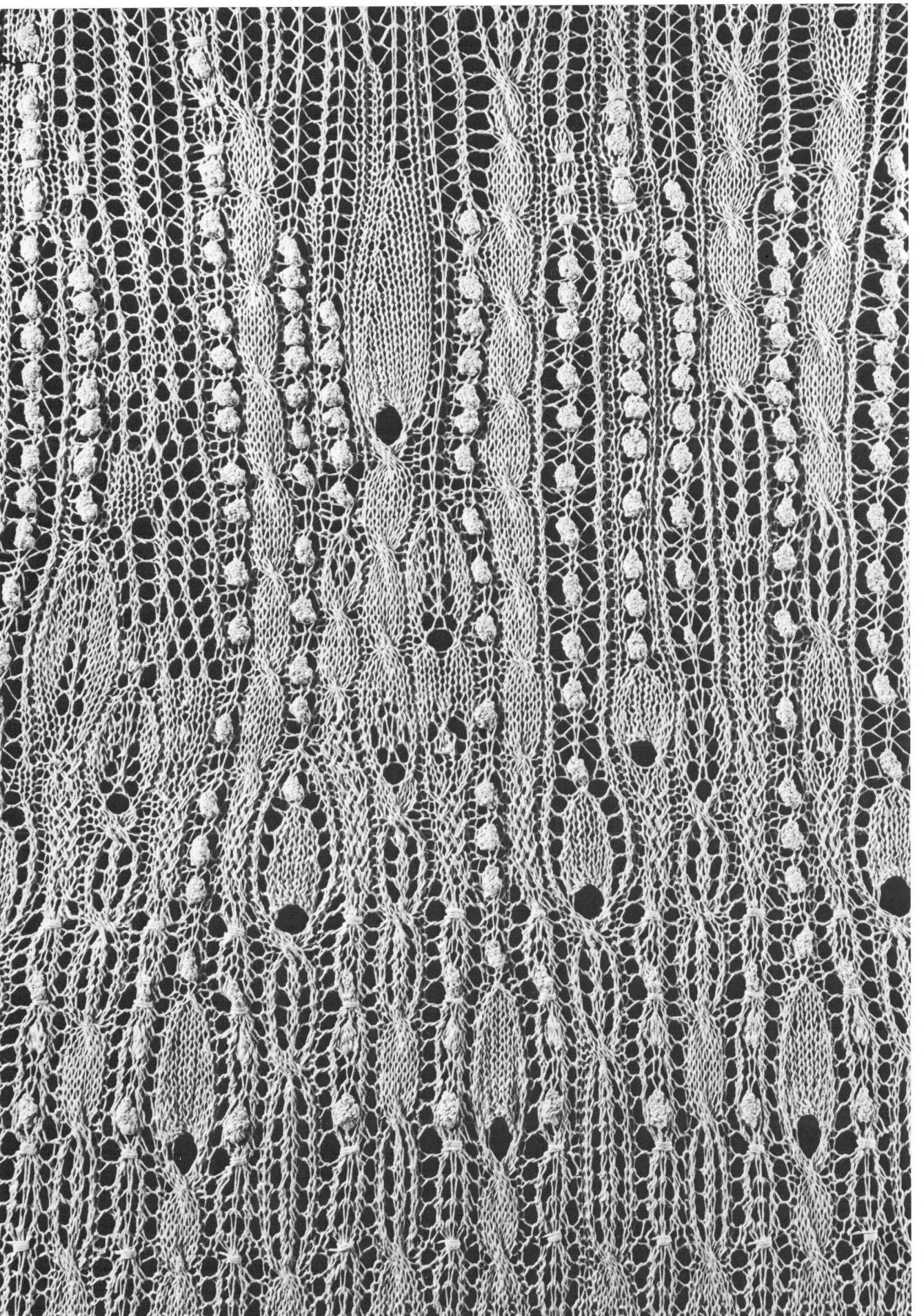

6. Experiments

There is great interest in the stitches used to create a knitted structure, and there is equivalent interest in the yarn and in the design possibilities presented by the combinations of yarns and stitches. Learning how they work together, exploring stitch variations, trying new materials, and discovering the effects on the stitches are all part of the excitement and challenge in experimentation.

An essential part of experimentation is building a knowledge of yarn—its characteristics, possibilities, and limitations. You can learn to recognize a unique personality in each yarn—the soft, the smooth, the fuzzy, nubby or rough. In my work, design is an outgrowth of the yarn being used. Other than that, my work is usually not planned and designs develop as I progress. Through such a spontaneous method of working, the yarn is not forced to follow a pattern it cannot adapt to; its various properties are acknowledged so that its personality can come forth honestly and naturally.

The differences in yarn challenge the craftsman to discover the most effective way of utilizing each one.

Experimentation will show in what ways texture affects the appearance of a stitch. Will fine yarns create thin surface-texture and soft-plied wool give a smooth texture? If you use wool instead of linen, how will the character of the finished design be altered—or will it be? If wool and linen are combined, what will the textured result be? Another consideration is the yarn's suitability for the piece being planned. Linen, for example, is excellent for wall hangings, but not for blankets. Loop mohair is suitable for blankets and stoles, but would not be my choice for wall hangings.

Part of experimentation is learning to achieve unity in the design, tying all components together for a harmonious total. This includes learning how to balance more than one yarn in the same piece as well as controlling a variety of stitches so that the design construction is a unified whole and not a series of unrelated sections. Different effects are assessed, such as, how a rough-textured yarn looks knitted together with a finer textured one, or a heavy one with a lighter one, and what happens when two yarns that reflect light differently are combined.

Achieving unity in design also means evaluating whether or not a pattern should be emphasized, and, if so, where and in what proportion. This includes visualizing how much variety to use in both stitches and yarn, and at what point that variety should be limited, and learning to save some design ideas for another knitted piece and not to crowd them all into one.

The needles are also experimented with in order to discover how different sizes can be used to vary design effects. By changing the size of the needle it is possible to vary a pattern so that size relationship between stitches is altered or the spacing modified.

A simple variation in pattern can be accomplished by using the same needle throughout the piece; you need only to throw the yarn around the needle more than once in order to introduce longer or more open stitches into the design. Through the use of this method, a lacelike effect can be achieved, and the original gauge is simply returned to on the next row. Such a technique also serves to keep the piece from becoming droopy.

Pieces that are knit too loosely will sag when they are hung, so that someone who has a tendency to knit a loose stitch will want to use smaller needles, and, of course, the person who knits a tight stitch will want to use larger needles.

From the start, my approach to knitting as a medium for creative expression was clear cut. I knew I had to have technical knowledge in order to be free to develop new ideas. The more research I did on the subject of knitting, the more fascinated I became, and the faster ideas came. My knitting to this point had been confined to sweaters and socks, but I changed my thinking quickly once I began to knit and experiment with my weaving materials.

My beginning experiments were samples. The first sample of every new pattern I tried was usually knit with 5/1 linen and a #7 needle. Each sample done was at least two pattern repeats in width and length. When only a few stitches were involved, I would cast on about thirty at the beginning. Each sample was blocked and then tagged with such information as material used, its source, and the needle size. Also included were comments for future reference, such as the suitability of yarn and needle size to the pattern used.

When samples were done in different weights of linen, whether slub or smooth, the comment on the tag would include my reaction to the yarn's appearance. The same held true when experimenting with wool, silk, glass, asbestos, metallic yarn, synthetic straw and others. If there is a great deal of pattern to the work, the end result will be more handsome if the yarn used is smooth rather than fuzzy or nubby, for the stitches are an important consideration. There is a beauty in them that is best expressed at times in simple yarns.

A good beginning exercise is to knit a sample of a set number of stitches and to progress from Garter Stitch to Stockinette to ribbings of various widths, then Plaited Basket, Cable Stitch, and Lace Stitch of several variations. Such an exercise presents the perfect opportunity for exploring the properties of yarn, its effect on the stitches, and the relationship of one pattern to another pattern.

By using the same yarn for the first sample of every new stitch tried, the various samples can be compared for gauge. Each stitch and each pattern varies in gauge. For example, 11 stitches knit in the Plaited Basket Stitch will be about half as wide as 11 stitches knit in either the Garter Stitch or the Stockinette Stitch.

On the following pages is a representation of some of my early experiments. I thought they might offer some guidance if illustrated and explained as to the effect of different yarns on the stitches and the variations of the stitches themselves. Some later experiments are also included together with prototypes that were developed into full pieces. In order to carry through still further into other areas of experimentation I handspun the yarns, ikat-dyed some, and handcut the leather that is used in a few of the samples shown.

After knitting samples of the basic stitches such as Garter, Stockinette, and ribbing, I experimented with the Fancy Crossed Throw. Directions were followed for a number of rows, then variations were made by winding the yarn around the needles more times to make a longer, more twisted stitch. While experimenting with this stitch, I tried many different types of yarns and combinations of two yarns. With each yarn used the stitch assumed a distinctive character.

Sample 1 was developed from the Fancy Crossed Throw and the Garter Stitch. The material used was 5/1 linen. The construction is basically a simple one of repeated long and short, twisted lengths with variations in the order of repetition, and it creates an interesting pattern of openwork. The practical result of this experiment was shown on page 13.

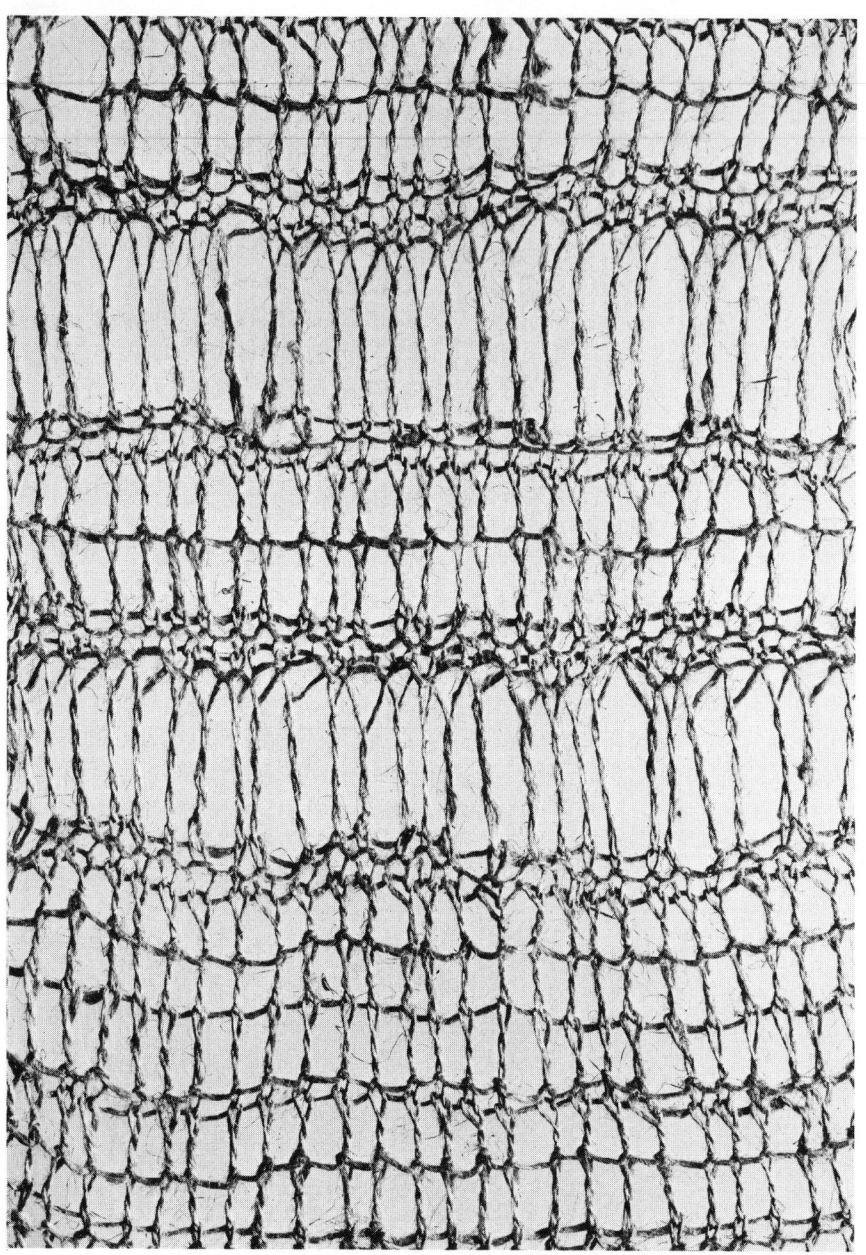

Sample 1. 5/1 natural linen, #7 needle. Fancy Crossed Throw and Garter Stitch.

Sample 2 has the same stitches as Sample 1, but there is less use of the Garter Stitch. By changing the yarn from linen to Fiberglas the character of the stitches was altered, and the linear pattern of the Fancy Crossed Throw achieved a more delicate quality. I do not recommend knitting with glass yarn, however, since the ruboff from the material can cause skin problems.

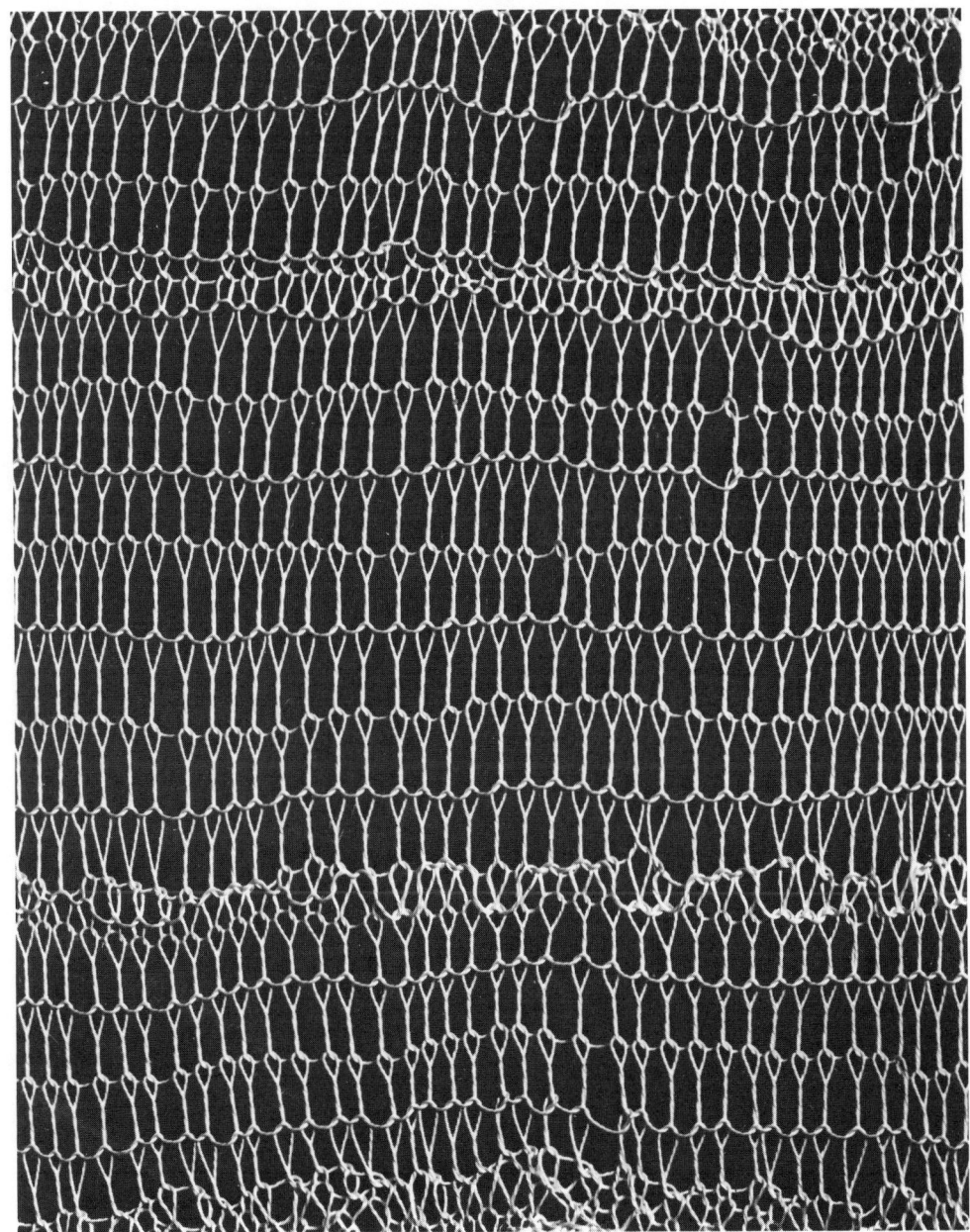

Sample 2. Fiberglass. Fancy Crossed Throw and Garter Stitch.

Sample 3 achieves yet another texture when two yarns—linen and a fine mohair—are combined. The stitches remain the same; but, here again, there is variation in their patterning.

The simplicity of the Fancy Crossed Throw Stitch and the possibilities in its linear tracery for still further design arrangements make it a natural one for further exploration. The piece shown in detail on page 44 has yet another variation of the Fancy Crossed Throw. By the addition of a three into three stitch (page 46) the threads are grouped into tentlike shapes instead of being twisted together as in the three samples shown here.

Still other variations on this stitch are shown in "Shells" and in its detail (page 81). The yarns used created their own bands of light and dark values. The light areas are in natural silk and the dark areas in natural linen.

The next experiment was the Lace Stitch, which also creates an open fabric—but one in which there is more of a circular pattern than a linear one. It is based upon a simple addition and subtraction of stitches.

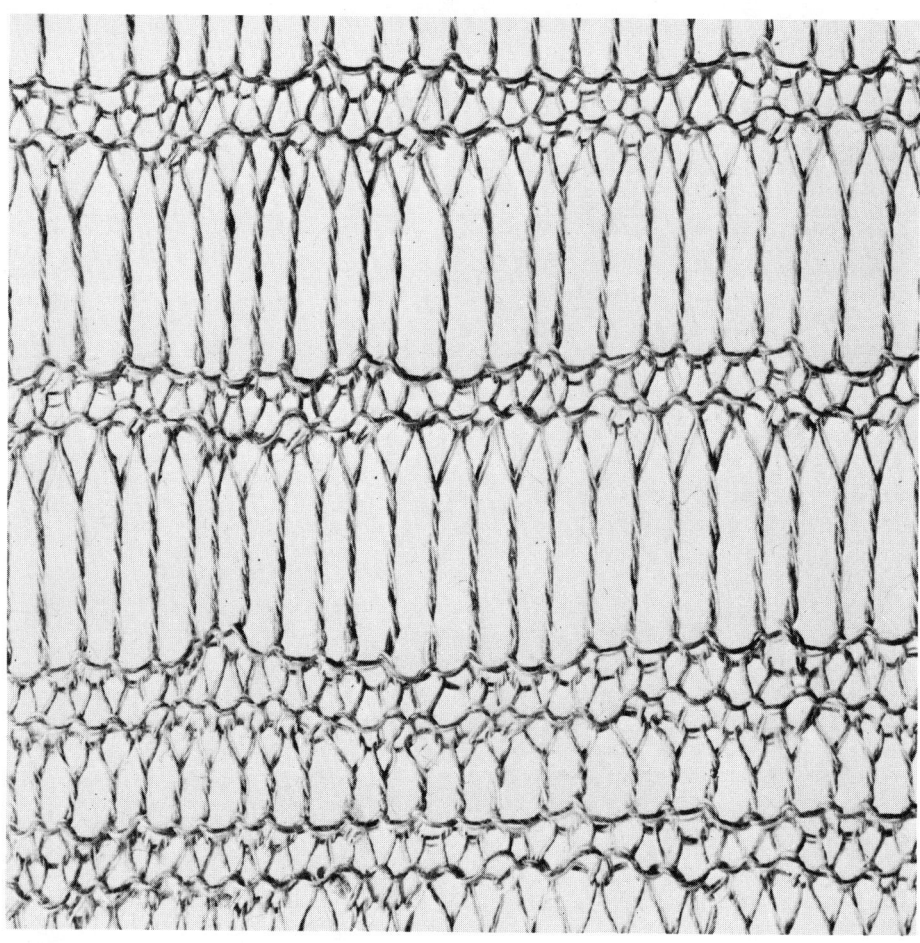

Sample 3. 5/1 natural linen and single-ply mohair. Fancy Crossed Throw and Garter Stitch.

Sample 4 is a variation on the simple Lace Stitch
(* YO, K2 tog *, repeat * to *, P the next row). The
material used was 5/1 linen. This stitch created nearly
rectangular forms within circular ones, which upon
constant repetition made for a rather strict, unified pattern. The back of the fabric is shown in this detail.

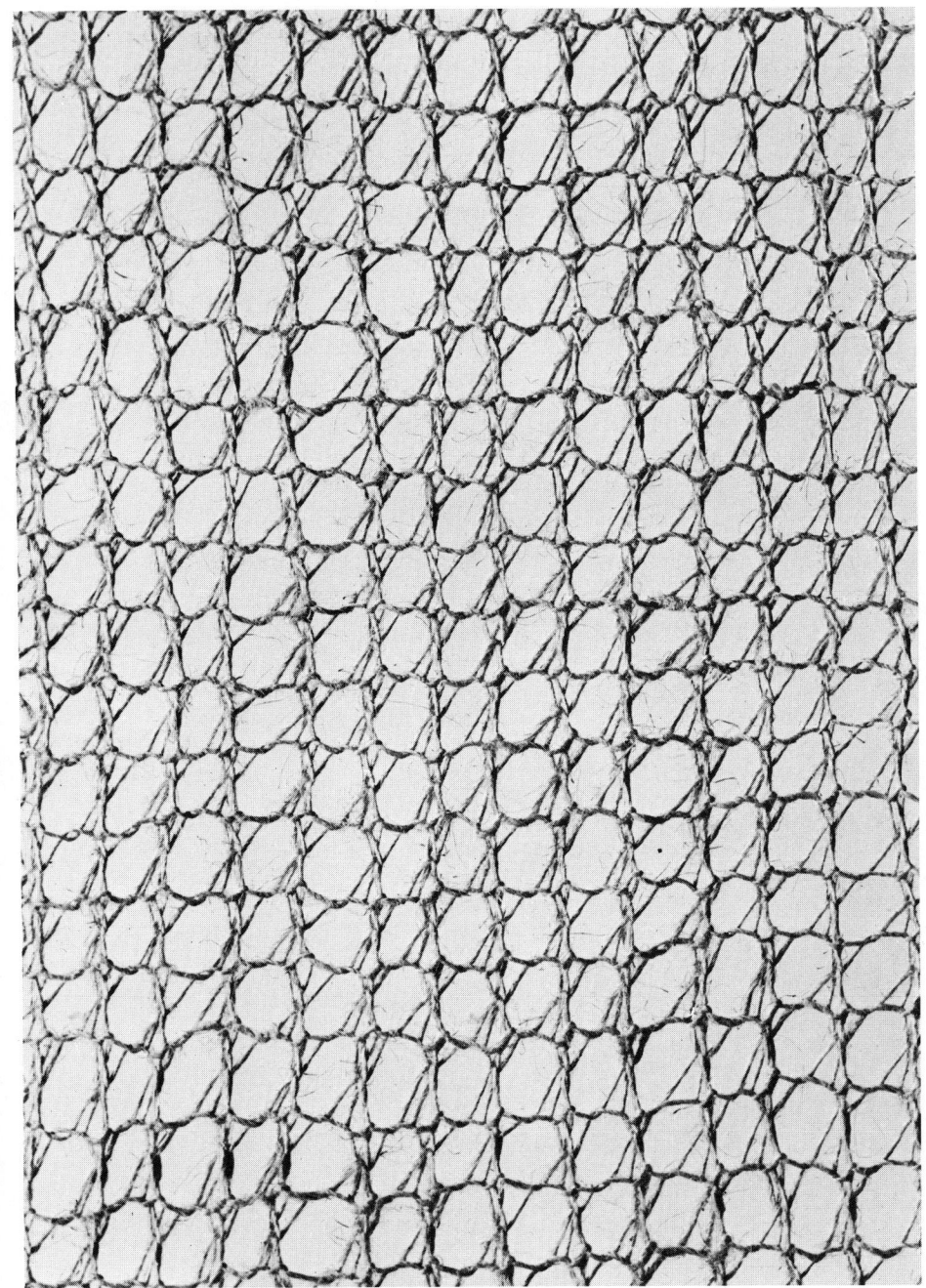

Sample 4.   5/1 natural linen. Lace Stitch. Back of fabric shown.

Sample 5 is the Lace Stitch knit with Rovana, a monofilament, and Lurex, a metallic yarn, both made by Dobeckmun Company. Note the different character of the stitch when knit with these yarns. The shape of the stitch is not as regular as in Sample 4, and there is more of a quality of crispness to it. In some sections, rows of Stockinette Stitch are used to vary the pattern; in others, areas of Stockinette Stitch are knit intermittently between areas of the Lace Stitch. By adding the Stockinette Stitch in a varied but still unified pattern, contrast was introduced. Compare this sample with number 4, which uses the Lace Stitch for a more repetitious effect.

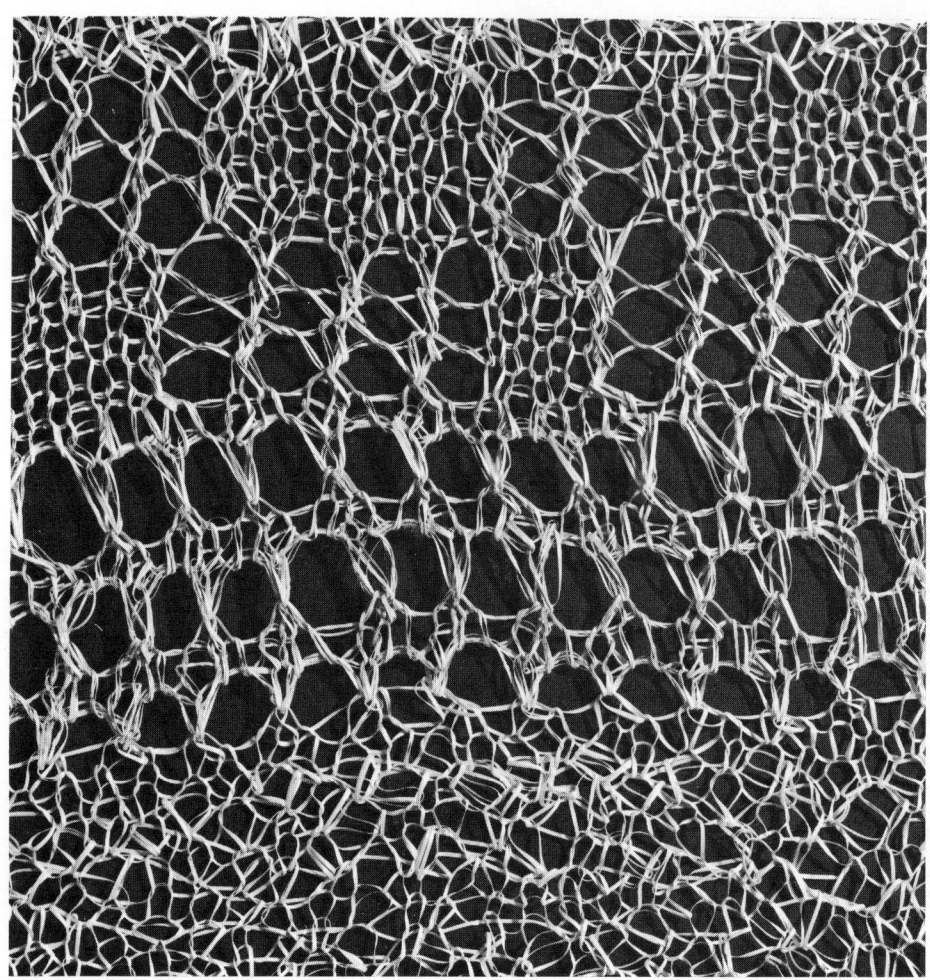

Sample 5. Rovana (a monofilament) and Lurex (metallic yarn). Lace and Stockinette Stitches.

Sample 6 is knit in synthetic straw and uses the Lace and Stockinette Stitches. Depth and texture are very evident here, as is the twisting and turning of the straw. A close-up view of the back of the fabric is shown so that the structure of the stitch can be very clearly seen. This sample was a prototype for a room divider.

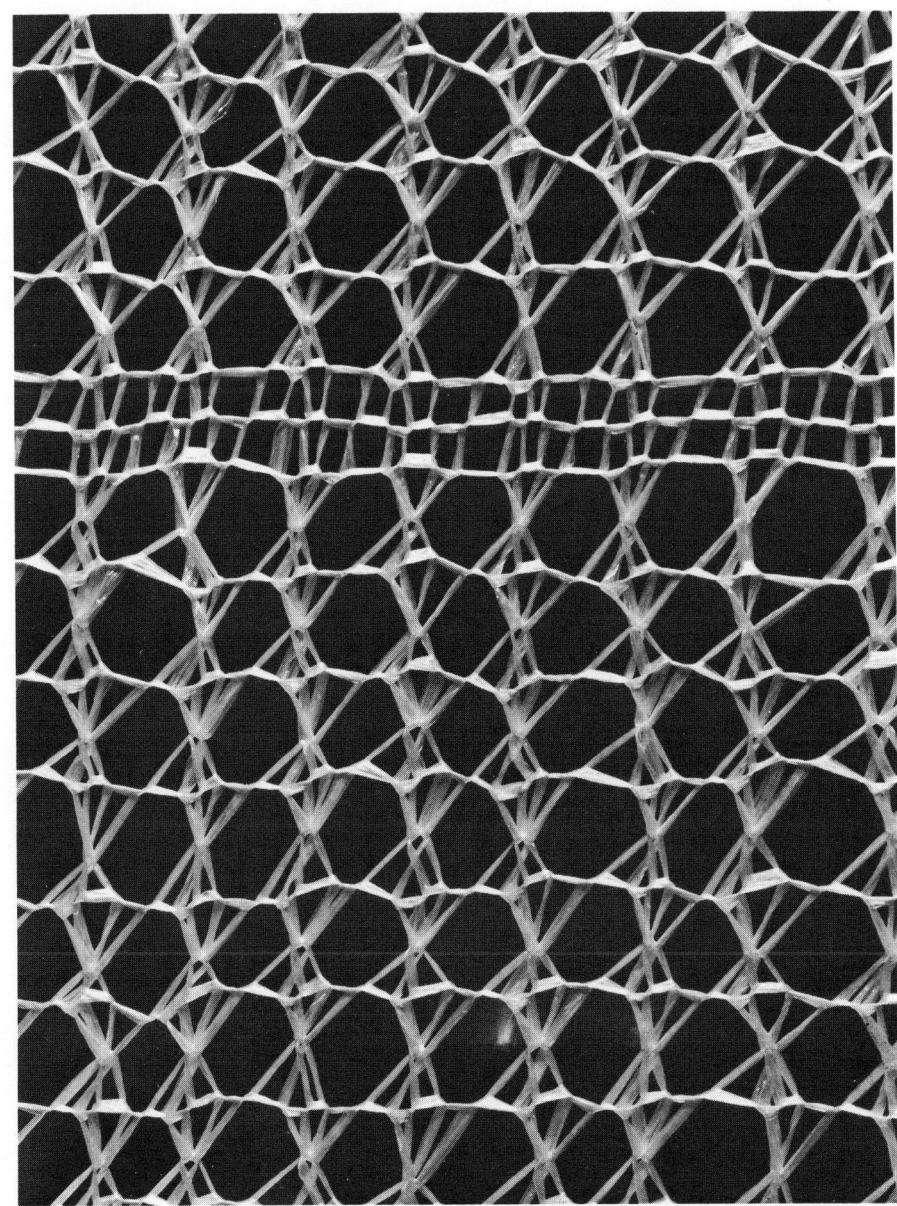

Sample 6. Synthetic straw. Lace and Stockinette Stitches. Back of fabric shown.

Sample 7 is a view of the front of the sample shown in number 6. The diagonals are more sharply apparent here than in the other samples using the Lace Stitch, and there is a crisp quality to the stitch that can be compared with Sample 5. Rows of Stockinette are used to separate the Lace Stitch and to create further design interest.

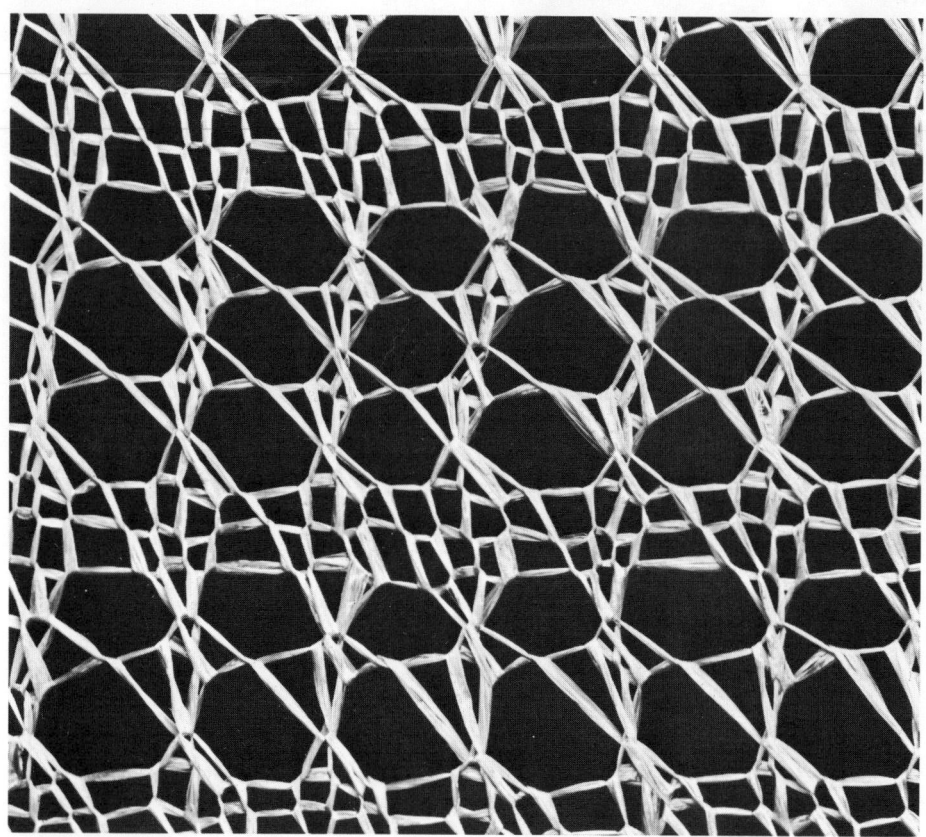

Sample 7.   Front view of Sample 6. Prototype for a screen.

Sample 8 shows the appearance of the Lace Stitch varied by the use of fine synthetic straw and gold metallic yarn. The yarns are combined in regular areas of the pattern, and the metallic yarn is used singly between these areas, creating a striped effect of thin, stranded shapes against thicker, textured ones. The subtle sheen of the fine metallic yarn produces still further textural interest. This sample, when compared with its fellows, shows shapes more circular than rectangular, and the diagonal is no longer as consistently apparent. The working of the Stockinette Stitch can also be noticed in areas of the pattern.

In searching for ways to exploit the use of synthetic straw, I tried imbedding a knitted straw sample in plastic. More experimenting will have to be done, but I believe there are possibilities here that would open up still other exciting avenues in knitting. Synthetic straw can also be used to make place mats. After being knit the mats are sprayed with a product, such as Krylon, to render them very stiff. The spray will also make them impervious to water so that they may be washed without their losing shape.

The Double Knit Stitch was also experimented with. A very versatile stitch, it creates scale and density and can be used to knit an openwork pattern or to make pockets for inserted objects. By textural play it can also define a shape. This is very explicit in the detail of "Cross" (page 68), where it defines a curve, and also in the full view of the piece (page 69), where it shapes the cross. In "Onward and Upward" (page 83), where it is used to create areas of tension, the Double Knit forms a pattern of shapes resembling a honeycomb. In "Circles" (page 47), it is used for the same purpose but with different results.

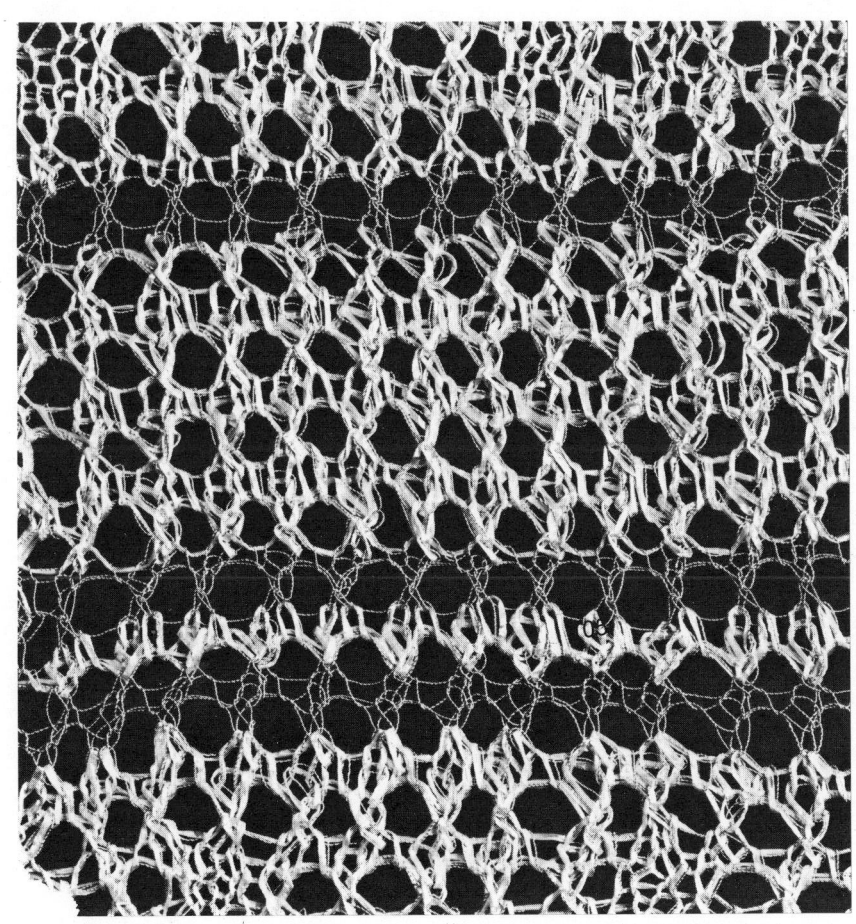

Sample 8. Synthetic straw and gold metallic yarn. Lace and Stockinette Stitches.

Sample 9 shows areas of Double Knit stripes alternating with areas of Garter Stitch. The materials used are 5/1 natural linen and natural, fine mohair. This is another way of creating a striped effect and should be compared with Sample 8. Double Knit can also be used with the Stockinette Stitch to make alternating circular areas as is seen in "Circles."

In the next three experiments the Stockinette Stitch was used to exploit the irregular surfaces of handspun yarns.

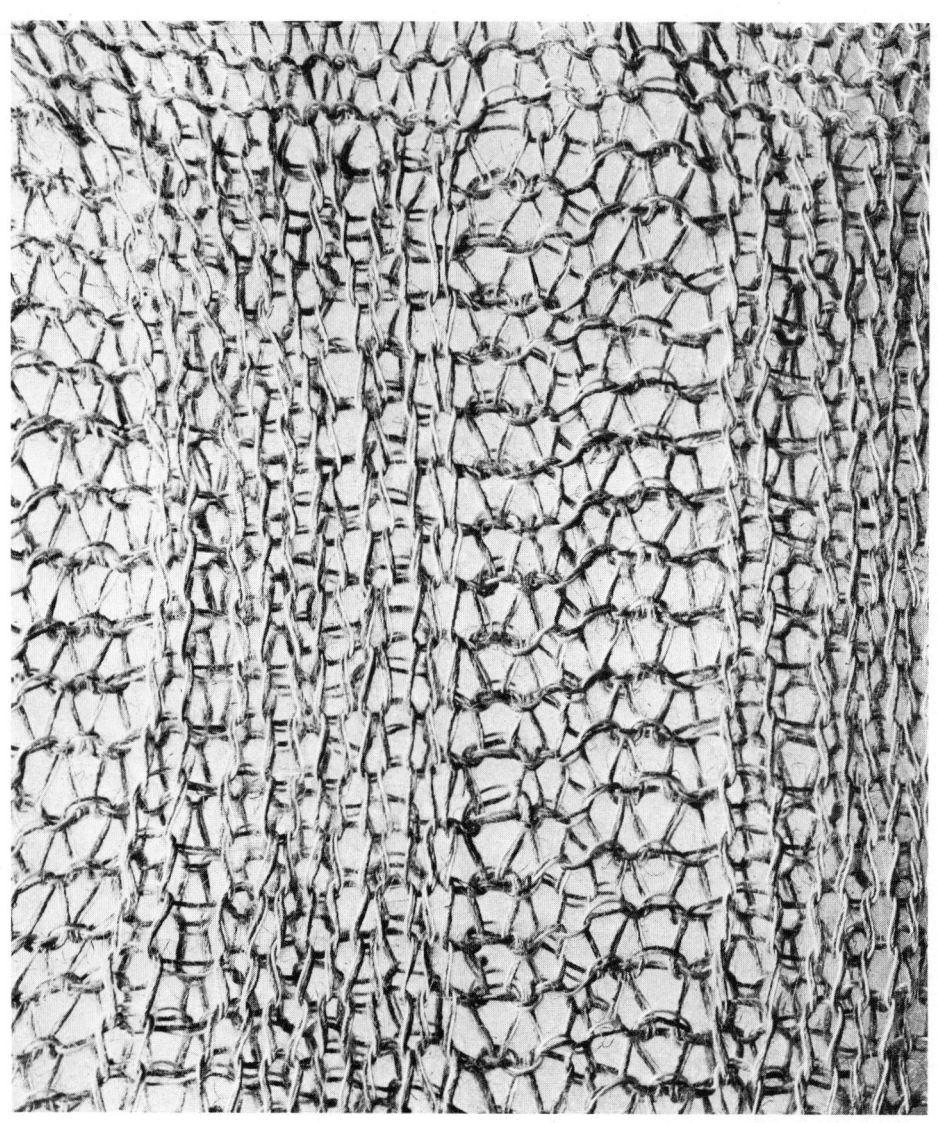

Sample 9. 5/1 natural linen and natural mohair. Double Knit and Garter Stitches. (Courtesy of *Craft Horizons* magazine.)

Sample 10 is a pillow cover knit with walnut-dyed handspun mohair and natural, handspun wool. The original sample proved so interesting that I carried it out to a full piece. This is a good example of how contrast is created by using two yarns of different textural value. The difference between the mohair's glossy sheen and the mat look of the less shiny wool was emphasized further by using the yarns individually in completely separate areas. Note here that, even though the surfaces of the yarns are irregular and bumpy, unity was achieved through the compact and close working of the Stockinette Stitch.

The thought of experimenting with a combination of leather and either handspun wool or handspun mohair intrigued me because of the possibility of creating unusual design effects. The unevenness in texture caused by the handspinning of the yarns would be in sharp contrast to either the rough or smooth sides of the leather. Since both sides of the leather provided such good contrast to each other, there was no attempt made to keep the leather flat while it was being knit.

Sample 10. Natural, handspun wool and walnut-dyed handspun mohair. Stockinette Stitch.

Sample 11 was knit with dahlia-dyed handspun wool and handcut, narrow leather strips in a matching color. The natural twisting of the leather while being knit revealed its two different sides with the result that three surfaces were juxtaposed although only two materials were being used. Two rows each of leather and wool alternate in the Stockinette Stitch. This sample was knit with wooden needles and its end result was a pillow cover.

Sample 12 was knit with natural handspun mohair and white, handcut leather strips, also with wooden needles. Mohair and leather alternate every two stitches in some rows while other rows are worked entirely in either mohair or leather. The Stockinete Stitch is used here also. This sample was eventually carried out to a finished pillow cover.

Further experimentation was done with methods that, like the Lace Stitch, created holes as part of the construction. Complex structures based on the addition and subtraction of stitches were tried, and, as always, many samples were made.

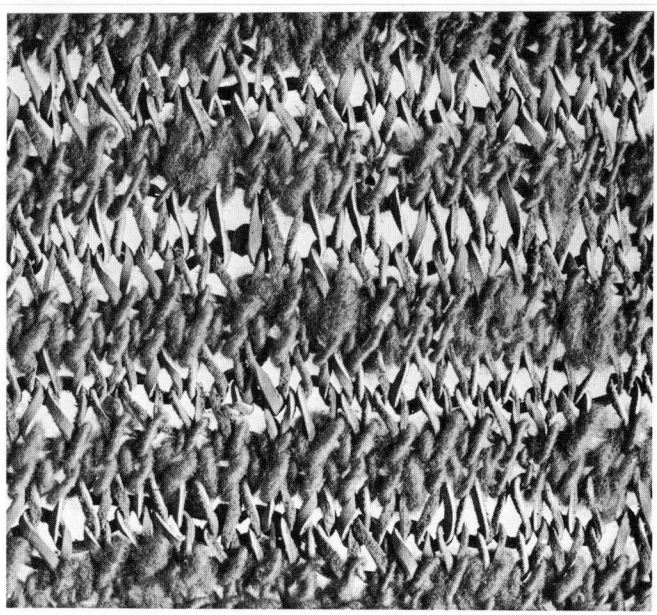

Sample 11. Dahlia-dyed handspun wool and handcut leather in matching color. Stockinette Stitch.

Sample 12. Natural, handspun mohair and white handcut leather, Stockinette Stitch. (Photograph by the author.)

Sample 13 is a detail showing the Bell Pattern, a construction that creates a pleasing visual form of round and tapering shapes. It was done in 5/1 natural linen with a #7 needle. This is a motif I have used again and again. It uses various multiples of stitches with what seems to be inexhaustible effects. The size of this pattern can be controlled by the number of stitches cast on and by the manner in which decreasing is done so that, if decreasing is done less often, the Bell motif will be larger.

In the sample shown here, the Bell motif is used as an overall repeat with the Garter Stitch forming the background. In the piece on page 63 a Bell-like motif with strong diagonal decreases is used. The almost carved-out appearance of the pattern can be more clearly seen in the detail (page 64). In Illus. 70 on page 89 and in "The Kings" (page 48) the Bell motif appears as a repeated insertion with many other varieties of stitches. This is an exciting pattern to create, and there are still other examples of its use throughout the book. It would be of interest and value to compare the differences in its appearance when knit with variations and with different stitches forming the background. Other stitches can also be compared in this fashion.

Once you have experimented with a large variety of samples, you will have a basis for beginning a piece of creative knitting, and, before too long, you might even devise an original pattern. The completion of either will give a feeling of satisfaction because the construction will really be yours—no one else will have done it before.

As mentioned previously I don't sketch my designs because I want as much freedom as possible to work directly with the yarns, but if you find it helpful to make a loose sketch with areas blocked off for different stitches and patterns, then by all means do so.

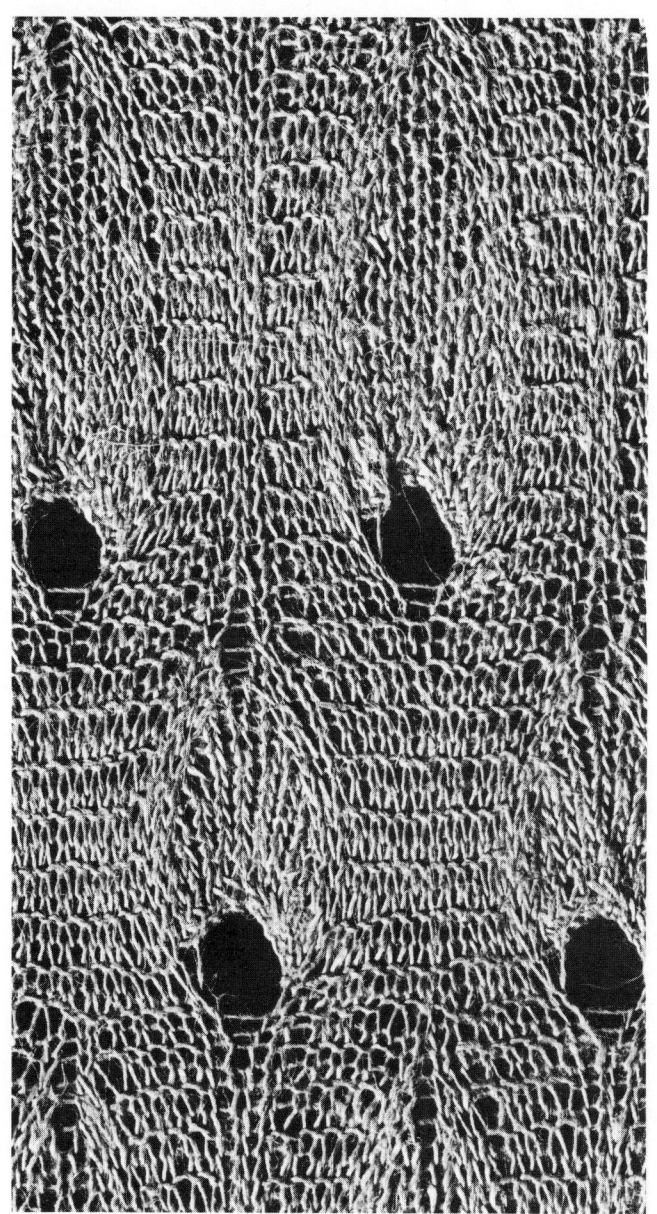

Sample 13. 5/1 natural linen, #7 needle. Bell Pattern and Garter Stitch.

Samples 14 and 15 are two examples of patterns that I devised through experimenting. They are included in the hope that they will stimulate the reader to undertake similar experimentation. There are no written directions for these patterns.

After a piece has been finished and blocked, there may be the feeling that the design does not balance well. When this happens a careful analysis will reveal the reason and will teach the craftsman more than a chance success that is not fully understood. Sometimes I will study a piece for days before I can decide whether or not it is a success. If I feel it is not, then I rip out the offending section and reknit with changes. Do not be afraid to rip—ripping is one of the things I have learned to do well. Most of the yarns used for creative knitting will not be damaged by ripping unless done excessively, for, unlike the usual knitting yarns, they do not stretch. Blocking the piece will take care of any kinks that result.

Another area for experimentation is ikat-dyeing. In this technique yarn is colored in an interrupted fashion. As the yarn is knit, the undyed areas form their own pattern and create fascinating designs in the fabric.

Those areas of the yarn that are not to be dyed are wrapped around with a resist wrapping, such as cord, and bound. The purpose of wrapping and binding is to keep the dye solution from penetrating the yarn. The wrapped yarn is placed into a dye bath and allowed to remain until the desired color is reached. If you want to dye it more than one color, then you must tie off more areas before redyeing in another bath. Overdyeing the yarns can produce interesting color blends. Remove the bindings when all the dyeing is completed and allow the yarn to dry.

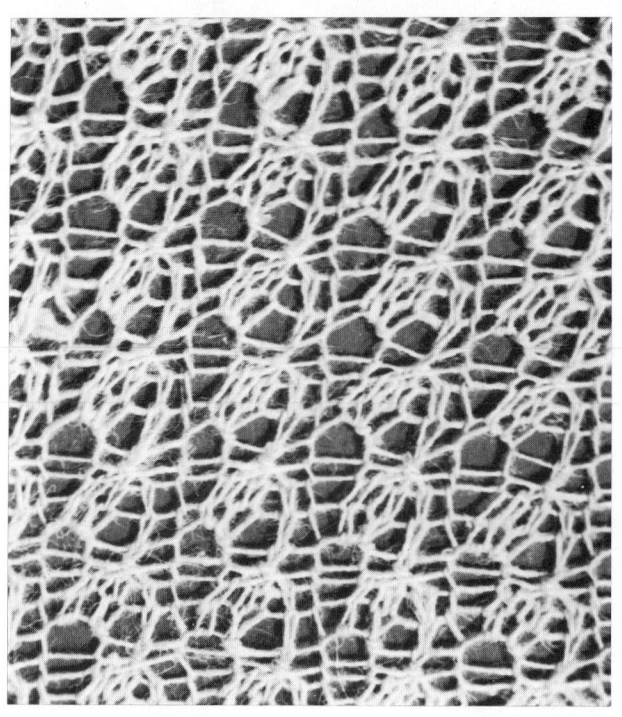

Sample 14. 5/1 natural linen. Detail of original pattern. Devised by experimentation with no written directions. (Photograph by the author.)

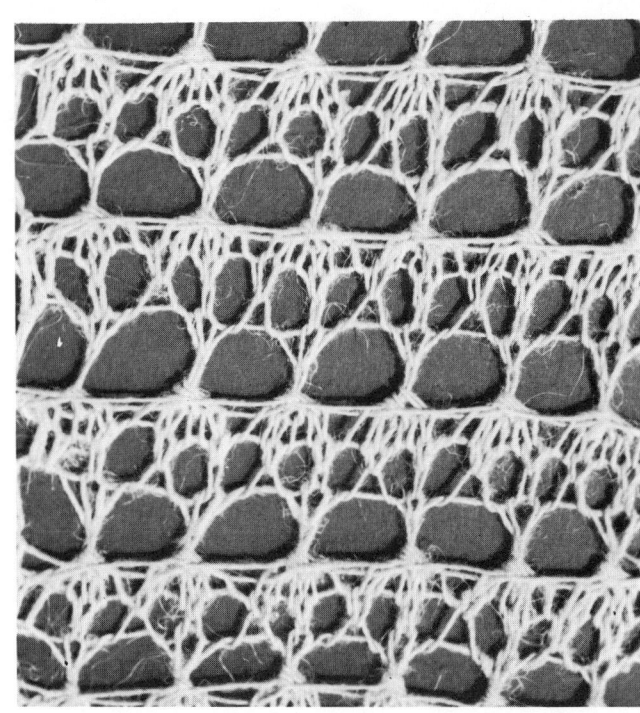

Sample 15. 5/1 natural linen. Detail of original pattern. Experiment with no written directions. (Photograph by the author.)

Sample 16 uses 5/1 natural and ikat-dyed blue linen. Only one tying was done for the yarn. Other examples of ikat are in various pieces throughout the book. Further exploration can lead to matching the color of yarn to found objects or dyeing the yarn a contrasting color. In a wall hanging on page 84, for example, the yarn was ikat-dyed red to match the red wooden beads also used in the piece.

A variety of stitches were used in Sample 16 for vertical, horizontal, and circular interest. This is another example of openwork patterning. By now you probably know the stitches so well that you could analyze the piece yourself. As you can see, two rows of Stockinette Stitch lead into a row of simple Lace Stitch producing a row of holes. The Ladder Stitch follows for several repeats and then another row of the Lace. More holes occur, this time as in the Lace Diadem Pattern, followed by decreasing. The Fancy Crossed Throw is at the top of the piece.

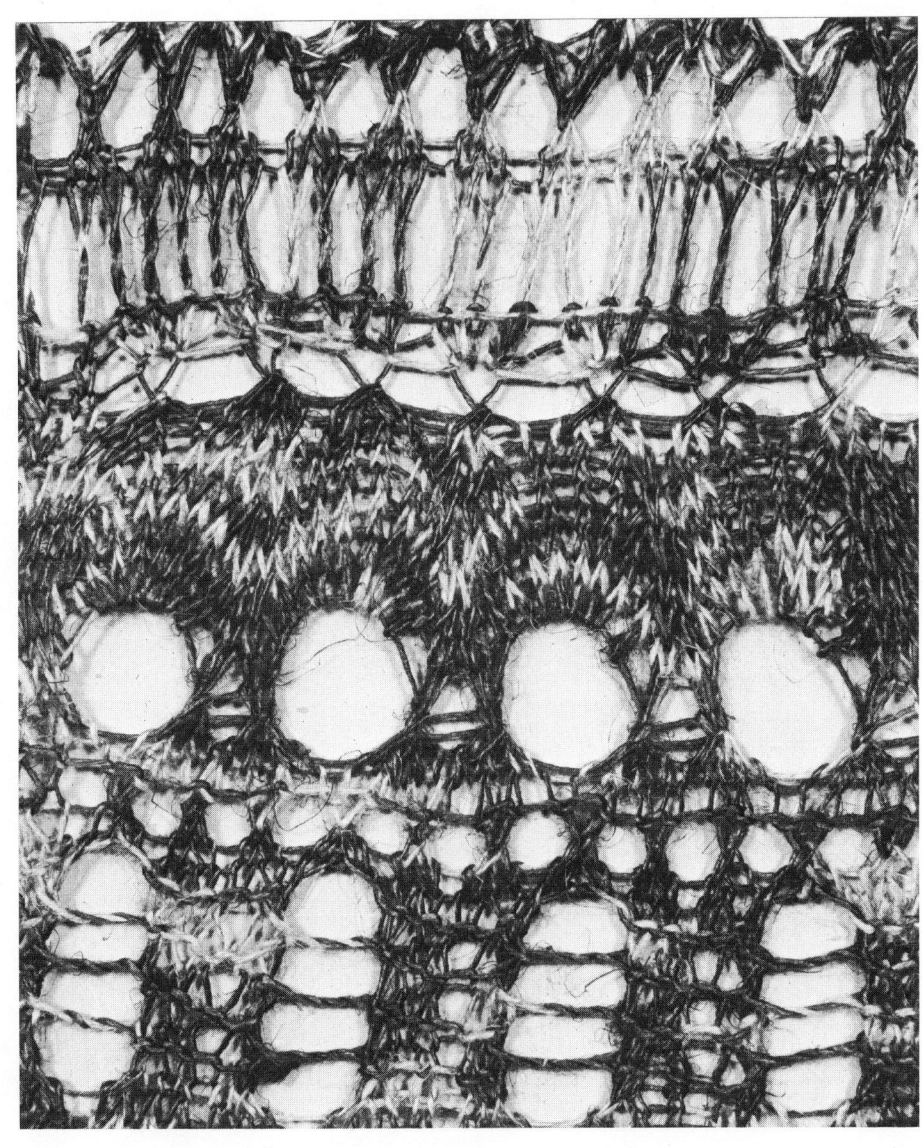

Sample 16. 5/1 natural and ikat-dyed blue linen. Ladder, Lace, and Fancy Crossed Throw Stitches. (Photograph by Gayle Smalley.)

The craftsman need know no limits in creating textural variety: Yarn can be ikat-dyed, holes can be knit in different sizes and shapes, and pockets can be made to hold found objects. The diversity of objects that can be added to fabrics is almost unlimited, and they can be incorporated into the design in a variety of ways and in endlessly variable arrangements. Such objects as beads, buttons, metal, shells, feathers, and small ceramic pieces can be experimented with. Also to be considered are coins, medals, bells, bits of mirror, and interesting pieces of polished stone. In Illus. 56 mica from North Carolina was inserted in the pockets and in "Peruvian Seeds" (page 49) seed pods from Peru were used. If beads or other found objects you plan to use are painted, test them for colorfastness. Perhaps the best guide is to make a test sample if you are in doubt about any materials.

Beads can be added onto a stitch by either of two simple methods. Remove a loop from the left needle and pull it up to lengthen it. Insert this loop through the hole in the bead and return it to the needle. Continue with the pattern. The stitch can also be knit first and then taken off the right needle. When the bead is put on, the loop is returned to the right needle.

If you have trouble pulling the yarn through the bead, put a length of sewing thread through the loop and insert the thread into the bead, pulling the yarn through with it. A jeweler's fine rattail file can be used to enlarge holes in wooden beads if necessary.

The rich variety of materials to knit with is so vast as to tantalize the imagination, and the ever-new ones appearing offer unlimited challenges to the knitter. Actually though, one can knit with practically anything. The more adventurous ones among us, who happen to have strong hands and shoulders, can knit with heavy rope, pliable wire, plastic tubing, and sisal. To knit the very heavy rope, circular needles can be fashioned from large dowels and plastic tubing.

Knitting with asbestos was one of my experiments, and I tried knitting it in a closely meshed fabric. It was a disappointment, though, since that mineral fiber has no character of its own. However, the important point to be learned is not to be intimidated by any material; if it is flexible, and you can make it work for you, try it. I am reminded of the saying: "He did it because he didn't know it couldn't be done."

Following are three prototypes, two of which were knit with paper. Paper material has had no great amount of experimentation done with it because it hasn't been that available. These prototypes were done for "Made with Paper," a traveling exhibition organ-ized by the Museum of Contemporary Crafts and the Container Corporation of America.

The first prototype is a hat (Illus. 79) and was knit with paper ribbon made in Japan. The basic Spiral Pattern was used for all the rows after casting on, and knitting was done on three needles. When the hat was about finished, decreasing was done every row. The finished piece was blocked on a hat form.

The second prototype (Illus. 80) is a wall covering and was knit with paper twine supplied by Enterprise, Incorporated. The piece is based on two patterns: the well-known Cable Stitch and the addition and subtraction of stitches. Instead of decreasing after the extra stitches were knit on, as is done in the Bell Pattern, a number of rows of Stockinette Stitch were done, then all cast-on stitches were cast off, which created a hole at either end of the increased area. The raised areas, which give a three-dimensional quality to the piece, were achieved by dowels inserted through the holes after the piece was stretched and pinned to the blocking board. The dowels remained until the piece was dry.

Illus. 79. Prototype of hat. Yellow paper ribbon made in Japan. Spiral Pattern. Shown in "Made with Paper" exhibit, Museum of Contemporary Crafts.

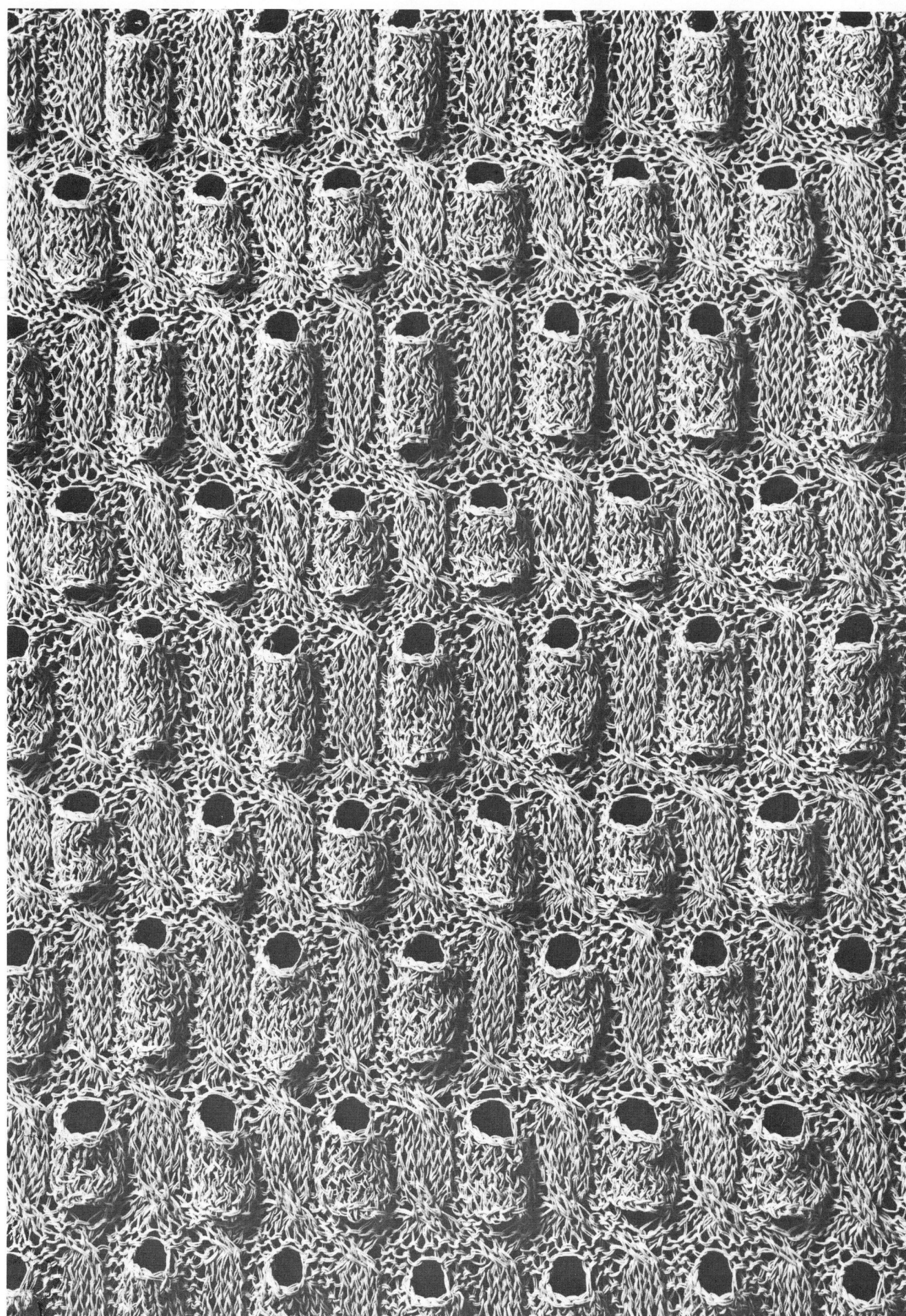

Illus. 80. Prototype of wall covering. Paper twine. Bell-like Pattern. Cable and Stockinette Stitches. Shown in "Made with Paper" exhibit, Museum of Contemporary Crafts.

The third prototype (Illus. 81) was knitted upholstery for a folding chair and was done in collaboration with designer Eva Zeisel for the Thirteenth Triennale in Milan, Italy, in 1964. The piece was knit of blue and turquoise nub wool in the Seed Stitch (K1, P1, odd number of stitches). It was knit on a circular needle and used the Spiral Rib principle. After the cover was on the chair, each end of it was sewn closed.

In this section, I have tried to present some of the possibilities in this creative medium; the search continues for still other ways to create designs, to pattern shapes, and for new ideas of combining them. Through it all, samples are made. One never really graduates from making samples; it is a continuous learning process, no matter how experienced the knitter.

Illus. 81. Prototype of full-fashioned, knitted upholstery for a folding chair. Blue and turquoise nub wool. Seed Stitch. Shown in American section at Thirteenth Milan Triennale, 1964. Chair designed by Eva Zeisel. (Photograph by Ancillotti Fotografie, Milan.)

Suggested Reading

BOOKS

Anchor Book of Lace Craft. London: B.T. Batsford, Ltd., 1961.

Bellinger, Louisa. "Patterned Stocking: possibly Indian, found in Egypt," in *The Textile Museum Journal*, 1954.

Bird, Junius; and Bellinger, Louisa. *Paracas Fabrics and Nazca Needlework*. Washington, D.C.: National Publishing Co., 1954.

Burnham, Dorothy. "Coptic Knitting, an Ancient Technique," in *Textile History*, Vol. 3, Dec. 1972.

D'Harcourt, Raoul et al, eds. *The Textiles of Ancient Peru and Their Techniques*. Tr. by Brown, Sadie. Reprint. Seattle: University of Washington Press, 1962.

DeDillmont, Thérèse, *Encyclopedia of Needlework*. Mulhouse, France: D.M.C. Corporation. Paperback edition Philadelphia: Running Press, 1972.

——*D.M.C. Library Knitting Series, O.P. 1–5*. Mulhouse, France: D.M.C. Corporation.

Emery, Irene. *The Primary Structure of Fabrics*. Washington, D.C.: The Textile Museum, 1966, 1980.

Fisch, Arline M. *Textile Techniques in Metal for Jewelers, Sculptors and Textile Artists*. New York: Van Nostrand Reinhold Co., 1975.

Harlow, Eve, ed. *The Art of Knitting*. Glasgow and London: William Collins Sons & Company, Ltd., 1977.

Knitting Dictionary. edited by the staff of *Mon Tricot*. New York: Crown Publishers, Inc. 1969.

Levey, S.M. "Illustrations of the History of Knitting: Selected from the Collection of the Victoria and Albert Museum," in *Textile History*, Vol. 1, #2, 1969, pp. 183–205.

Lyman, Lila Parrish. "Knitting, a Little Known Field for Collectors," *Antiques*, Vol. XLI, April, 1942, pp. 240-242.

Mackie, Louise. Paper #10. "Two Remarkable Fifteenth-Century Carpets from Spain." Textile Museum Roundtable, 1977, pp. 15–30. Washington, D.C: The Textile Museum.

Norbury, James. *Traditional Knitting Patterns*. London: B.T. Batsford, Ltd., 1962.

Norbury, James; and Agutter, Margaret. *Odham's Encyclopedia of Knitting*. London: Odhams Books, Ltd., 1957.

Özbed, Prof. Kenan. *Türk Köylü Coraplari. Istanbul: Birinci Baski, 1976. English edition: Knitted Stockings from Turkish Villages,* translated by Ahmet E. Üysal in collaboration with M. Fletcher, and Tahtakiliç. Istanbul: Turkiye Iş Bankasi Cultural Publications, 1981.

Pfister, R. and Bellinger, Louisa. "The Excavations at Dura-Europos conducted by Yale University and the French Academy of Inscriptions and Letters." Final report, IV, Part II, in *The Textiles*. Yale University Press, 1945, pp. 54–55.

Phillips, Mary Walker. *Step-by-Step Knitting*. New York: Golden Press, 1967.

Thomas, Mary. *Mary Thomas's Knitting Book. London: Hodder and Stoughton, 1938. Reprinted by Dover Publications, 1972.*

——*Mary Thomas's Book of Knitting Patterns*. London: Hodder and Stoughton, 1943. Reprinted by Dover Publications, 1972.

Walker, Barbara. *A Treasury of Knitting Patterns*. New York: Charles Scribner's Sons, 1968.

——*A Second Treasury of Knitting Patterns*. New York: Charles Scribner's Sons, 1970.

——*Charted Knitting Designs*. New York: Charles Scribner's Sons, 1972.

——*Learn to Knit Afghan Book*. New York: Charles Scribner's Sons, 1974.

——*The Craft of Cable Stitch Knitting*. New York: Charles Scribner's Sons, 1971.

——*The Craft of Lace Knitting. New York: Charles Scribner's Sons, 1979.*

——*Sampler Knitting. New York: Charles Scribner's Sons, 1973.*

Zimmermann, Elizabeth. Knitter's Almanac. New York: Charles Scribner's Sons, 1974.

——*Knitting Without Tears*. New York: Charles Scribner's Sons, 1971.

—— *Knitting Workshop*. Pittsville, Wisconsin: Schoolhouse Press, 1984.

PERIODICALS

American Craft. Published by the American Craft Council, 401 Park Avenue South, New York, NY 10016.

Bulletin of the Needle and Bobbin Club, selected issues. Can be found in Museum libraries.

Knitters, 126 South Phillips, Sioux Falls, SD 57102.

Textile Arts Newsletter, selected issues. 3006 San Pablo Avenue, Berkeley, CA 94702.

Textile History, selected issues. The best there is for history of knitting. Published by Butterworth Scientific, Ltd., Westbury House, PO Box 63, Guildford, England.

Threads, The Taunton Press, 52 Church Hill Road, Box 355, Newtown, CT 06470.

BOOK DEALERS

Bo & Co. Victoria's Orb, PO Box 162, Pomfret, CT 06258.

K.R. Drummond, 30 Hart Grove, Ealing Common, London, W5 England.

Dover Press, 180 Varick Street, New York, NY 10014.

Judith Mansfield, 60a, Dorton Rd, London SW12 9NE, London, England

Bette S. Feinstein, 90 Roundwood Road, Newton, Ma. 02164

Museum Books, 6 West 37th Street, New York, NY 10018.

Schoolhouse Press, 6899 Cary Bluff, Pittsville, WI 54466.

The Unicorn, Box 645, Rockville, MD 20851

Wooden Porch Books, Lois Mueller, Rte 1, Box 262, Middlebourne, W.V. 26149

SUPPLIERS

Frederick J. Fawcett, 1304 Scott St., Petaluma, CA 94952. (linen yarns).

The Niddy Noddy, 416 Albany Post Road, Croton-on-Hudson, New York, 10520. (yarns, books).

School Products Co., 1201 Broadway, New York, NY 10001. (yarns, books).

Straw Into Gold, 3006 San Pablo Avenue, Berkeley, CA 94702. (yarns, books).

Index

(Numbers in bold face indicate pages on which main knitting instructions and diagrams appear.)

Without doubt, Mary Walker Phillips is the most important figure in contemporary American knitting. The first person to explore knitting as an independent art form, she has given new meaning to a great folk craft, skillfully transforming yarn into objects of incomparable beauty.

Before turning her talents to knitting in 1962, Miss Phillips received acclaim as a designer of woven fabrics, in particular for her work in woven clothing fabrics. Her explorations in the fields of knitting and macrame have extended the boundaries of these crafts. Her work has been widely exhibited in the United States, Europe and New Zealand, and is in many private and museum collections, including the Museum of Modern Art, Museum of American Craft; Cooper-Hewitt, the National Museum of Design (Smithsonian); The Smithsonian Institution, Washington, D.C.; Objects U.S.A collection of Johnson Wax Corp; Cranbrook Academy of Art; the Royal Scottish Museum, Edinburgh; and The Art Institute of Chicago.

Miss Phillips received a B.F.A., Wool-clothing Fabrics, and M.F.A., Experimental Textiles, from Cranbrook Academy of Art. She has travelled extensively to teach and to do research on knitting in museums and historical collections in Europe, Great Britain, North America, Australia and New Zealand. She was named a Fellow of the American Craft Council in 1978 for turning knitting into an art form, and received a National Endowment for the Arts Fellowship grant in 1984.